Fight Your Way Out

Fight Your Way Out

The Siege of Sangshak, India/Burma Border, 1944

David Allison

Pen & Sword
MILITARY

First published in Great Britain in 2023 by
Pen & Sword Military
An imprint of Pen & Sword Books Limited
Yorkshire – Philadelphia

Copyright © David Allison 2023

ISBN 978 1 39905 631 1

The right of David Allison to be identified as
Author of this Work has been asserted by him in accordance
with the Copyright, Designs and Patents Act 1988.

A CIP catalogue record for this book is
available from the British Library

All rights reserved. No part of this book may be reproduced or
transmitted in any form or by any means, electronic or mechanical
including photocopying, recording or by any information storage and
retrieval system, without permission from the Publisher in writing.

Typeset by Mac Style
Printed in the UK by CPI Group (UK) Ltd, Croydon, CR0 4YY.

Pen & Sword Books Limited incorporates the imprints of After
the Battle, Atlas, Archaeology, Aviation, Discovery, Family History,
Fiction, History, Maritime, Military, Military Classics, Politics,
Select, Transport, True Crime, Air World, Frontline Publishing, Leo
Cooper, Remember When, Seaforth Publishing, The Praetorian Press,
Wharncliffe Local History, Wharncliffe Transport, Wharncliffe True
Crime and White Owl.

For a complete list of Pen & Sword titles please contact

PEN & SWORD BOOKS LIMITED
47 Church Street, Barnsley, South Yorkshire, S70 2AS, England
E-mail: enquiries@pen-and-sword.co.uk
Website: www.pen-and-sword.co.uk
or
PEN AND SWORD BOOKS
1950 Lawrence Rd, Havertown, PA 19083, USA
E-mail: Uspen-and-sword@casematepublishers.com
Website: www.penandswordbooks.com

Contents

Foreword		vi
Maps		viii
Introduction		ix
Chapter 1	Prelude, 15 March – On the Chindwin River	1
Chapter 2	50 Parachute Brigade	4
Chapter 3	Japan Strikes	14
Chapter 4	19 March – Attack at Sheldon's Corner	23
Chapter 5	20 March – The New Guinea Roadblock	40
Chapter 6	21 March – Race to Sangshak	60
Chapter 7	22 March – Consolidating the Box	71
Chapter 8	23 March – The Onslaught Begins	81
Chapter 9	23 March – Of Plans and Captured Maps	85
Chapter 10	24 March – Wearing down the Box	95
Chapter 11	25 March – The Church at Dawn	106
Chapter 12	26 March – 'A terrible day, never to be forgotten'	115
Chapter 13	26 March – Breakout	132
Chapter 14	The Prisoners	144
Chapter 15	The Aftermath	151
Appendix A: Ranks		160
Appendix B: Key Personnel		161
Notes		163
Bibliography		168
Acknowledgements		170
Index		171

Foreword
by Saul David

The heroic defence of Sangshak, a Naga village in the Manipur district of Assam, by the British, Indian and Gurkha troops of 50 Indian Parachute Brigade in March 1944 was one of the key battles of the Burma campaign. By holding up elements of two Japanese divisions for a week, the brigade had, in the words of its divisional commander Major General Ouvry Roberts, 'undoubtedly saved Imphal and Kohima from the danger of being immediately overrun by the Japanese spearhead troops'.

Yet the true significance of the battle has, until now, not been recognized. Instead historians have been preoccupied by minor details: such as the siting of the defensive position and the behaviour of the brigade commander who suffered a temporary nervous breakdown during the fight. David Allison's fine book considers all these debates, but never loses sight of the bigger picture. The battle, he concludes, had an effect on both combatants 'out of all proportion to the number of men involved, the casualties, its size or its geographical scope'.

He is able to show that the paratroopers stubborn defence caused a delay to Japanese plans to capture the vital communications hub of Dimapur from which they 'never recovered'. The Japanese commanders were also partly responsible for the delay by wasting valuable time and resources assaulting an isolated hilltop that could have been bypassed. Allison speculates that a combination of bulldog spirit and inter-division rivalry were to blame. The end result was the loss of up to 1,000 veteran soldiers that the Japanese were unable to replace. By June 1944, the daring Japanese offensive into British India – Operation U-Go – had failed. Thereafter, it was General Bill Slim's Fourteenth Army taking the initiative as it drove the Japanese out of Burma.

The 50 Parachute Brigade's achievement at Sangshak was not immediately apparent to the British troops defending Imphal. As the bedraggled remnants of the brigade – one battalion, the 152nd, had lost 90 per cent of its men – withdrew to Imphal, they fell victim to a malicious rumour: that the Gurkha and Indian battalions of the 50th had 'faltered' and 'run away'. The rumours, notes Allison, were fanned by a message from high command for all units around Imphal to look out for 'stragglers' from Sangshak. It is also likely that the commander of a support unit, the 4/5 Mahratta Light Infantry, exaggerated the contribution made by his own men to the defence of Sangshak, while at the same time diminishing the role played by the paratroopers.

Another factor was the arrival of the brigade commander, 'Tim' Hope-Thomson, at Imphal in a concussed and dazed state. Allison is able to show that Hope-Thomson did indeed suffer a short collapse during the battle and, though he quickly recovered, was no longer in a fit state to command the brigade, let alone defend its reputation to senior officers, by the time he reached Imphal.

Bill Slim repaired some of the damage when he issued his Special Order of the Day on 31 August 1944, congratulating 50 Parachute Brigade for the vital role it had played in stemming the advance of the Japanese and allowing the garrison of Imphal 'the vital time required to adjust their defences'. The Fourteenth Army had, as a result, been able to inflict on the Japanese their 'greatest defeat'.

Now, with the publication of Allison's deeply researched and fluently written book, we have the full story of 50 Brigade's heroics at Sangshak. They performed 'magnificently and courageously', he writes, in 'a crucial battle'. They did indeed.

Maps

Map 1: Regional Map   xi
Map 2: Operation U-Go   13
Map 3: Sangshak & Sheldon's Corner   22
Map 4: Sangshak Defence Plan   59

Maps designed by Rhys Davies

Introduction

The siege at Sangshak is an important but almost unknown battle in a previously little-known campaign. In early 1944, when much of the world was preoccupied with events in Europe and the upcoming D-Day landings, Japan implemented its audacious plan to invade northern India overland from Burma. Largely overlooked by both the Allied higher command and the public at the time, in recent years a number of historians have looked anew at the momentous series of battles that took place between Japanese and British Indian forces in March to July 1944.

Recent histories rightly focus on the twin battles of Kohima and Imphal, which between them halted the advance of the Japanese and wore them down to such a point that by the time the monsoons broke in May 1944, the three divisions who had boldly entered India in March had become a ragged, emaciated, diseased and shattered shadow of their former selves.

But this was the middle and end of the story. What about its start? When the Japanese surprised the British by launching two well-trained divisions of superb jungle fighters across the grain of the mountains and jungles of Manipur in mid-March 1944, there were few British formations to stop them. Almost by chance, however, the well trained but previously untested British, Indian and Gurkha troops of 50 Indian Parachute Brigade were undertaking advanced jungle training near the village of Sangshak. While the Japanese onslaught initially rolled straight through their forward line of troops, 50 Parachute Brigade's young commander, Brigadier Hope-Thomson, moved his men into a defensive 'box' atop the hill at Sangshak, where they endured wave upon wave of Japanese charges until, a week later, they withdrew from the position and made their way in small groups back to Imphal. This savage fighting not only blunted the enemy attack but also cost the Japanese precious time; time which allowed the British a breathing space to reinforce their positions at Kohima and Imphal, and arguably created the conditions for their eventual victory.

While most agree that Sangshak was a pivotal battle, it also generated a great deal of controversy, almost from the moment it finished. There has been much debate about the siting of the defensive position, the lack of water and defensive supplies, and the quality of the paratroopers themselves. Most insidiously, pointed questions and innuendo were aimed at the commander himself, Brigadier Julian Hope-Thomson, who in the later stages of the encounter suffered from battle exhaustion and a nervous breakdown.

While these matters have excited historians for decades, I believe that they have distracted many from seeing the big picture or remembering exactly what the paratroopers achieved.

So while this book will briefly examine the historical debates, my goal in writing is to revisit this essential battle and to tell the story, the whole story, about how a highly competent group of British, Indian and Gurkha soldiers held on against an equally determined and aggressive enemy force for over a week, causing a delay from which the Japanese never recovered and which contributed, in part, to the eventual British victory.

INDIA AND BURMA REGIONAL MAP 1944

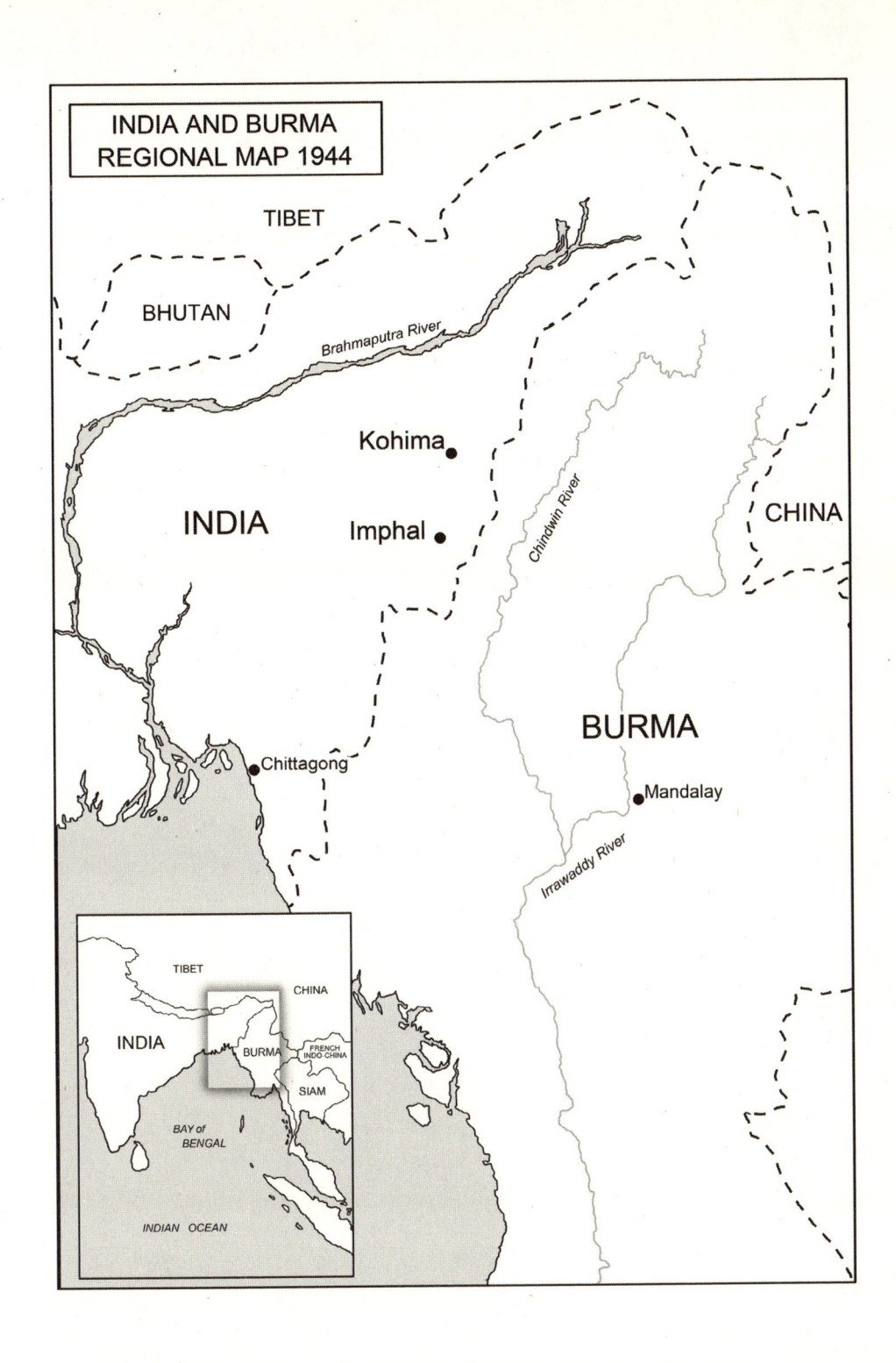

Chapter 1

Prelude, 15 March – On the Chindwin River

The early morning cool of 15 March 1944 saw the men of the Imperial Japanese Army's 31st Division spread out under cover of the jungle on the east bank of the brown, slow-flowing Chindwin River. They had moved up in small groups over the past week, carefully and under cover of night, trying to avoid detection by the British aircraft that regularly flew reconnaissance over the border between northern Burma and British India. The Japanese troops were making their final preparations, checking their equipment and readying themselves to cross the Chindwin River, the border between Burma and India, to begin their assault through Assam and Manipur.

Careful camouflage and concealment of their intentions from the British was crucial if their part in Operation U-Go, the secret Japanese plan to invade northern India, was to succeed. While their 33 Division comrades had already crossed the border far to the south on 7 March and were already marching northwards towards the regional capital of Imphal, the British were still largely in the dark as to the presence of 15 and 31 Divisions, still on the east bank of the Chindwin. The Japanese infantrymen making their final preparations to cross the river knew that total surprise and a lightning assault through the thinly held British lines to their objectives would be the key factors determining success or failure – just as they had been in the early campaigns of the war in Malaya, Hong Kong and Burma itself. A speedy assault, overwhelming an unprepared enemy and bypassing pockets of resistance, was the hallmark of the Japanese way of war, and it was hoped that these tactics would prove as effective during U-Go as they had in the past.

Just behind the front lines of the waiting infantry, newly arrived Lieutenant Hirakubo Masao was not resting but making frantic final preparations to supply his regiment. The 24-year-old, recently promoted supply officer had arrived at the front just two weeks earlier, when he was told that he would be responsible for the feeding and re-supply of 1,000 men. What became quickly apparent to the fresh-faced young man was that the regiment had almost no central supplies or pre-positioned supply dumps to speak of, and certainly no extra food rations. Accordingly, each man was required to carry his own rice and supplies for the duration of the operation. This amounted to a staggering twenty days of rice per man, which had to be hauled on his back along with all of the weapons, ammunition, combat stores and personal items that he needed for the entire operation. This was a huge load for any soldier to manage, particularly when he would be expected to travel, on foot, over some of the most difficult, mountainous and inhospitable terrain imaginable. But the Japanese infantryman was used to hardship. As a result of both tough training and an equally hardy spirit, most of these experienced men would bear this weight without complaint and still be ready to fight.

But while his comrades had the strength to carry their huge loads, Lieutenant Hirakubo knew that the men's rations and supplies were unlikely to be enough. The timetable for Operation U-Go was extremely ambitious – a mere twenty days from start to finish. Overly optimistic in the extreme, no contingency was allowed for delay, resistance by the enemy or the unforeseen vagaries of war. The fact was that neither were there any additional supplies nor was there any way of moving any supplies that miraculously became available to the forward troops, except by foot. Lieutenant Hirakubo was told in no uncertain terms that if for any reason his regiment required additional food or ammunition, it would be up to him to find it, scrounge it, steal or capture it from the British or from anyone else along the route to Imphal.

While Lieutenant Hirakubo fretted, the thoughts of the infantrymen quietly but anxiously resting under the thick jungle canopy turned to the task ahead of them. This section of the campaign – a thrust through the jungle-clad hills of Manipur to the main Imphal–Kohima trunk road and then on to Kohima itself, was to be an infantryman's war pure and simple. There were no bridges across the river and very few roads on the other side – just miles and miles of mountains running north–south, dotted with small hilltop villages connected by rough jungle tracks.

The crossing of the 600yd-wide Chindwin River would take place at night. Locally procured boats, carefully hidden along the river's edge, would be tied together in sections and overlaid with wooden and bamboo planks to make a temporary raft. Many of these rafts would then be joined together to form a rough bridge over which the troops, ammunition, mountain guns and supplies of the division would pass. The makeshift bridge would then be disassembled before dawn, so as not to draw the attention of the British and their spotter planes.

After crossing the river, the soldiers knew that the real work would then begin. They would face a gruelling few weeks of slogging through jungle-clad mountains before they reached their objectives. The terrain facing them on the western side of the Chindwin River was forbidding. A series of 3,000- to 5,000ft-high, energy-sapping mountain ranges, one after the other, stood in their path. While the mountain peaks could be almost bare of forest cover, the valleys in between were covered in thick, wet jungle. There were almost no roads, and the few mountain paths and tracks were barely accessible by mules, much less jeeps or larger vehicles. So it would be up to the infantrymen to make their way on foot over these ranges. The only comfort was that the pelting rains of the monsoon would not come for another month or so. Intelligence also suggested that the mountain ranges and villages were only very lightly held by British troops – just some small patrols, isolated units and early warning observation posts manned by British-led local tribesmen. The experienced veterans of the 31st Division were utterly unconcerned about these few British troops – they would certainly be swept out of their way, just as they had been in all previous campaigns. So the men continued to clean their weapons, adjust their packs and equipment and prepare themselves to move up to the river for the start of the operation when dusk arrived.

Chapter 2

50 Parachute Brigade

Five days' travel to the west, the men of 50 Indian Parachute Brigade (50 (P) Bde) were coming to grips with the same jungle and mountain ranges which occupied the imagination of the Japanese 31 Division. Unlike the Japanese, however, the British, Indian and Gurkha paratroopers training in the hills of Manipur were happy to be here, pleased to be finally in a front-line area of operations after so many years of training in the dry and dusty surroundings of Delhi.

The Brigade's young, ambitious 32-year-old commander, Brigadier Richard Julian 'Tim' Hope-Thomson, knew that it was not just luck that had got them assigned to this area. After yet another aborted parachute drop, Hope-Thomson had campaigned hard for the 'consolation prize' of some advanced jungle training in Manipur. He knew that it would be bad for his men's morale merely to revert disconsolately to endless rounds of training in the sterile surrounds of Delhi and so had actively pushed to have his Brigade brought forward. His wish was granted, and in late February 1944 he moved his two battalions, together with all of their support troops, from Delhi to Dimapur in Assam and then south towards Ukhrul.

Unlike many of the war-commissioned officers serving under him, Hope-Thomson was a pre-war regular. He was originally commissioned in 1931 into the Royal Scots Fusiliers and by 1936 had already been awarded the Military Cross for gallantry in Palestine. At the outbreak of war he was still only a Captain, which says more about the glacial speed of promotion in the inter-war army than either his experience or potential.

But with the coming of war, Hope-Thomson rapidly rose through the ranks. He was quickly promoted to Major (war service) and commanded a company in France with the British Expeditionary Force. After the British withdrawal from Dunkirk, he was lucky enough to be one of the first Army officers trained at Ringway in the relatively new art of parachuting. He was trained not only in individual parachuting but also in the staff and organizational aspects of commanding large bodies of paratroopers. Shortly thereafter, he was given a temporary promotion to Lieutenant Colonel.

But his star was to rise even further and faster when in 1942 a position suddenly became available to command the recently formed 50 Indian Parachute

Brigade, currently being raised outside Delhi. Thus, with no experience of India or the Far East, and only recently promoted to Lieutenant Colonel, Hope-Thomson found himself in India in charge of a newly raised Parachute Brigade, promoted a further two ranks and sporting a pair of Brigadier's red tabs.

Hope-Thomson was both fortunate and unlucky in equal parts in his new command. He was lucky to be leading a very fit and well-trained unit. This was no scratch Brigade such as had all too frequently been stood up in the hasty mobilization following the initial Japanese advances of a year earlier. Rather, he had been given a complement of excellent and highly motivated British and Indian officers commanding tough soldiers who were keen and ready to show their skills and mettle in combat.

While the quality of the men was excellent, their training, and in particular their parachute training, was routinely interrupted by a shortage of aircraft to perform anything more than the minimum required number of qualification jumps. Even when the battalions were warned out for operational deployment, their orders kept being cancelled at the last minute, due to lack of aircraft or last-minute changes of plan. This was extremely demoralizing for high-quality troops who were keen to test themselves against the enemy. During the whole of 1943 only a single parachute drop of one small detachment of men took place, in support of a Chindit operation deep inside Burma. Otherwise, no operational use had been made of the Parachute Brigade since it had been stood up, apart from the usual tasking to quell civil unrest which was familiar to all Army units serving in India in early 1943.

With the coming of the New Year, it appeared the unit's fortunes had changed. January 1944 saw the Brigade in a high state of excitement after they were suddenly put on standby for a full-scale Brigade parachute drop into the Arakan peninsula in Burma. This airborne assault was to be a spearhead inserted ahead of an enormous Allied amphibious operation to retake that vital part of Burma. But as had happened so many times before, at the last minute the operation was cancelled. The strategic situation had changed, with the result that the vital assault craft needed for the amphibious elements were diverted to Italy for the upcoming Anzio landings, and the transport planes were withdrawn and redirected to other theatres.

All the paratroopers, British, Indian and Gurkha alike, were despondent, upset that once again they had missed their chance to prove their worth in battle. Probably no one was more despondent than Hope-Thomson. 'Our Brigadier's heart was almost broken', was how a fellow officer described the state of their commander upon being given the news.[1]

Now in his second year of command of the Brigade, Hope-Thomson had spent the time furiously bringing his men to a high degree of readiness. Hard training, long route marches and frequent practice drops (when planes were available) had forged a unit that was fit, disciplined and extremely enthusiastic. But time and time again their planned operations were aborted at the last minute, and this had a crushing effect on morale – for both officers and men alike. What was the point of a highly trained, precision weapon if there was no prospect of it ever being used?

This time, however, after the Arakan operation was cancelled, Hope-Thomson had managed to get the Brigade assigned to do 'advanced jungle training' in Manipur around the strategic town of Kohima. It would not be the same as parachuting into enemy territory, but at least it was a 'proper' operational area, evidenced by the fact that the men all received an additional field allowance. Hope-Thomson knew that working in an operational area, close to the border with Burma, would do a great deal for the men's morale – certainly more than being stuck in the dusty surroundings of their base at Campbellpore. So they traded their parachute smocks for jungle green uniforms and left behind their distinctive red berets in favour of the broad-brimmed, floppy slouch hat worn by all regular infantry units in Burma. They then prepared themselves and their equipment for the long train ride from dry Campbellpore to the jungles and mountains of Manipur.

All the men of the Brigade were enthusiastic about going. The grant of 'batta' or field allowance of one rupee per day[2] for working in an operational area may have been an incentive to some, but more importantly, the men were hungry to get on with 'a real operation' rather than endless barrack and training 'schemes', as military exercises were referred to at the time. Even those with minor injuries pulled every trick in the book to be allowed to travel with their units rather than be left behind. For example, Major John Fuller, the enthusiastic Officer Commanding (OC) of C Company, 152 Battalion still had his leg in plaster from a previous parachute training accident when the orders came through to move out to the jungle. But he was determined to go and would not remain behind while the rest of his Company went out east. It is not known whether he needed to hide his injury or whether it was just ignored by the accompanying medical staff. But we do know that when the trains pulled out, he was ready at the platform and boarded the train, with his men, for the journey east.

Parachuting in the British Indian Army

Parachuting into combat was a very new concept in 1941, and very few men in the British Army knew anything about it. In the Indian Army, no one knew anything about it at all. Nevertheless, after observing the Germans' spectacular use of parachute troops in Belgium and Crete in 1940 and 1941, the British soon identified a need for their own parachute troops. Shortly thereafter, India's only parachute unit, 50 Indian Parachute Brigade (50 (P) Bde), was born. From its beginnings the Brigade was singular; not only because of its novel method of going to war or because of its tough and intense training, but also because of the almost unique multi-ethnic makeup of its men. Whereas most Indian combat units of this time were relatively homogeneous in terms of race, caste or religion (for example, a battalion would consist exclusively of Sikhs or Rajputs or Marathas, etc.), the Parachute Brigade was, to an extent, and very progressively for the time, a blended multi-cultural unit.

The Brigade was in theory comprised of a headquarters, three Battalions and various supporting troops (for example, a field ambulance and field engineers). By early 1944, the fighting battalions were 152 Battalion (Indian) and 153 Battalion (Gurkha). Originally, the Brigade also had 151 Battalion, an all-British unit, but this Battalion had already been deployed for service in the Middle East in 1943 and so was no longer part of the Brigade. Its replacement, 154 Battalion, another Gurkha Battalion rather than all-British, had only just been raised and was still conducting initial training at the Brigade's base at Campbellpore. As such, 154 Battalion would miss out on the jungle training in Manipur.

The Indian 152 Battalion was commanded by Lieutenant Colonel Paul 'Hoppy' Hopkinson. Hopkinson has been described thus: 'Though small and slightly built … [he was] a giant of a man who gained the immediate trust of all who knew him. He looked more like a scholar than a military man, diffident, self-effacing, quiet, [with] a sense of humour … but without doubt a supremely competent soldier.'[3] Hopkinson was a regular Indian Army officer who had served in India for many years, including with distinction on the North-West Frontier. Like Hope-Thomson, Hopkinson was fortunate to be in England in 1941 and had also been selected to undertake parachute training with a view to taking what he had learned back to India to establish a parachute unit.

While Hopkinson's 152 Battalion was very progressive in that it contained men from all races and castes, there was still a clear dividing line between Hindu and Muslim soldiers, with individual platoons being comprised exclusively of one or the other. This division was based in part on practical considerations, foremost of which was the very different food that needed to be provided to each. It was also founded on the realization that there was only so much that would be accepted at this time in terms of integration.

There were no difficulties of integration or rations, however, in 153 Battalion. This was comprised exclusively of Gurkhas, hardy men from the hills of Nepal who had been an extremely important source of manpower to the British in India for generations. Sharing background, religion and language, the Gurkha Battalion was much more homogeneous than 152. In addition, the men were drawn almost exclusively from a single Gurkha regiment, who had joined en masse two years previously. These factors helped to give their commanding officer, Lieutenant Colonel Willis, an extremely tight and well-knit fighting battalion.

While the Brigade was to an extent multi-cultural, or at least more so than most of the Indian Army at this time, all the senior officers of the Brigade were British, as were most of the junior officers. The exceptions, however, were a number of ethnically Indian or Gurkha junior officers. With the growing push by 1943/44 to 'Indianize' the Army, an increasing number of Indian officers were filling some of the platoon commander roles. Often these were extremely experienced men who had worked their way up through the ranks. They were on the whole very competent officers who took their soldiering seriously. These men were known by their Indian rank of *Jemadar* (equivalent to Lieutenant) or *Subedar* (Captain).

But while Indianization was coming to the Army, in early 1944 it was still very much the *British* Indian Army, and as such, British officers continued to dominate all major positions. Likewise, the vitally important signals section at Brigade headquarters was comprised exclusively of British soldiers.

David Atkins, the author of *The Forgotten Major* fondly remembers seeing the Parachute Brigade officers in Delhi. He said:

> I had known the 50th Indian Parachute Brigade when they were stationed in Delhi. They were made up of every major race and caste in the Indian Army except for the Sikhs, who were not included as their turbans prevented them using the parachute helmet. The young officers in Delhi looked magnificent and were at all the parties. They were wearing at that time the blue parachute wings on their right pocket. I remember a memsahib at the club looking at a group of them and misquoting:
>
> > Young Apollos, golden haired,
> > Magnificently unprepared
> > For the long dirtiness of war[4]

The quotation, whilst poetic, was wrong on several counts, in particular the memsahib's view on the paratroopers' preparedness for war. While they had not seen active duty in Burma over the past few years, they had been rigorously and continually trained, to the point that when they finally made their way to the Burma front they were probably some of the best trained troops available in the theatre. This fact was often glossed over or completely forgotten by their detractors, who in the first few days after the battle at Sangshak spread wild and unsubstantiated rumours that the Brigade's failures were due to the fact that the paratroopers were new, green and insufficiently trained. This was not the case.

When Brigadier Hope-Thomson took over the Brigade, it was keen but still operating somewhat languidly, more like a unit of the pre-war Indian Army than one that could be sent to face the Japanese at a moment's notice. This 'gentlemanly approach to soldiering' changed immediately upon the new Brigadier's arrival, and both the frequency and intensity of training saw a marked uptick. Also, while parachuting training remained important for the Brigade (when aircraft were available), Hope-Thomson also placed a premium on honing basic infantry skills.

The focus on ground skills was important to Hope-Thomson, and this was reflected in an operational Instruction to the Brigade in which he laid out his thinking:

> The most important thing about operational training from the point of view of 50 (P) Bde, is that the actual transportation by air and the parachute descent should diminish in relative importance in everyone's mind. Up to now, it has been inevitable that, in the minds of the troops, and perhaps of some of the officers also, the gymnastic feat of making a parachute descent has been given primary importance.[5]

After telling his officers and men to stop obsessing about the parachuting element of their work, he then went on to lay out instructions that all sub-units must conduct daily training in physical exercises and unarmed combat, regular field firing, battle drills and night movement. This was essential foundational warfighting, and Hope-Thomson's insistence that the Brigade master these skills would prove invaluable during the upcoming struggle at Sangshak.

The Move to Manipur: Order of Battle and Equipment

As the Brigade moved to Manipur for its 'advanced jungle training', a certain amount of secrecy accompanied its movements, perhaps to deceive any Japanese spies or 'fifth columnists' as to the whereabouts of India's only Parachute Brigade. This secrecy extended not only to their whereabouts but also to what the men wore and carried into battle.

Instead of its usual distinctive parachutist dress and equipment, the Brigade was kitted out for the jungle like all regular infantry battalions. An order was given that all parachute designations were to be taken off their uniforms and no one was to wear their distinctive red berets or the embroidered 'wings' on their uniforms. Rather, all soldiers wore the standard jungle green uniforms, with a 'patch pocket' on the front right leg, and carried the jungle green version of the 1937 pattern webbing. The newly issued jungle green uniforms, made of breathable 'aertex' material, were well suited to the jungles of Manipur and a considerable improvement on the previously issued khaki drill which Indian units had worn during the early days of the war. It was light and comfortable and, most importantly, deep green in colour, better suited to camouflaging men in the hills and jungles of Burma. The only complaint most men had was that the blouse was cut far too short (modelled as it was on the conventional European battle dress), which meant it often 'rode up', exposing the midriff and becoming generally uncomfortable.

The pouches and webbing, in which the men carried their ammunition, Bren gun magazines and grenades, was an Indian-manufactured version of the standard 1937 pattern webbing familiar to all British troops. However, having already trained in the jungle for some time, the paratroopers uniformly dispensed with the cross braces of the webbing, which was felt to be too constrictive. In its place, they fixed a water bottle on their belts, slung bandoliers of ammunition around their waists and kept everything else in their packs.

On their heads, only the mortar troops wore steel helmets. Everyone else either wore the Gurkha broad-brimmed felt hat or the slouch hat, often with the left brim turned up. Some of the men, particularly during the cold nights up in the hills of Manipur, wore the ubiquitous 'cap comforter woollen warm' instead. A mainstay of the British Army, the cap comforter was a sort of khaki scarf-like tube which, when folded in on itself, turned into a rather warm beanie-style woollen hat.

With regard to weapons, 50 Parachute Brigade was armed in the same way as most British infantry operating in Burma at this time. The rifle 'section' was the smallest unit of the Brigade and comprised 8–10 men. It was led by a *Naik* (equivalent to a corporal) armed with a 9mm Sten gun. The Sten was a very simple weapon, short and stubby, with its 30-round magazine jutting out horizontally from its left side. It was made of pressed aluminium and was a sub-machine gun capable of a high rate of fire. While it was of little use at long range, its compactness and high rate of fire made it a popular weapon for airborne troops and very effective in jungle fighting.

The rest of the section were armed with the standard .303 Lee Enfield rifle, except for the section gunner, who sported the Bren light machine gun (LMG). The Bren was one of the standout weapons carried by the British during the war, very accurate and capable of a high rate of fire. While it was fed by 30-round curved box magazines rather than relying on a linked belt of ammunition, it was a light machine gun built for sustained fire. It had a heavy barrel which could be changed with minimum fuss if it overheated.

Besides the section's small arms, all men carried a stock of grenades, whilst the officers were equipped with revolvers. Added to this, the men carried either a bayonet, or in the case of the Gurkhas a *kukri*, their famous curved fighting knife. Even some of the non-Gurkha troops preferred to carry a *kukri* since it was an invaluable tool in the jungle for clearing scrub, cutting bamboo or, in extremis, digging slit trenches. But in close combat it was the Gurkhas who made best use of these knives, relishing the opportunity to get up close to the enemy and slashing at the Japanese during close-quarter fighting.

* * *

As the trains rumbled eastwards towards the railhead at Dimapur, and Manipur beyond, Hope-Thomson reflected on the numbers of men he had at hand. While his formation was termed a Brigade, it was in truth a Brigade on a very light scale indeed. Instead of the three Battalions which made up its official order of battle, Hope-Thomson was only taking two Battalions to Manipur. Also, a typical parachute Battalion was more lightly manned than a typical British infantry battalion – being only three companies strong (plus attachments) instead of the usual four. He did, however, have the services of the dedicated Machine Gun Company as well as a troop of the sappers of 411 (Royal Bombay) Field Engineers. Together with his headquarters and a collection of minor support staff, HQ Defence Platoon and the like, his Brigade totalled approximately 2,000 men – many fewer than the usual 3,000 or so found in a regular Brigade. On the other hand, 2,000 trained paratroopers was a formidable body of men, and as they entered Manipur, Hope-Thomson most likely felt satisfaction, pride and quiet anticipation, feelings justified by the training, discipline and toughness of his men, rather than any sense of unease or concern.

Manipur – the terrain

The Brigade was allotted an area of operations in the eastern portion of Manipur, centred on the town of Ukhrul and wedged north-east of Imphal and south-west of Kohima. It was wild, mountainous country, with peaks frequently rising to between 1,000 and 2,000 metres (3,000–6,000ft) or more running north-south through the area from the plains of Imphal to the Chindwin River in the east. The mountains were invariably heavily forested, jungle-like in places – particularly on the lower slopes – but with less dense vegetation at higher elevations. Between the hills and mountains were row upon row of deep valleys, often containing thick jungle, water courses or small rivers.

While the area of operations was remote it was not uninhabited, and small villages of local Naga and Kuki tribesmen dotted many of the hills of Manipur. Villages were usually small affairs, traditionally sited on a hilltop and consisting of numerous small thatched houses, firewood stacked under rough shelters to protect it from the rain, and perhaps a rough open area for village gatherings and the like. The villages would typically have some small gardens for vegetables and pens for pigs and chickens. However, due to the mountainous terrain, the villagers did not engage in large scale farming as in lowland areas. Surprisingly, considering the reputation of Naga tribesmen as fierce warriors and head-hunters, most of the Naga villages sported their own Christian church, which was usually the largest and most substantial structure in the village. The many churches throughout Manipur were testament to the persistent efforts of American Baptist missionaries, who had expanded into the region for several decades before the war, converting a great many of the Nagas to Christianity.

Communication between the villages was by way of a series of jeep tracks and roughly hewn jungle paths, often precariously hugging the side of hills and mountains with steep falls '*khudside*'[6] down to the valleys and ravines below. There were few roads in the Brigade's area of operations, the exception being the key Manipur Road running along the western edge of the Brigade's area of operations and intersected by the important 'Finches Corner' road marker at Mile 36. Finches Corner was named after Major John Finch, Bombay Sappers and Miners, who prepared that section of the Ukhrul Road in 1942. A stone commemorating the achievement still stands today, and it marked an important spot for travellers up and down the busy trunk road. It would also be a focal point for the Brigade headquarters in the days to come. Off the trunk road, however, it was down to jeep tracks and jungle paths, passable only by small jeeps but more usually by mule or foot traffic. As a consequence, almost all of the Brigade's movement off the trunk road and further into the hills had to be undertaken on foot.

The jungles of Manipur were teeming with life – river fish, birds, deer, wild pigs and more. Reports of the rich wildlife had encouraged some of the more hopeful junior officers to bring along their fishing gear and shotguns in the hope of enjoying a bit of fishing and shooting after the training had concluded. As fate would have it, the Brigade would soon engage in a great deal of blood sports, during which hunting horns were frequently blown – but their quarry was a lot more dangerous than deer or wild pigs.

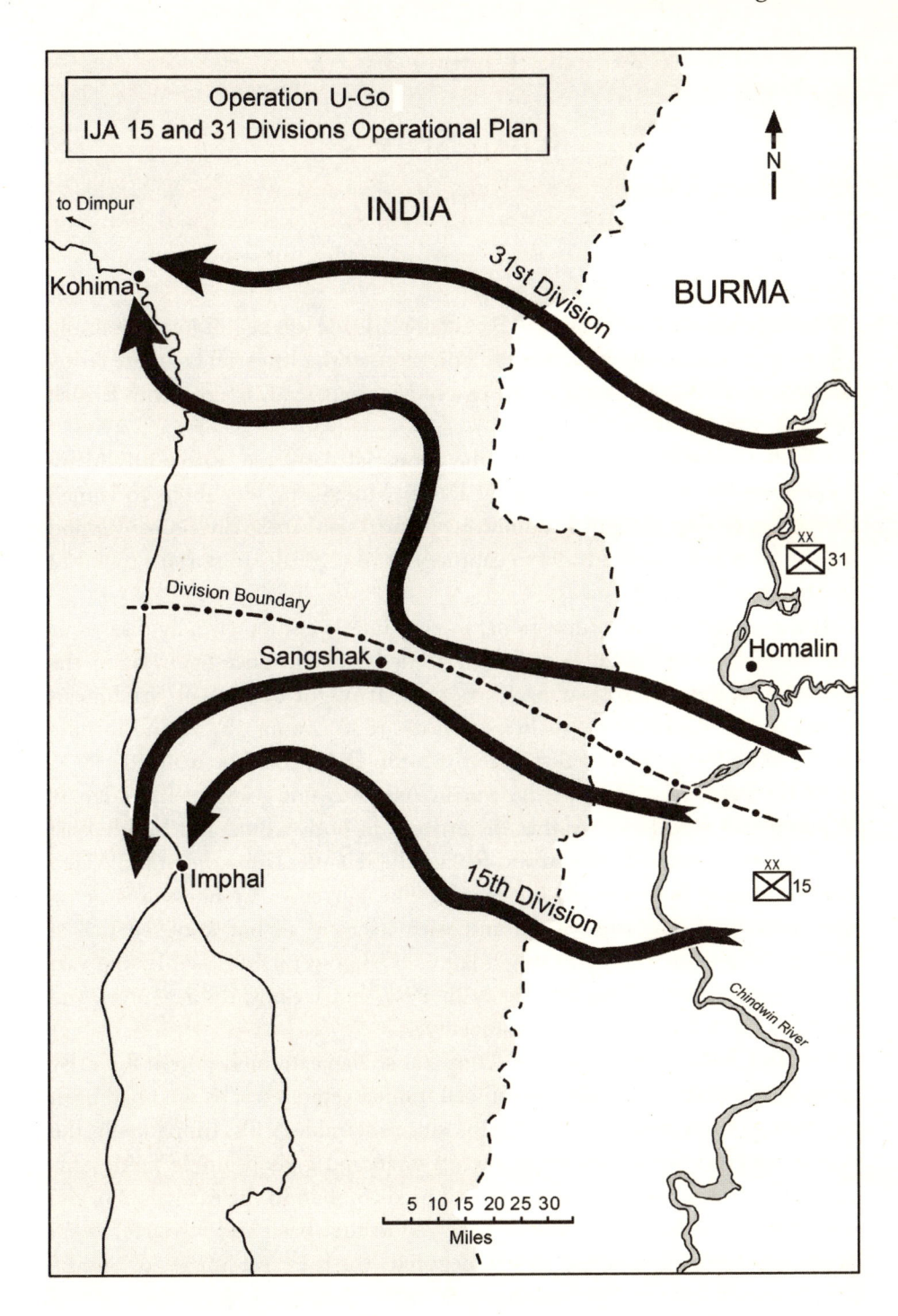

Operation U-Go
IJA 15 and 31 Divisions Operational Plan

Chapter 3

Japan Strikes

In early March 1944, just as 50 Parachute Brigade was beginning its training programme in Manipur, three full divisions of the Imperial Japanese Army were secretly converging to the east of Manipur, ready to cross into British India for the first time.

Unbeknownst to the British, the Imperial Japanese Fifteenth Army, commanded by Lieutenant General Renya Mutaguchi, was about to launch Operation U-Go, a mightily ambitions plan to send these divisions overland from Burma into British India to capture the strategically important towns of Imphal and Dimapur.

It was a plan of epic proportions, soaring hubris and potentially disastrous consequences if it failed. But if it succeeded it could once again hand the initiative in the eastern war back to Japan. It might even push Britain out of the war in Asia if Mutaguchi's secret desire to conquer India and instal a sympathetic Indian Nationalist government in Delhi could be realized.

At the beginning of 1944 the war in Asia was not going well for Japan. While it still held large swathes of territory in both China and South-East Asia, including all of Burma, it was feeling the relentless pressure of the Allied island-hopping campaign in the Pacific. The Japanese Air Force was being steadily eroded into irrelevance, and with its navy all but knocked out of the war, Japan was fast becoming a landlocked power, tied down by the vast territory which it had won so easily in 1942, but lacking the resources and ability to hold it or continue to manoeuvre.

On land, however, the Japanese Army was still an extremely potent force. By early 1944 it had a large number of well trained veteran troops who had been engaged in constant fighting in China since the mid-1930s. Individually, the Japanese soldier was an excellent infantryman and a good jungle fighter, his skills forged in often brutal training and hard combat. In the early days of the war, British troops were constantly amazed at the speed and resourcefulness of the Japanese, who seemed able to negotiate the toughest jungles of South-East Asia to outflank, surround and annihilate their trapped enemies. It was this lightning speed, skill and determination which had enabled Japan to seize Malaya, Singapore and Burma in quick succession in early 1942.

But by the beginning of 1944 the strategic advantage had swung decisively away from Japan. The Imperial Japanese Army and Navy were being strangled, imperceptibly slowly, but just as certainly. As its empire was slipping away, thoughtful minds in Japan were just starting to realize that sooner or later, Allied forces would smash through the various island chains which protected Japan and then assault the Japanese home islands themselves.

As surrender was unthinkable, Japan needed a decisive victory, something to break the Allies' will and to turn the tide of the war back in their favour. As the navy no longer had the ability to deliver such a decisive event at sea, it would have to be a land victory, with the chosen target being the apparently sleeping giant of British India.

* * *

Mutaguchi's plan was not the first time that the Japanese had considered a strike through northern Burma into the north-east Indian state of Manipur. Operation-21, as it was initially known, had been discussed by the Japanese Imperial staff in early 1943. However, the plan was soon abandoned after serious analysis was undertaken of the challenges that an invading army would face if it took the overland route into India. Ironically as it turns out, Mutaguchi himself did not favour this earlier plan. At the time it was presented, he strongly believed that the mountains and jungles of north-west Burma were impassable to large formations of troops, and thus it would be impossible to invade via this route.[1]

Firstly, the Chindwin River, which formed both the border and a mighty barrier between northern Burma and India would need to be crossed. This long river, a major tributary of the Irrawaddy, is brown, muddy and 300–500ft wide in its northern reaches. In 1944 there were few bridges, and thus provision would need to be made to transport the troops to the western bank by barge or by building bridges – both of which options were slow and would leave the assault troops vulnerable.

Mutaguchi knew of the difficult terrain, soaring mountains, thick jungle and paucity of roads which characterized most of Manipur. In addition, Japanese planners (like their British opponents) were acutely aware of the effect of weather on any large-scale operation, and in particular the debilitating nature of the monsoon, which starts in early May and lasts until October. The monsoons were rightly feared by all soldiers in Burma, Japanese and British alike, since monthly rainfall of over 1,200mm (47in) would destroy all but the best all-weather roads and make off-road travel virtually impossible. Significant military operations would grind to a close during the monsoon season, and both sides, unable to move or take any offensive action, would be forced merely to wait in their rain-sodden, mud-filled camps until the rains abated in late October.

The ability to supply a large army in such difficult terrain and weather appeared insurmountable to Japanese planners. Accordingly, the plan to invade northern India was quietly shelved until one particularly ambitious Japanese general picked it up, dusted it off, added a few touches of his own and then presented it again to the high command in late 1943.

That enterprising and endlessly self-promoting general was 55-year-old Lieutenant General Renya Mutaguchi. He had had a solid, rather than exceptional, Army career, first in China and later in the invasion of Malaya and Singapore. He would often claim that, as a Colonel, he was the man who had 'started the war with China' by firing the first shots in the Marco Polo Bridge incident north of Beijing in 1937. Whether this claim was true or not, Mutaguchi frequently played it up in an attempt to boost his credentials as an aggressive, go-getting officer.

What was real, however, was the extent of his ambition. He believed that he was destined for great things, and a grand sweep into India appeared to be just the sort of action needed to show to the world his potential. He allegedly commented: 'If I could decisively influence the Great East Asia War with an offensive operation against India, since I triggered it with the Marco Polo Bridge Incident, it would be very honourable for me.'[2]

In 1943 Mutaguchi was in command of the Fifteenth Army in Burma under the ultimate command of General Masakazu Kawabe, the heavily-moustached Commander-in-Chief of the Burma Area Army. Mutaguchi was certainly aware of the previous Operation 21 plan and the reasons why it was not pursued, including the difficulty of crossing the Chindwin River and the jungle-clad mountains beyond. But in 1943 a bold British initiative made him question previous assumptions and start to think that the plan might just be workable.

Mutaguchi's inspiration was the famous Chindits raids of 1943 and early 1944. The brainchild of the eccentric British General Orde Wingate, the Chindit operations consisted of long-range penetration by raiding parties that moved overland deep into Japanese-held Burma to carry out reconnaissance, sabotage and attacks. After the war, serious questions were raised about the effectiveness of the Chindits when compared with the vast expenditure of manpower and resources lavished on them. Lieutenant General William 'Bill' Slim himself, Commander of the Fourteenth Army, wrote in his book *Defeat into Victory* that 'the Chindits gave splendid examples of courage and hardihood. Yet I came firmly to the conclusion that such formations ... were wasteful. They did not give, militarily, a worth-while return for the resources in men, material and time that they absorbed.'[3] But while the Chindits may not have contributed much in a strictly military sense, the psychological and morale-raising effect they had on the British was immeasurable, representing one of the first successes scored against the Japanese.

But for the Japanese, the Chindit operations demonstrated what was possible. Mutaguchi said after the war: 'I had not foreseen the Wingate operation. I believed that the jungles of north Burma were not suitable for large scale warfare but I changed my conception after his first operation. I thought it better to launch a sudden attack on the enemy base, rather than wait to be attacked.'[4]

Inspired by Wingate, Mutaguchi was now convinced that a sudden attack, overland through northern Burma into India, could work. Speed and daring had propelled the Japanese to victory in 1942, and Mutaguchi now believed that the feat could be repeated. His revised plan, now named Operation U-Go, envisaged a diversionary attack in the Arakan by one Division from the neighbouring 28 Army (ultimately 55 Division) and then a thrust by three divisions from his own Fifteenth Army across the Chindwin and then overland towards Imphal and Dimapur. While the British were fighting the diversion in the Arakan, the three invasion divisions would mass secretly on the Chindwin, cross the river, then travel, mostly on foot, across the jungle-clad mountain ranges and strike.

Mutaguchi's plan called for the Japanese 33rd Division, the heaviest of his divisions, together with what armour he had, to move first from around 7/8 March in a long south-westerly sweep through the Imphal plain, before attacking Imphal from the south. Then, while the British were engaged with 33 Division, 31 and 15 Divisions would strike due west across the Chindwin and the hills of Manipur, before moving to take the strategic hill station of Kohima (31 Division) or to attack Imphal from the north (15 Division).

As had been identified under the old Operation-21 plan, supply and logistics would be the key restriction. However, unlike the British Chindits, there could be no hope of re-supply from air, and given the difficulty of the terrain, overland supply would also prove extremely difficult. Accordingly, Mutaguchi decided that all troops should carry everything they would need, including supplies for up to twenty days. They would then supplement this by capturing British ammunition and supply dumps. He also came up with the novel idea, apparently inspired by Genghis Khan, of having his troops drive thousands of head of cattle along the route, in effect supplying food 'on the hoof'. While imaginative, this plan paid no heed to the uncooperativeness of Burmese oxen, many of which failed to move at any speed and most of which perished when falling over steep-sided ravines and into treacherous mountain passes.

Japanese headquarters were aware of the limitations in Mutaguchi's plan. Major General Inada, a senior staff officer commented:

> The Mutaguchi Plan is full of fond hopes. He counts his chickens before they are hatched. The Mutaguchi Plan goes like this: the Army crosses the Chindwin River and goes over the Arakan Mountains, where there is no road, with as much ammunition and food as it can carry. And then when rations run out, food and ammunition are to be gained in Imphal and supplied to the divisions, using as much transportation as necessary captured there. Such an operation might have been possible in the spring of 1942. But now that the enemy is preparing for a counter-attack, this plan is senseless … In any case, the Mutaguchi Plan lacks flexibility.[5]

Yet despite these misgivings, the plan was approved by Japanese Prime Minister Tojo, in somewhat strange circumstances, apparently while he was having a bath! The official orders to begin the operation were then issued on 7 January 1944 by Japanese Imperial General Headquarters.

After the plan was approved, Mutaguchi worked quickly to assemble his army, until in early March 1944 his three divisions were massed on the east bank of the Chindwin and ready to strike.

The Japanese infantryman

The responsibility of realizing Mutaguchi's ambitious plan fell mainly on the shoulders of the Japanese infantryman. An October 1944 US Army Intelligence report into Japanese Strategy and Tactics in Burma presented a short word picture of the Japanese soldier as he appeared to the Allies:[6]

> He is a well-trained soldier. He is able to endure hardships and privation. He has a fanatical and fearless conception of death on the battlefield. This feeling of the individual soldier of a personal honour in death, has enabled the Japanese soldier to be aggressive in battle and perform almost unbelievable feats.
>
> It can however, by no means be said that the Japanese infantryman is super-human. In many cases, imminent death has caused him to panic. He is just as subject to hunger and disease as is his enemy. Physically he is only another soldier, sometimes well-trained, sometimes not. Mentally and spiritually he often conducts himself in a very inhuman manner. Although he will often continue to fight, even with a club after all his

arms and equipment are gone, yet he is only an effective fighter when he is well equipped with supplies, arms and ammunition.

This intelligence summary, prepared shortly after the Imphal campaign in 1944, neatly summarizes and analyzes the characteristics of the Japanese fighting man in a relatively objective manner. While comments about 'fanaticism' were commonly used at the time to describe Japanese soldiers (this being the only contemporary explanation as to why the Japanese appeared to often fight to the death in otherwise hopeless circumstances), this has now given way to a more nuanced view of the Japanese soldier's motivations. He was on the whole a tenacious fighter, and the strength of the Japanese Army lay in its individual soldier and small teams, rather than in firepower, heavy weapons, combined arms or air superiority. It was on the shoulders of individual Japanese infantrymen that success or failure of Mutaguchi's plan firmly rested.

Structure of the Japanese Infantry

In early 1944, a Japanese infantry platoon consisted of four sections of about thirteen men. The Japanese infantry soldier was typically equipped with the Arisaka Type 99 rifle. This was a robust 7.7mm bolt-action rifle which sported a particularly long bayonet, useful for the close-quarter fighting embraced by the Japanese. Hand grenades were plentiful, and each section was supported by a Type 99 Nambu Light Machine Gun (LMG). The LMG was also a 7.7mm calibre weapon and was fed by a top-loading 30-round curved box magazine. Officers carried both a sword and a pistol, the former often used prominently in attacks, given that it was a point of honour for an officer to advance using his sword.

Three platoons made a company (commanded by a Captain) and four to five companies comprised a battalion of approximately 1,100 men. Companies and battalions were supported by heavier weapons, including heavy, tripod-mounted machine guns and light 50mm mortars capable of firing both high explosive rounds similar to a grenade and illumination rounds.

On paper, a regiment was made up of three battalions plus supporting arms and totalled around 3,800 men (of which just 100 were officers). In practice, and especially during Operation U-Go, however, the regiments were often smaller. The main attacking unit at Sangshak, 58 Regiment, was estimated to contain only just over 2,000 men.

In addition to the infantry, the most important supporting arm for the operation was its integral artillery. During the U-Go Operation this mainly came in the form of the venerable but still highly effective 75mm mountain gun. Unfortunately for the Japanese, these mountain guns were in short supply; the whole of 15 Division had a mere eighteen (nine type 41 guns and nine of the older type 31) at its disposal.[7]

The Indian National Army

Mutaguchi planned that his men would be supported by troops of the Indian National Army (INA), in order to maintain the pretence that the Japanese were entering India to 'liberate' it from the British.

The INA was a curious organization, formed after the fall of Singapore and led by the enigmatic Indian nationalist, Subhas Chandra Bose, whose aim was to drive the British out of India. The force was made up of several thousand Indian soldiers captured in Malaya and Singapore who had now agreed to fight for the Japanese. Some did so willingly, although for many it was a simple case of self-interest, the alternative being to spend the remainder of the war in a prison camp.

While the Japanese did arm the INA, they did so only with light infantry weapons and certainly gave them no artillery, mortars or armour. During the entire U-Go campaign, the INA saw little large-scale fighting and were regarded by the Japanese more as a useful propaganda tool than an effective fighting force.

The INA were known to the British as 'JIFS' (Japanese Indian Fifth Columnists), and they were roundly hated by the British Indian troops, who considered them traitors and cowards.[8] There are reports that Indian soldiers would often kill captured INA troops rather than send them rearwards as PoWs. Furthermore, while several thousand INA soldiers trudged their way into India as part of U-Go, there is no evidence that they achieved their goal of convincing British Indian troops to defect or turn on their British officers. Overall, despite their vaunted propaganda value, the INA made little impact on the outcome of the U-Go Campaign.

* * *

By early February Mutaguchi was nearly ready. Orders had been given for the three Divisions to move towards the border, and soon they would cross the Chindwin on their way to strike India. Mutaguchi felt that his destiny was soon to be realized, and he issued a Special Order of the Day to all of his troops:

> The Army has now reached the stage of invincibility and the day when the Rising Sun shall proclaim our definite victory in India is not far off ...
> I will remind you that a speedy and successful advance is the keynote of

this operation ... When we strike we must be absolutely ready, reaching our objectives with the speed of wildfire despite all the obstacles of the river, mountain and labyrinthine jungle. We must sweep aside the paltry opposition we encounter and add lustre to Army tradition by achieving a victory of annihilation.[9]

With his army nearly all assembled, the invasion commenced on 7/8 March, when 33 Division crossed the river and started its long march northwards towards Imphal. The troops, tanks and supporting arms of 33 Division moved quickly towards their objectives, initially meeting little resistance. For several days the British did not seem to fully understand the scale of the threat and put up comparatively limited opposition. It would be several days before they became fully aware of what they were facing, whereupon they began to deploy more and more troops to the south of Imphal to block the advancing Japanese.

All the while, 31 and 15 Divisions were still moving stealthily up to the east bank of the Chindwin, ready to make their move on 15 March. The 58th Regiment of 31 Division and the 60th Regiment of 15 Division were camped almost parallel to each other along their respective divisional southern and northern boundaries. Despite their excellent camouflage, they were spotted by elements of the British V Force – the light screen of observation posts manned by British-led local Naga tribesmen. However, the V Force warnings appeared to have been largely ignored, and so on 15 March the Japanese commenced their crossing of the river, meeting almost no resistance.

Once on the west bank, the Japanese infantrymen shouldered their enormous packs, picked up their weapons and commenced the trek westwards. Captain Shosaku Kameyama, a company commander in the 58th Regiment recounted:

We went up and then climbed down the steep mountains, undisturbed by British troops or planes. After six days hard march we poured into Ukhurul ... British troops seemed to have evacuated it only a few hours before and the village was burning. We then realized that the enemy had destroyed all of their food and supplies, to our great disappointment.[10]

Despite seeing their hoped-for supplies go up in smoke, as dawn came on the morning of 19 March, both the 58th Regiment and its counterpart the 60th were in good spirits. They had faced very little opposition on their journey so far, their supplies were still plentiful and morale was high.

It was, however, at just around this time that lead elements of 58th Regiment would encounter a large concentration of British Indian soldiers a few miles to the east of Sangshak and just south of Ukhrul. Their previously unopposed trek through the mountains of Manipur was about to end.

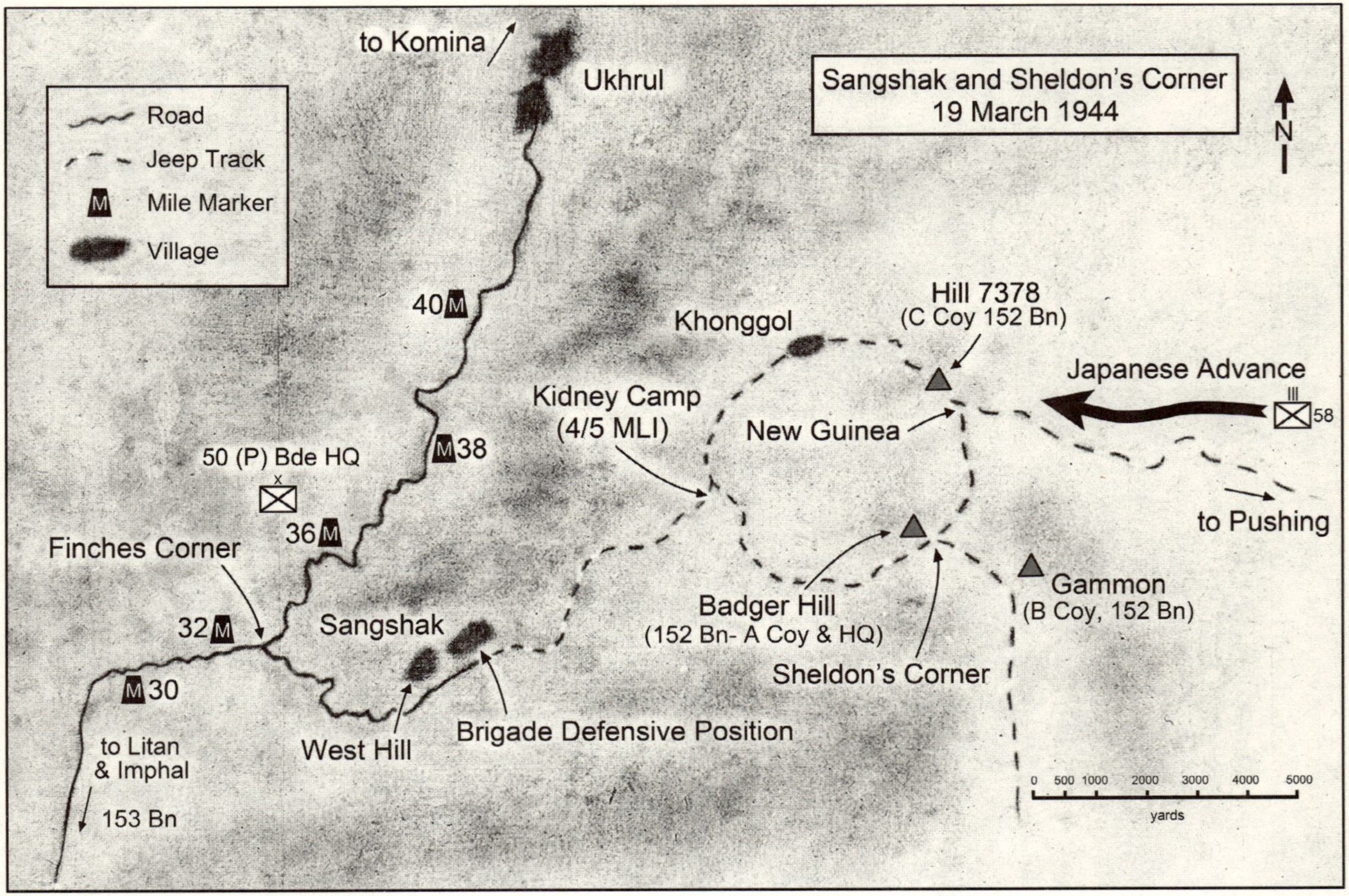

Sangshak and Sheldon's Corner
19 March 1944
N
Road
Jeep Track
Mile Marker
Village
to Komina
Ukhrul
40
38
36
32
30
50 (P) Bde HQ
Finches Corner
Sangshak
West Hill
Brigade Defensive Position
to Litan
& Imphal
153 Bn
Khonggol
Kidney Camp
(4/5 MLI)
Hill 7378
(C Coy 152 Bn)
New Guinea
Japanese Advance
58
to Pushing
Badger Hill
(152 Bn- A Coy & HQ)
Sheldon's Corner
Gammon
(B Coy, 152 Bn)
0 500 1000 2000 3000 4000 5000
yards

Chapter 4

19 March – Attack at Sheldon's Corner

In early March the paratroopers of 50 Parachute Brigade were shaking out and moving to their designated defensive positions along the jungle tracks and villages north-east of Imphal, unaware that the enemy was massing, in great strength, a mere five days' march to the east.

Shortly after arriving in Manipur around 9 March 1944, Hope-Thomson received orders from the commander of 23 Indian Division, Major General Ouvry Roberts, to take responsibility for the areas around Sheldon's Corner,[1] Ukhrul, Kharsom and Jessami. The previous occupants of this section of Manipur, 49 Brigade, had just been moved south with orders to shore up the defences around Imphal. The British were also busily withdrawing all remaining lines of communication soldiers, men who usually formed the bulk of troops in this area ferrying stores, clearing tracks, building roads and fulfilling the myriad other tasks necessary to bring this wild country into the fold of India's growing defensive structure and to build the foundation for future offensives over the border into Burma. By the time the Parachute Brigade had assumed control of this area, very few other British troops remained, with the exception of columns of trucks ferrying troops up and down the main Manipur Road between Imphal and Kohima. By mid-March, 50 Parachute Brigade was the only sizeable fighting unit left in this sector.

As the main fighting force in this area, and despite officially being on 'training manoeuvres', the Brigade's task in reality was to prevent Japanese scouting and infiltration by way of the various tracks that interlaced the region. The Brigade was also ordered to take over and further develop the various half-built defensive positions which 49 Brigade had started to prepare over the previous weeks but had not yet finished prior to their withdrawal.

The paratroopers' first few days in Manipur were punctuated by unseasonably heavy rains. The constant downpour turned the few passable tracks into sodden, muddy slides, which slowed all vehicle travel to a painfully slow crawl. But the Battalions made the most of their muddy encampments and endured the rains with quiet resignation. All the while, their energetic Brigade commander conducted multiple reconnaissances of the area and travelled to and from Headquarters at Imphal to receive further briefings and orders.

While at 23 Division headquarters, Hope-Thomson learned that a column of Japanese had been spotted moving from Pushing (to the east of the Brigade area of operations) and had attacked a V Force HQ element. Intelligence suggested that this column was likely to continue westwards and might well 'bump' (come in contact with) forward elements of 152 Battalion in the vicinity of Sheldon's Corner sometime over the next few days. This exciting intelligence immediately put paid to the fiction that Hope-Thomson's Brigade was engaged in a mere 'training exercise', and it was now highly likely that his men would soon meet the Japanese in battle. Nevertheless, at this stage no one believed that the Japanese would send much more than a few small reconnaissance patrols into the Brigade's area of operations (AO). Once again, and despite the example recently set by their own Chindit operations far behind enemy lines, the British had fallen into the familiar trap of believing that it is was impossible for large numbers of Japanese troops to traverse the hills and jungles of this part of Manipur.

Hope-Thomson was also provided with the welcome news that his Brigade would be augmented by the 4th Battalion 5th Regiment Mahratta Light Infantry (4/5 MLI), as well as two Companies of Khali Bahadur soldiers (Nepalese State troops), currently defending the eastern approaches to the village of Sangshak. The addition of 4/5 MLI substantially increased Hope-Thomson's manpower and firepower and fleshed out the otherwise under-strength Parachute Brigade. They were also a very experienced and battle-hardened Battalion, led by their commander Lieutenant Colonel Jack Trim.

The Khali Bahadurs on the other hand, while of the same Gurkha stock as the men of 153 Battalion, were not officially part of the Indian Army but were placed under command of the British for the duration of the conflict. Little is known about these men. They were probably tough as individual soldiers but lacked the leadership of professional British or Indian officers and NCOs. That said, the extra manpower was a great relief and assistance in defending the approaches to Sangshak village.

19 March 1944

The early morning cool of 19 March gave no inkling that 50 Parachute Brigade's peace was about to be shattered and its isolated forward screen located on Hill 7378 at Sheldon's Corner was soon to be engaged by lead elements of the advancing Japanese forces.

Rather, the early morning found Hope-Thomson considering the disposition of his troops and the continued implementation of the Brigade training programme. He was aware that the core of his Brigade was stretched over an area in excess of 30 square miles, a little too much for a Brigade which lacked sufficient motor transport. This arrangement was acceptable if the Brigade was only to provide early warning and act as a screen, but the men were too thinly spread to form a consolidated fighting force. His Brigade HQ was located on the trunk road at the 36-mile post (near Finches Corner), whereas his nearest Battalion, 152 Battalion, was occupying a number of hilltop positions near Sheldon's Corner, several miles to the east. And 153 Battalion was even further away, still on the road at the 10-mile post and moving slowly in the aftermath of the recent rains to regroup with the Brigade.

Hope-Thomson had further stretched his Brigade by placing his Medium Machine Gun (MMG) Company, sporting their old but still highly capable Vickers machine guns, to defend the important town of Ukhrul. The Mahrattas of 4/5 MLI were located in their old jungle base, the so-called 'Kidney Camp', located approximately halfway between Sheldon's Corner and Sangshak. Finally, the newly attached Khali Bahadur Regiment was still stationed in Sangshak, occupying the same positions they had held since 49 Brigade controlled the area.

Later that morning, Hope-Thomson received a visit from his commanding officer, Major General Ouvry Roberts, the commander of 23 Division. Roberts informed the assembled Brigade officers of the presence of the Japanese far to the south of Imphal. Intelligence reports suggested some small Japanese infiltration teams were operating south of Imphal, but fortunately none had been detected in 50 Parachute Brigade's sector. In Roberts' view, any Japanese attacks would inevitably come from much further south, since the mountains and jungles of this part of Manipur were deemed 'impenetrable' to large groups of enemy.

While Roberts' address was probably good for morale, it proved to be a wildly inaccurate statement from a senior officer who ought to have known better. As the IJA troops had showed again and again in the early days of the war, in the Malayan and Burmese campaigns, they were extremely adept at moving through 'impassable' jungle to envelop and cut off British troops, and the British should have been in no doubt about the Japanese ability to traverse difficult terrain. As would happen over the next few days, this apparently 'impassable' terrain would become the highway for two full Japanese divisions thrusting into eastern India. Hindsight is a remarkable thing, but even at the time, the British intelligence reports and assessments either appeared incredibly naïve or demonstrated wilful blindness in the face of what was already widely known about the IJA.

Providentially, however, 23 Division Intelligence issued a message later that afternoon to all Brigade and Box commanders, clarifying the situation around Imphal:

It is now clear that the Japs have embarked on a foolhardy [and] ambitious plan for the capture of IMPHAL. Japs may be expected to infiltrate in the IMPHAL plain any day and JIFFS will be used. Unless otherwise ordered, positions must be held to the last man as mob[ile] troops will come to their assistance. This is our opportunity to inflict a decisive defeat.[2]

The message showed that by now, both Division and higher headquarters had finally realized that the Japanese thrust to the south of Imphal was no mere infiltration but rather an all-out push to take the regional capital.

What the message omitted, however, was any mention of the two divisions of Japanese troops that were moving quickly westwards over mountain passes and tracks through the jungles of Manipur towards Ukhrul, Litan and Kohima. This was because the British did not know they were there and, as Roberts had confidently told 50 Parachute Brigade earlier in the day, even if there were any Japanese in their sector, it was believed they were likely to be small infiltration parties only and certainly nothing to be too concerned about.

Sheldon's Corner

Approximately 10 miles to the east of Finches Corner (but considerably further by foot), 152 Battalion formed the easternmost screen of both the Brigade and 23 Division. It was also the closest sizeable British unit to the Chindwin River and the border with Burma. Lieutenant Colonel Hopkinson, Commanding Officer of 152 Battalion, ordered his C Company to occupy defensive positions on Hill 7378 overlooking a track junction known as 'New Guinea'. Hopkinson then placed B Company approximately 1½ miles east of his HQ on a hill known as 'Gammon'. His final company, A Company, was situated with Battalion HQ roughly equidistant between the two forward companies and a little to the west, behind a feature known as 'Badger Hill'.

Each of the positions occupied high ground and overlooked important jeep tracks. They were sited partly for their excellent fields of observation and partly because they already possessed some limited defensive works, bunkers and trenches, left behind by the recently departed 49 Brigade.

Whilst the Battalion positions dominated the high ground, the Company positions were not mutually supporting.[3] They were quite spread out, the result of this being that an attack on one position could not immediately be responded to with effective fire from any of the others. Accordingly, if the Japanese managed to surround a Company position, it was at risk of being cut off and would need to fight on alone, unless or until additional men could be brought in from one of the nearby positions. These limitations on Gammon and New Guinea were known to Hopkinson, who deemed the risk acceptable in the circumstances, based on what he thought were the likely Japanese intentions in his area. In any event, there was little else that could be done to defend such a large expanse of hilly and jungle-clad territory with the relatively few troops at his disposal. Thus, each independent company would have to look to itself in case of an attack.

For his part, Hope-Thomson was not overly concerned about the tactical disposition of his forward Companies. Encouraged by both the very positive briefing from Roberts and the earlier briefings he had received at Imphal over the past week, he did not believe that extensive fixed defences were needed. Rather, he outlined an aggressive patrolling plan for the Brigade which he believed would be the best means of detecting the Japanese patrols that he expected to be infiltrating his area of operations in the near future.[4]

C Company – 152 Battalion

C Company, under Major John Fuller (the officer whose leg was in plaster from his previous parachuting accident), occupied the most north-westerly position of the Brigade on Hill 7378 overlooking 'New Guinea' (apparently so named because the vegetation in this area was so lush, complete with luxurious orchid blooms, that it reminded some previous traveller of that country's jungles.)[5] The defensive 'box' was located on a relatively steep, vaguely triangular hill, cut by numerous gullies and small watercourses. Most of its sides were heavily wooded, before the vegetation thinned out near the top. The base of the southern slope of the hill also marked the corner of the dry-season jeep track, where the track from Pushing to the east turned sharply south towards Sheldon's Corner, which itself was located about 1½ miles to the south and just past the Badger's Hill Battalion HQ box.

By 19 March 1944, C Company had been in place for two days, occupying the hill and improving their defensive positions. Since taking up their post, the men had been busy laying up stores of ammunition, food and water. As this position had previously been occupied by elements of 4/5 MLI, some initial defensive works had already been completed. The MLI positions were not, however, heavily fortified or reinforced, and this again reflected the thinking of the time that any Japanese who made it over the Chindwin and into this sector would probably consist of isolated patrols only. Slit trenches and minor defensive works would be more than sufficient! Indeed, before the Parachute Brigade took over the hill, many of the MLI units had been living in '*bashas*' (temporary huts constructed above ground and made from bamboo and other local materials) beside the tracks, clearly 'camping' in peacetime style rather than preparing for an imminent conflict in which the *bashas* would only serve to draw enemy attention and fire. However, once C Company took over, the *bashas* were removed, and the men lived and slept in their trenches and dugouts, preparing their positions for anything that might come their way.

Major Fuller, following the main body of his men, arrived at the C Company position on the evening of 17 March and took command of the Company. Remarkably, his leg was still in plaster, the result of the parachuting accident that had nearly sidelined him from this operation. The injury did not appear to slow him down in the least, and as his actions over the following few days would show, he lived up to the description of him as an enthusiastic, cheerful and confident officer. He was determined that nothing as trifling as a gammy leg would stop him from being in the thick of the action or from commanding his men.

Also arriving with Fuller was some much-needed 3-inch mortar ammunition. Besides its primary purpose in supplying the small mortar detachment of two mortar tubes which were co-located with the Company, some of his more enterprising men would filch a mortar bomb or two from the stockpile in order to put them to good use over the next few days in a number of very inventive ways.

While C Company was taking over the previous MLI positions, much work remained to be done to develop the position into a proper defensive 'box'. The term 'box' had become ubiquitous within the British Army in Burma over the past twelve months and was now used to refer to any sizeable defensive position. It is not known where the term originated, but the concept of what a 'box' should be was relatively simple and well known to all British troops in the theatre. In short, if the Japanese attacked in strength, instead of merely falling back and conducting a fighting withdrawal to a new defensive line (which had been the standard British practice early in the war), a unit of any size would form a defensive 'box' by going into all-round defence to stay and fight. The defending unit would then be re-supplied by a higher formation, probably from the air, until the enemy had spent all of its strength battering itself on the hard edges of the box.

Terrance Lane, a British Gunner deployed in Manipur at this time describes what he understood the defence of a box to mean: 'You were to stay where you are; it's your territory; hang on, no matter what happens, and we will supply you by air.'[6]

While the men were keen, C Company's digging and defensive works were slowed down considerably by the lack of motorized transport to bring in stores and by a lack of basic tools and equipment such as picks, shovels and wire.

19 March – Attack at Sheldon's Corner

By the morning of 19 March it is likely that weapons pits had been dug, machine guns sighted along likely enemy routes and food and ammunition stored up. While there are references to a 'bunker' in some of the war diaries, this structure was probably more modest than its name would suggest, at most just a more substantial dugout for the Company HQ and the important radio equipment.

The water point is one piece of C Company's field works which deserves particular mention. On arriving at New Guinea, and despite being surrounded by lush wet jungle, they found precious little drinking water nearby. This necessitated the digging of tanks, or large pits, in the ground and lining them with tarpaulins to trap and contain water. Thirst would be a recurring theme in all survivors' stories of the battles of Sheldon's Corner and Sangshak, and the lack of water would become critical over the next few days.

On the other hand, Fuller had slightly better luck when it came to his communications; these were good with both Battalion Headquarters at Badger and the MLI Battalion further back at Kidney Camp. When 49 Brigade had occupied the area it had laid signal cable between the various positions, and this had thankfully been left intact, ready for Major Fuller's signallers to tap into. In an era when wireless communications were still relatively new, and in an area where the terrain and atmospherics would often play havoc with radio signals, this land line allowed communications to be maintained between the key fixed locations and meant Fuller could remain in contact with his higher headquarters throughout the upcoming battle.

On the evening of 18 March, C Company was joined by a three-man patrol from A Company, led by Lieutenant Bill Gollop. The patrol had been sent down from A Company to check a previously unmarked mule track that the CO wished to investigate. Arriving at dusk, Gollop was astonished to see a line of fires in the distance, across the valley and in the direction of Pushing to the east. As no British or Indian troops were located near Pushing, the fires could only have one source – the Japanese! Sensibly, Lieutenant Gollop and his patrol decided to remain within the C Company perimeter for the night rather than risk being caught out alone in the jungle.

Gollop was not the only one to note that the Japanese had crossed the river and were on their way west. V Force patrols had been pulling back from their observation posts overlooking the Chindwin and started to send through reports that small groups of Japanese had crossed the river. As night fell, an exhausted V Force officer made his way into Fuller's position and told the C Company officers that the Japanese had now crossed the Chindwin in strength and were moving rapidly towards them. The V Force officer said that his men had been forced to hastily abandon their positions near Pushing to avoid being captured. They had no time either to move or to destroy the considerable stocks of ammunition and material they had cached in Pushing, with the result that they had been forced to leave a number of jeeps, ammunition and equipment to the Japanese.

Seeing the fires in the distance and hearing the V Force reports, Fuller became concerned about the men he had placed to man observation posts four miles to the east in the direction of Pushing. Not wanting to leave them exposed in the face of a likely enemy advance, Fuller obtained permission from Hopkinson to pull back his observation posts to the main C Company position.

A little before dawn on 19 March, Fuller ordered a number of patrols to move forward of the Company box on Hill 7378 and reconnoitre towards the east in the direction of Pushing. Fuller wanted to confirm whether there really were any Japanese coming towards him.

Fuller was in good spirits that morning, despite all the evidence that strongly suggested a sizeable force of Japanese soldiers could soon be approaching. He turned to his surprise guests and invited Lieutenant Gollop and his patrol to stay and have breakfast. But as Gollop's men were Muslim and the men of C Company were all Hindu, the former would not have been able to eat with C Company. So Gollop declined the offer, rounded up his patrol and started walking back up the track towards Badger.

However, just as he started to move back up the main track, the excited observation party, mounted in a jeep, came driving back at full speed into the Company position. Lieutenant Faul, the commander of the observation patrol, jumped out of the jeep and reported spotting a large group of about 200 Japanese in the vicinity of Pushing moving quickly westwards and closely following them. Faul said he had left a few booby traps as 'surprises' for the Japanese and to slow their advance. There are no records of exactly what booby traps he set, but we do know that they did almost nothing to slow the advance of the Japanese, who were by now very close behind him.

Lieutenant Gollop needed no second warning and pushed his patrol to move back to Badger as quickly as possible. As he said later, 'I took the decision that my chaps, being Muslim, would rather fight or die with their own kind, and we shot off back to A Company. For that reason I am alive today: you will know what happened to C Company.'[7]

Lieutenant Faul's report was completely accurate, and C Company's first contact with the enemy was reported to have occurred around 0830hrs. Clearly, this was not the minor reconnaissance patrol suggested by Divisional intelligence (or indeed by Roberts' briefing a few short hours earlier), but a substantial Japanese infantry element. When the Japanese hit the forward slopes of Hill 7378 they did not hesitate, but let off a furious fusillade, to which the men of the Parachute Company responded in kind. It was reported that the initial firing was so intense that it was even heard by elements of 4/5 MLI, who at that time were camped over three miles to the west at Kidney Camp.

Upon encountering the C Company position, the Japanese utilized their standard tactic of trying to get around the flanks, feeling for the edges of the position. At this stage, they attacked mainly with small arms including rifles and light machine guns. British reports also noted the use of 'grenade dischargers', a type of mini-mortar (sometimes erroneously referred to as a 'knee mortar') commonly carried by front-line Japanese infantry that could lob a standard Japanese hand grenade much further than a man could throw it and with a higher trajectory, making it useful for attacking weapon pits and dugouts.

The initial attack, although fierce, was a relatively short and sharp affair lasting no more than ten or fifteen minutes. It appeared to be a classic first encounter and had obviously surprised both sides, as this was the first serious opposition that the Japanese had met in this area. It was also C Company's first taste of battle.

The surprise wore off quickly, and the Japanese set about methodically probing and then attacking the C Company position, which blocked the track junction north towards Khangoi and the substantial stores and ammunition dumps at Ukhrul. Being such an important location, the Japanese could not merely ignore or bypass it. Hill 7378 needed to be taken.

In front of C Company, down in the jungle at the foot of the hill, the Japanese were calling out to each other, forgoing silence for the need to coordinate their troops. Not content with mere skirmishing, the Japanese were now determined to take the position and lined up their men accordingly. At 0930 hrs, just one hour after the first shots were fired, the Japanese resumed their attack in earnest, assaulting a forward position of C Company from two directions simultaneously in order to pin down then destroy the defenders. Eventually, the Japanese put in a charge, racing uphill out of the jungle with a sword-wielding officer at their head. C Company's forward line was completely overtaken by this charge, which led to the deaths of one British officer and about twenty men. The Japanese then poured into the forward pits and took control of the position. The attack had been so ferocious that only a single Indian had survived, a lone messenger who had luckily been sent back to the main Company position with a report just prior to the attack.

While commanding the unfolding battle from the middle of his Company position high on the hilltop, Fuller remained in constant contact with his

Battalion HQ on Badger, who in turn regularly relayed his reports back to Brigade HQ at Finches Corner. When his report eventually reached the Brigade Commander, Hope-Thomson said that he was initially stunned. 'Incredulity' was the word he used to describe his reaction upon receiving the initial report,[8] since attacks of this scale and ferocity had not been foreseen in the sector. Quickly regaining his composure, and after considering the implications of the report, Hope-Thomson immediately set off towards Badger to confer with his Battalion Commander and to review the unfolding situation at first-hand.

Less than two miles to the south of Fuller in his Battalion Headquarters on Badger, Hopkinson also became concerned at this sudden attack on his forward Company. Needing to get a better view of the battle, he decided to move up to the summit of his hill in order to establish what he termed 'a forward Battalion HQ'. While only a few hundred yards away, the summit gave him a much better view of the surrounding country, including Hill 7378, than his bunker on the other side of the hill. He was soon joined by a number of Brigade officers, including the Brigade Commander, the Brigade intelligence officer, Captain Richards, Lieutenant Colonel Trim, CO of 4/5 MLI and his intelligence officer, Lieutenant Pyara. They had arrived quite quickly by jeep from Brigade HQ and the MLI position at Kidney Camp.

As soon as the command team moved up to the newly established forward Battalion HQ, they wasted no time is assessing the situation and discussing how best to support Fuller and his men. But while they were pointing at their maps and discussing the available options, the officers started to sense that there was something moving in the distance somewhere to the east of them. Following the trail from west to east with their binoculars, it soon became apparent that a large party of Japanese soldiers, perhaps 700- to 900-strong, were marching quickly along the track from Pushing towards the C Company position. Incredibly, and despite the risk from Allied aircraft, the Japanese were making no attempt to conceal their movements, marching in the middle of the day and clearly prioritizing speed over stealth.

Ordinarily, such a large and obvious mass of troops would have been an absolute gift to British attack aircraft or artillery fire. Unfortunately, none of the Brigade's artillery or mortars were in range, and aircraft were not currently available. Thus there was little that Hope-Thomson could do except watch the growing mass of Japanese move towards them with concern and a certain amount of incredulity.

Back on Hill 7378, and buoyed by their initial success, the Japanese put in a further series of quick charges uphill against the main C Company position. This time, the Indian troops were ready for them. Fuller's men fought back steadfastly and, instead of seeing the forward pits overrun, the Indian paratroopers were successful in repelling the Japanese charges. This time it was the Japanese who suffered heavy casualties, with only minimal Indian casualties in response.

Despite having their blood up after their initial success, the repeated charges were starting to take their toll on the Japanese, and after four hours of battle, by about 1300 hrs, their attacks had run out of steam. Sensing that they could not break in at this stage, the Japanese commander pulled his men back into the jungle to reorganize and regroup. He also knew that additional troops were coming to support him, and thus a short pause would give him the ability to launch a bigger and more aggressive attack. However, while the main body of soldiers pulled back into the undergrowth, the Japanese placed several snipers high up in the trees in order to harry Fuller's men and pick off any C Company defenders who raised their heads above the top of their weapon pits. The Japanese snipers were lethally efficient and proved to be a constant thorn in the British side, both at Hill 7378 and over the ensuing few days at Sangshak. By mid-afternoon the snipers had claimed a further two Indian soldiers.

* * *

While C Company was busy keeping at bay the Japanese, who seemed to be mounting more attacks from multiple directions, the command group on Badger were developing a plan to relieve C Company and counter-attack the Japanese. It is notable that, even at this early stage, Hope-Thomson's instincts were to have his men in contact form a box and then counter-attack when and where they could. This was a very active and aggressive form of response, much in keeping with the forward-leaning style of paratroopers, and if executed well, offered the best chance of repelling Japanese attacks.

Having considered the options, Hope-Thomson agreed with Hopkinson's plan to commit 152 Battalion's only reserve, namely A Company, commanded by Major Gillett. Rather than march directly into the C Company position, and therefore straight into the middle of an active firefight, A Company was to move generally north-east towards but slightly to the rear of New Guinea, and then swing behind the Japanese and attack them from the rear. It was this intended hooking manoeuvre that earned A Company the moniker of 'the swingers' in the official 23 Division War Diary. Meanwhile, D Company 4/5 MLI, commanded by Captain Steele, was tasked to move north from their current hide at Kidney Camp and establish an ambush in the vicinity of Khangoi, cutting off access to any Japanese who attempted to bypass the C Company position or try to move further westwards.

It was a solid plan but also a dangerous one which would rely on A Company achieving complete surprise and taking the Japanese unawares. Ordinarily, an attacker should have a three to one numerical advantage over his opponent. Hope-Thomson knew the enemy strength was at least 200–300 at this time, while the *combined* strength of A and C Companies was only about 200 men, not taking into account that C Company was pinned down and had already taken significant casualties. C Company at least had some defensive works to rely on, whereas A Company, if discovered prior to successfully hooking in behind the Japanese, would have little protection except for the trees and scrub of the jungle itself.

While the Command team on Badger were developing their plan, the rest of the Brigade was responding to a flurry of signals that the Brigadier was at the same time dictating for dispatch to his HQ. Brigade HQ was instructed to immediately take up hasty defensive positions around the 36-mile marker, while 4/5 MLI was ordered to move a Company from its hide at Kidney Camp to Nungshong to protect the Battalion's left flank.

It was also decided that Trim would send A Company to move quickly down the track towards the Badger HQ position and provide additional protection for the now largely defenceless 152 Battalion HQ. Upon receipt of their orders, A Company 4/5 MLI made hasty preparations and left Kidney Camp at about 1500hrs to commence the three-hour march to Badger.

Having outlined his plan and given his orders, Brigadier Hope-Thomson bade farewell to Hopkinson, wished him luck and then started the trek back to his HQ at Mile 36, stopping for a brief meal at Kidney Camp at 1630hrs. At around the same time, A Company 152 Battalion moved off through the jungle towards New Guinea, guided in part by the sounds of rifle and automatic fire which intermittently still punctuated the usual sounds of the jungle. By 1700hrs Hopkinson was left alone again on Badger with only a small protection party and his signals detachment.

Fortunately, A Company 4/5 MLI under command of Major Holland made very good time and arrived at Hopkinson's headquarters on Badger just before dark at around 1800hrs. Hopkinson didn't know it, but he was lucky to have Holland's men to protect his HQ. They were an impressive group of very experienced jungle fighters who in 1943 had acted as the demonstration Company at Fourteenth Army's Jungle Warfare School.[9] They knew their business and would have been a great comfort to Hopkinson, who was probably feeling very exposed, since all of his own Companies were already committed to the battle, leaving no troops to protect his headquarters or to act as a reserve.

But even with the arrival of Holland's soldiers, Hopkinson remained worried about the Japanese he had earlier seen moving to the east. To these

19 March – Attack at Sheldon's Corner

initial sightings there was now added an increased amount of noise, together with the lights of several motor vehicles bouncing up and down the track from Pushing. The vehicles were very likely the British jeeps captured from V Force outposts near Pushing, and the Japanese were putting them to good use to ferry ammunition up to their forward troops. This could only spell further trouble for 152 Battalion.

* * *

While C Company was fighting its gallant defensive battle at New Guinea, Brigade HQ continued to update 23 Division and organize the rest of the Brigade. Staff officers at 23 Division expressed some surprise at the sudden appearance of a large group of enemy out from the jungle as if from nowhere to mount an aggressive attack on 50 Brigade. 'The enemy strength was about 200 and their rate of advance over difficult country was most surprising', ran the understated narrative in the official 23 Division War Diary. As if to try and explain, however inadequately, the sudden and unexpected appearance of the Japanese, the War Diary went on to say, 'Their camouflage was good'![10] Recognizing the growing threat, 23 Division ordered the entire Ukhrul position to be evacuated and the supply dumps to be destroyed.

Meanwhile, at around dusk on 19 March, the Gurkhas of 153 Battalion had just arrived at Imphal by motor transport, completely unaware of the unfolding battle at New Guinea. General rumours about possible Japanese infiltration had been circulating in the rear areas, including a rumour that the Japanese had already cut the main Manipur Road. This last news was known to be false by 153 Battalion, as they had just driven along that very road. Nevertheless, besides a short air raid, the Battalion was largely unperturbed by the rumours as it set about taking up overnight lodgings in several abandoned government buildings. This nonchalance would quickly evaporate, however, as they learned that their sister parachute battalion 'was in difficulties'[11] around Sheldon's Corner. Orders came through, and a Company of 153 Battalion was ordered to move immediately to Ukhrul – notwithstanding that Ukhrul itself had just been abandoned.

* * *

Back at Hill 7378, shadows lengthened and the inky darkness of a jungle night fell soon after 1800hrs. The men of C Company, crouched low in their weapons pits, were straining their ears for any sounds of the enemy who they knew were only a few hundred yards away down the hill and hidden in the thick jungle.

No one dared light a fire or cook any food, and all thoughts and senses were focussed on the attacks that they knew were sure to come sometime that night.

The Japanese welcomed the coming of night, confident that the darkness would provide them with the cover they needed to move up unseen close to the British positions before charging and breaking in. As the night wore on, the Japanese resumed their probing attacks and fired brief fusillades at Fuller's men, testing the boundaries of their defences as well as trying to find an opening between the small bands of tired Indian troops. This methodical and constant action on the part of the Japanese steadily wore down the defenders.

However, the constant attacks would also negatively affect the Japanese and distract from their overall campaign objectives. As all the Japanese officers and men knew, Mutaguchi's plan called for great speed and replenishment of supplies from the enemy. While still adequate at this early stage of the campaign, the men's supplies were not so abundant as to permit them the luxury of wasting time on minor engagements. Instead of bypassing what was a relatively small British position, the Japanese poured significant troops and ammunition into clearing Hill 7378, which had the effect of slowing their overall advance in this sector by at least a day.

This was a delay that the Japanese could ill afford.

Further up the hill, and despite the constant firing and pressure which was kept up throughout the night, Fuller reported back to Battalion HQ that his Company was still holding on. He seemed to be in good spirits, and while Fuller's apparent confidence may have heartened Hopkinson somewhat, it did not eliminate his worry. Hopkinson had no artillery to support C Company, and by now B Company, located to the east on Gammon, was also starting to take sporadic fire from Japanese patrols moving from Sheldon's Corner towards them. Fortunately, the Japanese did not follow up their potshots at Gammon, and their firing in that sector quickly died down.

Notwithstanding the frequent firing into C Company, Fuller was able to keep in close contact with Battalion HQ throughout the night as his wireless sets continued to work well, not something to be taken for granted in this area. It was because of this open line of communication that we have a relatively clear picture of what happened during the night of 19 March. We know that Lieutenant Andrew Faul once again displayed his enthusiasm and skill at booby-trapping, when he silently moved out about 200 yards in front of the Company position and set up a trap consisting of a series of eight mortar bombs tied together with a trip wire. Having set his trap, he crept quietly back to the safety of the Company lines. Unfortunately, when the Japanese launched their next fierce assault at around 0200hrs, the bombs failed to go off. Whether the trap was faulty or the Japanese were just lucky is not known. But in any event, C Company was once again able to beat back the latest Japanese assault, mainly by the skilful employment of rifle and Bren gun fire.

Fuller was now under no illusions as to the size of the enemy arrayed against him, and he estimated that there were at least several Battalions of Japanese attackers surrounding his position. This was very likely an inaccurate count, but it is thought that at a minimum there was a Battalion of Japanese in the immediate vicinity of his hill. Thankfully, the Japanese had not yet hauled up any artillery, and thus Fuller's men were spared a bombardment. Nevertheless, the weight of attackers was great, and the volume of grenades, rifle and machine gun fire meant that the already strained defenders would soon be overcome.

At around 0200hrs the Japanese renewed their charges en masse on the C Company position, achieving a breakthrough at around 0230hrs. By this time, the Indian paratroopers were in a bad way, and Fuller radioed back to Battalion HQ that their perimeter had been breached by large numbers of the enemy and that reinforcements were desperately needed.

The battle was not a one-way street, however, and Fuller estimated that Japanese casualties must have been significant, in large part due to the way that they attacked 'in close formation with the attackers very bunched offering good targets'.[12] This style of frontal charge, led by a sword-wielding officer and accompanied by much yelling from the following soldiers, bayonets held level as they ran, was to be a constant feature of the Japanese style of combat in this area. Lieutenant John Weaver, an officer of 153 Battalion who would himself be on the receiving end of similar charges in the days to come, remarked that 'the Japanese were extraordinarily brave' and had a 'terribly aggressive spirit', but for all that they were very impulsive. The tactics were reminiscent of the First World War, charging trenches over open ground, with the inevitable result that the attackers often suffered significant casualties. And so it was here on the slopes of Hill 7378, as Japanese casualties started to pile up on the forward slopes and among the recently captured forward pits.

But despite the casualties they were taking, the Japanese were wearing the British and Indian troops down. During the night a further twelve Indian Army soldiers had been killed, including two British officers, and a similar number sustained wounds. The high number of officers killed and wounded would be a constant feature of the fighting over the next week, the result of which was that command and motivation of the troops often devolved to and depended on the Indian and Gurkha NCOs. To illustrate this, after the loss of his British officers on Hill 7378, Havildar Makmud Din did not hesitate to take up the baton and lead his men. He was particularly noted for tirelessly darting from pit to pit to transport ammunition to the forward troops or to help to drag a wounded soldier to cover. These gallant actions helped to steel the men in the forward trenches but they also put this senior NCO in constant danger until, almost inevitably, he too would be struck down during the fighting in the early morning. Suffering from serious wounds, Makmud Din would himself need to be dragged to join the growing band of wounded lying in a covered position at the makeshift Company aid post. He eventually died from his wounds later in the morning.

Another British officer killed during the night-time attacks was Lieutenant Ronald Bolton, a 22-year-old native of Essex who had been with the Battalion for just over a year. Photographs of Lieutenant Bolton show a young man full of promise and pride, obviously relishing his posting to India. During periods of leave, he took the opportunity to travel around India and seized many chances to be photographed with young ladies. The most captivating photograph of Bolton is a rather irreverent shot of him sitting on the ground in his summer uniform, clutching his knees to his chest and sticking out his tongue at the photographer – probably one of the young ladies who accompanied him on his travels. It is a childlike and innocent photo, full of fun, and captures the playful side of this young man.

But play was far from Bolton's thoughts on the night of 19 March, with reports showing that he was last seen leading his men at the front of the Company position, fending off yet another Japanese attack. As the fighting intensified, and with his men unable to hold their ground, Bolton covered them as they moved past him and withdrew back up the hill towards the main Company position. Taking up a grenade to fling at the enemy, Bolton was hit by rifle fire and severely wounded. His men had already completed their withdrawal, but when Bolton was hit he was already too far from them to be pulled back to safety. Later, when there was a lull in the fighting, one of his men was able to crawl back to where Bolton lay. But it was too late, and as they had feared, by the time they found him, Lieutenant Ronald Bolton had already died from his wounds.

* * *

C Company was now running dangerously short of able-bodied men to man the defences. Including the initial attack that had overrun the forward position, subsequent attacks and sniping, and the main frontal charge at 0200 hrs, C Company had now lost approximately three British officers and thirty-four men, with a further two officers and seventeen men wounded. At full strength, a parachute company would only comprise about 120 men at most. Thus Fuller's losses so far were approximately 30 per cent killed and another 15 per cent wounded. These were significant numbers for a small unit, and ordinarily such losses would render a unit 'combat ineffective', unable to put up any further effective resistance. One can imagine the thoughts of the surviving troops, surrounded on all sides by their dead and seriously wounded comrades, with a large number of unseen Japanese attackers hidden in the trees, jungle surrounding them, and nowhere to retreat to and no other option but to fight on.

Fortunately for C Company, and without warning, at around 0300hrs the Japanese suddenly broke contact. The most likely reason was that their men needed to rest and regroup. The doggedness of C Company's resistance had taken the Japanese by surprise, and they had also suffered significant casualties of their own during their repeated charges at the entrenched positions. Although they knew that they had killed or wounded a large number of defenders, the Japanese had still been unable to effectively break through. So, about three hours before dawn on 20 March, the attackers withdrew into the jungle surrounding the lower slopes of the hill. C Company noted that a great deal of noise was made by the Japanese as they tried to remove their casualties, which by now littered the slopes of Hill 7378. The noise was inexplicable given the reputation of the Japanese as stealthy and efficient jungle fighters, but several sources note the Japanese's apparent lack of noise discipline when not immediately facing the enemy.

After a short pause, the Japanese also started calling out to the defenders in Urdu and Punjabi, using a megaphone. Apparently, the calls in Urdu were 'extoll[ing] the virtues of Japanese rule',[13] and it is likely that this propaganda was delivered by the INA JIFs who accompanied the force. It is not known whether C Company replied, but since the JIFS were generally hated by most of the British Indian troops, it is likely that their calls were either ignored or may have sparked some colourful insults in response.

Thus the first day of fighting came to an end, with the men of C Company grimly holding on to Hill 7378 while listening to the sounds of the Japanese dragging off their dead and assailing them with propaganda. The Indian soldiers were quiet as they caught their breath, restocked their ammunition and waited for the next charge that they knew would come, sooner or later.

Chapter 5

20 March – The New Guinea Roadblock

Throughout the early hours of the 20th, Hopkinson continued to receive intermittent reports from his beleaguered C Company on Hill 7378. He could hear the sounds of the battle drifting over the valley towards him on Badger and was relieved when the Japanese attacks appeared to slacken and then stop at around 0300hrs. But he knew that this was only a temporary reprieve, and that the enemy was certain to resume their assault come the dawn.

Unfortunately for Hopkinson, his options and freedom of manoeuvre were limited. He was painfully aware that C Company was facing a great onslaught on its own and he was desperate to relieve them, but he had very few troops at hand to send into the fight. Despite having left several hours earlier, nothing had been heard from A Company. Had they bumped the enemy and been destroyed themselves? Had they got lost in the thick jungle? Or was it merely a case of poor communications – an all-too-common occurrence in this part of Manipur? In any event, with A Company unaccounted for, this only left him with the remaining elements of the MLI Company that had come up earlier to help secure his HQ.

With few options but needing to do something to assist Fuller, Hopkinson decided to dispatch one of the few remaining platoons that he had on Badger, 8 Platoon under Lieutenant Ghayal, whose orders were to take a wireless set and to get as close to C Company as possible. They were then to create something of a diversion and report back on enemy positions and movements in the vicinity of Hill 7378. While Ghayal readied his Platoon for their dangerous mission, Hopkinson contacted Kidney Camp and requested yet more support from 4/5 MLI to be sent forward as soon as possible. Trim immediately agreed to send his own C Company up to Badger. But even if they left immediately they could only hope to arrive at around 0700hrs at the earliest.

It was a case of robbing Peter to pay Paul. By sending his C Company up to Badger, Trim was leaving himself and his HQ at Kidney Camp dangerously short of men and vulnerable to any attacks that struck his sector. Realizing the danger, Trim pulled in his remaining men from Khangoli to reinforce his own Battalion HQ. Both Battalion commanders knew that they were facing significant danger and started to pull in their outlying troops in order to 'circle the wagons'.

In the early light of the false dawn (around 0450hrs), Fuller reported to Hopkinson that the Japanese appeared to be forming up and getting ready to renew their attacks. Hopkinson had nothing to give Fuller in response, as still nothing had been heard from A Company or from the recently dispatched 8 Platoon under Lieutenant Ghayal.

Knowing what Fuller would soon be facing, Hopkinson had a difficult choice: should he keep his remaining troops to man the defences at Badger or should he throw them in now to try and help C Company? In the end, Hopkinson decided to try and help Fuller, and so ordered the remainder of the MLI Company under Holland to move out immediately to support C Company. It was to follow the same route as the MLI Platoon had taken the night before, and it too was ordered to try to get through to C Company. One senses the grim desperation of a commander with no further options; no reserves to commit and no artillery or air support. As Hopkinson would later remark, 'There was little else I could do to help C Company as all reserves were now committed.'

Back at New Guinea, and knowing that no further help would be immediately available, Fuller decided to counter-attack with the troops he had left. It was a bold move given the depleted number of men he had available, but it worked. The short sharp thrust at the Japanese took them by surprise, and the paratroopers' sudden rush pushed the enemy back and allowed the Indian troops to reclaim some of their forward positions. It was yet another example of the tough and gallant efforts of the men of C Company to hold on to their hill. It is clear that they were no mere passive defenders, stuck in their holes and waiting for the inevitable, but were actively and aggressively engaged, using everything at their disposal to eject the Japanese from their positions. Unfortunately, the sheer weight of Japanese numbers told against them. At around 0600hrs the see-saw of the battle had again tipped back in favour of the attackers. After their latest charge, an urgent call was made to Battalion Headquarters and the bad news was relayed to Hopkinson – both Fuller and the Company 2IC, Captain Roseby, were wounded, and the enemy had once again broken into the perimeter. Shortly afterwards, a follow-up message confirmed that both Fuller and Roseby had died from their wounds. By this point, C Company was almost leaderless, left under the command of the pitifully few remaining officers and NCOs.

In the early morning gloom, the fighting became closer and more personal. The Japanese had advanced right up to the British lines and weapon pits, meaning that this was not longer an exchange of long-range sniping but a close-quarters battle of sword, bayonet, rifle and grenades.

Despite the losses on the British side, by some miracle the men were still holding on. Radio and telephone messages continued to be relayed to Battalion HQ, but these were becoming less and less frequent as every man left in C Company was now engaged in desperate attempts to hold back the enemy.

Back on Badger, Captain Tom Monaghan, Hopkinson's adjutant, was monitoring the radio traffic. He listened to the hurried reports coming in which told how one of the Platoon commanders, Lieutenant Andrew Faul, was encouraging his men and continuing to take the fight to the Japanese. Unfortunately, Faul, too, was soon killed, leaving even fewer British officers to lead the remnants of C Company.

* * *

Roadblock

Two overladen jeeps left the Badger Hill headquarters at around 0600hrs, hurrying towards the sound of gunfire and the beleaguered C Company at New Guinea. The dusty green vehicles were commanded by a signals officer from 152 Battalion, accompanied by a protection party of fifteen men from the MLI's A Company, 9 Platoon. The remainder of A Company under their OC, Major Holland, received orders from Hopkinson to 'proceed forthwith to New Guinea to do what was possible to relieve pressure on C Company, 152 Bn'. With no more vehicles (or MT, Motor Transport, as vehicles were usually described) available, Holland and his remaining platoons moved out on foot, hoping to link up with their own 8 Platoon, who had been sent out a few hours previously.

An hour into their march, however, and just as they were approaching the New Guinea corner and the foothills of Hill 7378, Holland was literally 'stopped in his tracks' by a strong roadblock that the Japanese had established between the Badger position and New Guinea. The two jeeps that had been sent out just before Holland left Badger had been shot up and lay wrecked at the side of the road. The signals officer and three of his men were found lying dead on the track, riddled with bullets. They had been ambushed before they could even get to Hill 7378, while the rest of the protection party were nowhere to be found.

* * *

The roadblock was a tactic that the Japanese frequently used and had all but perfected throughout the South-East Asian area of operations. In their lightning drive down through Malaya to Singapore in 1941, the Japanese would frequently employ roadblocks against the largely road-bound, vehicle-borne British. As Lieutenant General William 'Bill' Slim (then commander of the XIV Army) would write in *Defeat into Victory*:

> Being tied to a road proved to be our undoing. It made us fight on a narrow front, while the enemy, moving wide through the jungle, encircled us and placed a force behind us across the only road. The Japanese had developed the art of the road-block to perfection; we seemed to have no answer to it. If we stood and fought where we were, unless the road were reopened, we starved. So invariably we had turned back to clear the road-block, breaking through it usually at the cost of vehicles, and in any case making another withdrawal.[1]

* * *

Here at New Guinea, the Japanese had established a hasty roadblock consisting of a number of felled trees placed across the road, supported by firing positions and snipers on both sides of the track. It was simple but lethally effective. A sketch of the roadblock prepared by Holland shows it to be just a few hundred yards in front of the Hill 7378 position, just forward of where the track bends to the south. At this point the track ran along a cutting, with hills and knolls rising sharply from the trackside to the east. Also to the east of the track was a series of three small knolls running in a line roughly north to south. Machine guns or LMGs were sited on the southernmost knoll facing down the track – straight along A Company's line of advance and overlooking the main roadblock from the second knoll. Each of the other knolls had Japanese soldiers manning LMGs. To the west of the track was thick scrub or jungle, where the Japanese employed yet another favourite tactic, placing a number of snipers up in the tree canopy. Rounding out the ambushers' armoury were either light mortars or soldiers holding grenade dischargers immediately behind the middle knoll, and more LMGs to the north beyond New Guinea and on the slopes of Hill 7378 itself. All in all, this constituted a formidable obstacle, a massive amount of firepower in a classic Japanese ambush position.

Pulling up just short of the roadblock, and confronted by the sight of the dead British and Indian troops in front of him, Holland knew he was in trouble. He had little time to plan and so decided just to dive in and assault the roadblock and the knolls in a 'blitz'-style attack. At this stage he still had hopes of quickly breaking through the roadblock and reaching the surrounded paratroopers beyond, but he knew that only speed and daring could get his men through. He quickly yelled orders, forming his 9 Platoon on the right side of the track and 7 Platoon to the left. Both 8 Platoon and the headquarters platoon were placed directly behind 7 Platoon in reserve. Once the order was given, the platoons moved forward, heading for their respective objectives under the 'crump, crump' of light covering fire provided by the 2-inch mortar section attached to Holland's Company.

But almost as soon as they started to move forward, all platoons encountered heavy fire from both LMGs and the snipers perched up in the trees. With little time for tactical creativity or finesse, 9 Platoon rushed forward and attacked the first knoll, over the relatively open ground, in a strong frontal assault. It was a fast and aggressive action which saw 9 Platoon sweep over the knoll and quickly silence the Japanese section holding it. But just as they cleared this position they started to come under more intense fire, laid down by the Japanese holding the subsequent knolls, and this quickly brought their advance to a halt.

Over on the left side of the track, 7 and 8 Platoons punched straight ahead and parallel to the track before turning to attack the second and third knolls from the flank. 7 Platoon, under command of Jemadar Laxuman Desai, initially blitzed 100 yards to their front. Accounts show that the MLI Platoon held its fire until it was just 15 yards from the forward Japanese LMG positions. They then opened fire, silencing two LMGs and clearing several tree snipers with a furious burst of fire from their rifles, Brens and sub-machine guns.

Following this success, Holland yelled out to Jemadar Desai to attack towards the right and try to support 9 Platoon, pinned down on the other side of the road. What this meant, however, was that 7 Platoon would need to cross the open track – a highly dangerous manoeuvre given that the Japanese had set up the ambush to take advantage of the clear lines of sight down the track. Also, the other side of the road had a deep base cutting, which would make scrambling up the steep and wooded knoll very difficult for the attacking troops.

Nevertheless, 7 Platoon immediately obeyed and turned to the right to support 9 Platoon on the first knoll. As they crossed the road, however, intense fire was directed at them from the third knoll just to their north. This fire came directly down the track, in enfilade, in exactly the manner that all infantry soldiers are taught to use against an attacking enemy. Then, as 7 Platoon stepped out to cross the track, grenades started to rain down from the second knoll. The attack stalled, and 7 Platoon started to take casualties.

The mortar section, commanded by Subedar Shripat Vishwashrao, attempted to provide some covering fire as 7 Platoon formed up for another attack. This attack was also repulsed, and the intense fire from the Japanese positions even disrupted Company Headquarters, who were following 7 Platoon at some distance to the rear. Holland and his command party scattered and attempted to find some cover.

On their third attempt, 7 Platoon managed to cross the track and scramble up the steep bank, but not before Jemadar Laxuman Desai himself was hit and seriously wounded. He and number of his men had been hit whilst crossing the tracking and fell right in the middle of the road. Despite being seriously wounded, Laxuman continued to encourage his men forward, and several managed to haul themselves up through the scrub and reach the top of the second knoll. Under covering fire of his runner, Lance Naik Appa Desai, the young Indian officer continued to call out encouragement to his men even though he was badly wounded and still lying exposed in the middle of the track.

Fire continued to be sent straight down the track towards the wounded men. Despite this, Lance Naik Desai refused to leave his commander. He continued to fire up towards the top of knoll, attempting to suppress the enemy LMG and displaying amazing bravery and loyalty to his commander, for which he was later awarded the Military Medal. His citation reads in part:

> With complete disregard of enemy fire he helped drag his platoon commander off the road and returned to carry another wounded man from the same place. He himself was wounded in doing so but nevertheless again returned to the road and alternately hurled grenades and fired his tommy gun into the Jap post not 10 yards to his front, thus enabling other casualties to be evacuated. When his ammunition was exhausted, from his exposed position he shouted abuse at the enemy and encouragement to his platoon. He had finally to be ordered to retire, refusing assistance.[2]

For his part and for his 'outstanding leadership and courage' in leading this attack, Jemadar Desai would later be awarded the Military Cross.[3]

Having succeeded in scrambling up the steep cutting, the remaining men of 7 Platoon quickly cleared the second knoll of all Japanese except for an elusive soldier with a rifle and grenades who, despite 7 Platoon's best efforts, was never found. He was a very lucky man!

While 7 Platoon was engaged in their brutal charge across the road towards the second knoll, 8 Platoon and Company headquarters were engaged in their own blitz parallel to the track and up towards a position parallel with the third knoll. They moved steadily forward, clearing tree snipers with bursts from their tommy guns. However, they were surprised when they came parallel to the third knoll and found themselves in relatively open ground. This space afforded little cover and was in fact the start of the southern slope of Hill 7378 proper. Holland had originally hoped to link up with the forward troops of C Company here, but it quickly became very clear that the only troops to their front were Japanese. As they hit the edge of the open ground, Holland's men started to be fired upon from both their front left and front right. Looking up the hill, C Company was nowhere to be seen; the only troops to their front were now Japanese. Holland saw movement to his right and on the other side of the third knoll which suggested to him that the Japanese were moving up their reserves to reinforce the fight at the roadblock.

Quickly assessing the situation at the forward edge of the battle parallel with the third knoll, Holland realized that his position was untenable. While his Company had performed magnificently in clearing both the roadblock and the Japanese positions on the surrounding knolls, Holland was unable to consolidate his position. He could not go any further, and with the realization that the C Company paratroopers had been overrun, Holland decided to pull back his troops to New Guinea proper and form a defensive box. This would enable him to collect and care for his wounded and provide a strong enough base to protect his Company while he waited for further orders.

C Company's final stand

Back on Hill 7378, Lieutenant Easton, the last surviving British officer, was composing a message to headquarters. At around 1015 hrs he radioed C Company's last message to Hopkinson, saying that the Japanese had attacked in great strength and had killed many of his men. Ammunition was practically exhausted, and the few survivors were attempting to withdraw to Badger. C Company had been completely overrun, and no further resistance was possible. After sending the message he presumably destroyed the radio before making his way down the southern slope of Hill 7378, towards the scene of the roadblock battle, together with a handful of his men.

No one knows exactly what happened during the last hour on the C Company position, but it was certainly desperate. Several accounts note that the Company was short of men and, critically, ammunition. Following Easton's final message the official War Diaries are silent. However, Harry Seaman in his account of the battle quotes from a Japanese Regimental memoire which supposedly records the final moments of C Company's stand as follows:

By mid-morning the enemy's fire slackened considerably. Suddenly, from the top of the hill, a small group of about twenty men charged down towards us, firing and shouting in a counter-attack. However, between us was a wide ravine which they had been unable to see, and of those who were still alive some fell into it in their rush onwards while the rest had no choice but to surrender. A few escaped. At the very top of the position an officer appeared in sight, put a pistol to his head and shot himself in full view of everyone below. Our men fell silent, deeply impressed by such a brave act ... At Point 7378 the 3rd Battalion [the attacking Japanese battalion] suffered 160 casualties in the action, with one company and two platoon commanders killed and another four officers wounded ... The enemy had resisted with courage and skill.[4]

Whether this account is true or not will never be known. It is certainly true that in the early morning the British defenders were desperately short of ammunition, and the charge down the hill described above may well have been the counter-attack mentioned in the earlier radio reports to Hopkinson. But what of the apparent suicide of an officer at the top of the hill? While it is certainly *possible*, it seems very unlikely, given that by this time almost all the British officers had already been killed and the remaining officer, Lieutenant Easton, would soon make his escape. A brave officer dramatically taking his own life rather than being captured certainly fits the Japanese way of war at this time and their conception of how an honourable officer should behave. If the situation had been reversed, it is almost certainly what the majority of Japanese officers would have done. But for a British officer, the description does not quite ring true.

In any event, Easton and a handful of men managed to slip through the Japanese cordon during the confusion and make their way down the south slope towards New Guinea. Fortunately, they were able to evade the remaining Japanese troops closing in on Holland's Company and reach the MLI troops just after they had finished clearing the roadblock. These were the lucky ones, the few who had survived, while nearly eighty or so of their comrades lay dead around the slopes of Hill 7378. While they would later learn that up to twenty-four C Company soldiers had been captured either that morning or over the next few days, at midday on the 20th this was unknown.[5] As far as Hopkinson and the whole 50 Parachute Brigade knew, C Company had been wiped out, nearly 100 men had perished and the Japanese had been victorious in their first major encounter with the Parachute Brigade.

* * *

For 152 Battalion, the loss of C Company was a grave blow. Parachute battalions were already smaller than a typical British infantry battalion, fielding only three companies and support troops as opposed to the standard four companies of a regular infantry battalion. Accordingly, the total annihilation of C Company effectively meant that Hopkinson's strength had been depleted by at least 25 per cent in just the first 24 hours after meeting the enemy.

On the other hand, C Company's defence of Hill 7378 had cost the Japanese valuable time and significant casualties. They could ill afford a delay of 36 hours when time, rations and ammunition were limited. The Japanese appear to have sustained at least 160 casualties, as against the roughly 100 men who died from C Company. Battles are not, however, a matter of mere arithmetic. The winner is not always the side which loses the fewer men. The loss of C Company was a terrible blow to 152 Battalion and the entire 50 Parachute Brigade.

Major Holland withdraws to Badger

While C Company was in its final death throes, Holland's Company was performing a series of textbook leapfrogs back to New Guinea: 8 Platoon withdrew first under cover of 7 Platoon, then 7 Platoon under the watch of 9 Platoon, and finally 9 Platoon moved back into the hastily formed defensive box.

One of the immediate difficulties facing Holland was how to evacuate the large number of wounded men lying out in the jungle along the line of the previous platoon blitzes on each side of the track. This exercise would prove particularly arduous since at this time approximately a quarter of the Company's entire strength were wounded. That the retrieval of the wounded men was successful was in large part due to the calm direction of Subedar Shripat Vishwashrao, the officer who had previously commanded the 2-inch mortar section. While some were 'walking wounded' and could largely take care of themselves, others, including Jemadar Dasi, were much more badly hurt and needed to be carried. To collect each of these men from where they lay out in the jungle was no easy job, and for his 'personal command, efficiency and general cheerfulness' in accomplishing this task, and other examples of courage, Subedar Shripat Vishwashrao was later awarded the Military Cross.[6] The records show that every single wounded man was collected successfully and brought back to the Company defensive box.

At around 1000 hrs, while they were busily bringing in their wounded, Holland's men heard intense fire coming from the Hill 7378 position to their front. The bursts of fire continued for some time before sputtering out and then abruptly stopping. Then, to everyone's amazement, a short time later, Easton and a handful of his men somehow stumbled into Holland's Company box at New Guinea. The breathless Easton confirmed what Holland had already guessed: that C Company had been completely overrun, no longer able to repel the enemy since almost all their ammunition was gone and most of the Company were dead.

Hearing this news, Holland knew that his Company would soon be swamped by the large numbers of Japanese now streaming down from Hill 7378 towards him. He immediately sent a runner back to the 152 Battalion Headquarters on Badger, requesting further orders. At the same time, Subedar Shripat Vishwashrao commenced reconnaissance of a series of fall-back positions so that the Company could move back towards Badger in an orderly fashion if required. Small patrols of three men under an NCO were also sent out to the front of the Company box to act as early warning, in case the Japanese pressed their advance towards them.

These prudent battle preparations proved their worth. Just before noon, the Japanese commenced an attack on the Company box, with assaults coming down each side of the track supported by a flanking party far out to the left of Holland's position. Fortunately, this attack was disrupted and fell apart in confusion, most likely due to the fire of the forward warning positions which disorientated the Japanese and confused them as to Holland's actual position.

When the Japanese finally put in an attack, it was quickly repulsed and the attackers pushed back. In response, Holland ordered 8 Platoon to conduct a limited counter-attack off to the left of the track, which succeeded in forcing the Japanese to retire from the box.

The aggressive infantry tactics employed by Holland and his men were highly successful in repelling everything the Japanese had to throw at them. But dash and skilful use of tactics could only get them so far. Ammunition was running low, and the fighting strength of the Company was down to about thirty-nine men of all ranks, about a third of a full-strength company. The temporary position in the jungle would not withstand a determined assault when the Japanese had regained their bearings, and so, under cover of fire from the 2-inch mortars, a carrying party together with escorts was immediately sent back down the track to take all casualties rearwards to the 152 Battalion HQ. After the casualties had safely got away, and under the cover of mortar fire, the remainder of the Company started to withdraw, moving back to the first fall-back position previously reconnoitred by Subedar Shripat Vishwashrao.

Meanwhile, back on Badger, Hopkinson learned from the runner of the sizeable engagement that Holland was facing at the roadblock. Surveying the dwindling supply of reserves still available to him at Badger, Hopkinson decided to immediately dispatch a troop of mortars from 582 Battery RA in light trucks and two jeeps down the track towards Holland. Unfortunately, these reinforcements met Holland just as he was performing his fighting withdrawal back up the track to his third fall-back position. The trucks and jeeps, coming to a sudden halt in the jungle, soon clogged the single-lane dirt track, and confusion reigned until the traffic jam was cleared. While some of the men busied themselves sorting out the vehicles and turning them round to face back up the track, the 3-inch mortars of 582 Battery were quickly taken from the trucks and brought into action. They started to lay down effective covering fire for the retiring soldiers, forcing the Japanese to keep their distance and giving Holland a critical breathing space to sort out the traffic jam and get his wounded rearwards. Under cover of this much heavier mortar fire, the Japanese advance slowed and finally halted. Subsequently, only occasional movement was seen in the jungle, accompanied by the odd bit of sniping, as the defenders withdrew towards Badger and the newly formed Battalion box.

* * *

Holland's action at the roadblock and his withdrawal to Badger has not received much attention in any of the post-battle accounts of Sangshak. This is not surprising, since at the time it was a fairly typical example of the short, violent encounters that were taking place all over Imphal and indeed the entire Burma theatre. On the other hand, and putting it into perspective, the roadblock battle was an excellent example of how just far the British Indian Army had come since the disorderly retreats of just over a year ago. By early 1944 the British Indian troops were in no way intimidated by the Japanese and showed themselves to be highly skilled jungle fighters and masters of quick, aggressive infantry tactics. They were more than a match for the enemy. While this action has never got the attention it deserves, the intensity of the fighting and the bravery of the men who fought is clear from the award of two Military Crosses and a Military Medal in the space of just a few hours. The roadblock action also served to give the respective Battalion headquarters at Badger and Kidney Camp precious time to reorganize themselves and bring reinforcements forward.

After the battle, Major Holland is reported to have said, 'The chaps were splendid. They went on just as if they were on a training scheme. They could not have been better.'[7]

Brigade HQ – pulling in the edges

Despite the misplaced optimism of only a week earlier that the Brigade would only meet 'small reconnaissance patrols', it was now clear to Hope-Thomson back at Brigade HQ that a very sizeable enemy force would soon be moving through 50 Parachute Brigade's area of operations. The Brigadier realized that if he wished to avoid having his units picked off one by one, he would need to consolidate his forces and do so quickly.

By mid-morning on 20 March, Hope-Thomson found his Brigade was stretched over an area of many square miles. Few of them possessed jeeps or trucks to allow rapid movement in case of emergency, and none of the dispersed units was able to support another. Each was essentially isolated. Taking stock, he saw that his key units were deployed as follows:

Unit	Location
Headquarters	
HQ	36-mile post (on Manipur Road)
MMG Coy	Ukhrul
152 Parachute Battalion	
HQ	Badger – advanced command post
A Coy	Ridge east of Hill 7378 – out of communication
B Coy	Defending Gammon. No enemy contact except for minor sniping
C Coy	Overrun. Survivors withdrawing to Badger
153 Parachute Battalion	
All sub-units	Imphal
4/5 Maratha Light Infantry	
HQ	Kidney Camp
A Coy	New Guinea roadblock – in action
B Coy	Kidney Camp
C Coy	Kidney Camp
D Coy	Khangoi – no communications

Hope-Thomson had been busy throughout the day, frequently communicating with Hopkinson and Trim around Sheldon's Corner as well as providing SITREPS (situation reports) to his higher commander at 23 Division. He was also desperately trying to contact each of his sub-units, warning them to be prepared to move and consolidate near his headquarters.

Critically, he needed to bring 153 Battalion up from its current location in Imphal, where it had only just arrived the night before. With both 152 Battalion and the MLI committed at Sheldon's Corner, 153 Battalion was the last fighting battalion and manoeuvre element that Hope-Thomson had under his command, and it was vital that it rejoin the Brigade as soon as possible. Having just got out of their vehicles after a long ride from Kohima to Imphal, the Gurkhas were now told to get ready to reboard the trucks and make their way quickly to join Hope-Thomson at Brigade Headquarters.

As well as receiving the signal to move, mid-morning was when 153 Battalion started to get the first hints of what had befallen Major Fuller's C Company. Captain Eric Neild, 153 Battalion's Medical Officer, describes hearing the news while his Battalion was still in the vicinity of Imphal:

> During the night the mess-havildar arrived with the mess staff and equipment in *yakdans*, leather mule-portable crates. This enabled us next morning to sit down to an ample breakfast, which was our first proper meal for twenty-four hours and, as it turned out, last one until we returned to Imphal. We had barely finished breakfast when the incredible news arrived. The two leading companies of 152 had been overrun. Where had the Japs come from? If 'I' [Intelligence] was correct they should be some hundred miles on the other side of the Chindwin. The situation was roughly comparable to a Londoner being told that the Germans had appeared at Tonbridge, and not by parachute either. We were flabbergasted.
>
> It was obvious that something grave was afoot and that our own time would soon be coming. We began to put detonators in our grenades.[8]

While Neild incorrectly stated that two Companies had been overrun, his comments capture the feelings of shock and utter surprise that must have been spreading through the entire Brigade. Hastily re-boarding their trucks, they set off for the equally bumpy and dusty return journey to Brigade Headquarters at Finches Corner. It would take them the best part of a whole day, bumping along the same road they had just come down the day before. It would not be until 1800 hrs, just before nightfall, that the first elements of 153 Battalion rounded the last bend to enter Finches Corner. One platoon was then immediately sent further along the road to Ukhrul to relieve a platoon of the medium machine gun company which was required back at Mile 36 to bolster the defences around the headquarters.

* * *

By now, Hope-Thomson would have realized that his dispersed Brigade was facing a large enemy force of possibly two Regiments. As the only fighting unit in this part of Manipur, 50 Parachute Brigade was effectively alone. With most available elements of Fourteenth Army already committed to defending Imphal or facing the supposed main Japanese thrust south and south-east of Imphal, there were no troops to spare to reinforce 50 Brigade. Hope-Thomson knew he could not leave his units dispersed and so determined that the best strategy would be to draw all units into the centre and consolidate them in a strong defensive box. He reasoned that such a box would give the Brigade a fighting chance.

Hope-Thomson was aided in his decision by directions received over the radio from 23 Division. He was told that 50 Brigade was tasked to 'destroy the Japs moving West and if unable to do so owing to superior enemy strength, to ensure security of [your] force by conc[entreating] it … into a close defensive box or boxes in general area of SANGSHAK and SHELDON'S CORNER. If the enemy bypass them, to cut the enemy's L of C (line of communication).'[9]

But where should he place his box? Sangshak? Sheldon's Corner, as suggested by Division? Or Finches Corner, where his headquarters was already located, soon to be bolstered by his Machine Gun Company? Given that 152 Battalion was already in contact with the enemy at Sheldon's Corner, he quickly discounted that as a viable option.

In the end, it came down to a choice between the village of Sangshak and Finches Corner. Neither position was ideal. Finches Corner was astride the main arterial road between Imphal and Ukhrul and so would be useful in bringing reinforcements and supplies, assuming any were available. But it was otherwise a poor defensive position. At Sangshak, some initial defensive positions had been established by the prior occupants, 49 Brigade, and it was also held by two companies of the Khali Bahadur Regiment. However, it had an extremely small perimeter surrounded by jungle on two sides. Importantly, both of the proposed positions suffered from a shortage of drinking water. At Sangshak, the few water points were to be found outside the current Khali Bahadur defensive position. This lack of water was to be an issue that would plague the Brigade throughout its time at Sangshak and is something all veterans would continue to comment on, often many years after the event.

Having considered his meagre options, Hope-Thomson radioed through to 23 Division HQ with an update of the enemy situation and his proposed defensive options – either Finches Corner or Sangshak. No decision was made immediately, although the Division prudently decided that whatever the choice, the Brigade would need additional fire support. Accordingly, the Division immediate allocated artillery support in the form of 15 Mountain

Battery to 50 Parachute Brigade. The Battery was currently located in the vicinity of Litan and, despite being mule-mounted only, could reach Finches' Corner relatively quickly. Accordingly, it was ordered to move the next morning, first towards Finches Corner and then on to Sangshak if required.

The Mountain Battery was commanded by Major John Lock, a very experienced mountain gunner who went into battle wearing a trademark, and certainly non-issue, 'fore and aft' deerstalker hat. Lock was at that time located in Litan, several miles away from Sangshak and Finches Corner, commanding the Litan Box (known by its code name of 'Gnat'). When Lock had arrived at Litan just a day before he too had been told by Division that 'it is not anticipated that anything larger than enemy parties of 30–40 can reach your box at present'.[10] Under his command were four 3.7-inch mountain guns, manned by approximately forty-eight men, all of whom were experienced in jungle fighting. The Battery also had a generous supply of Bren guns and small arms. Most importantly, it was well supplied with radios, the vital link between the forward observer parties, the guns themselves and the Artillery nets of higher headquarters.

Mountain batteries had been used in India for generations, particularly in the North-West Frontier region, where their relatively compact size and excellent mobility made them a great asset in the numerous border wars and raids that the British had been almost continuously engaged in for over a century. A mountain battery was a light artillery unit. It was highly mobile; traditionally, an entire battery, together with its ammunition, could be disassembled and packed onto just forty-eight war mules, while a single gun could be broken down into its component parts and packed onto eight mules. Although an increasing number of British artillery units in the theatre had been converted to motor transport by this time, 15 Mountain Battery had not abandoned its trusty mules. The animals had distinct advantages over jeeps among the steep hills, knife-like ridges and valleys of Manipur, since a mule could travel almost anywhere that a man could walk. The war mules were also almost silent, having had their voice boxes cut out at a young age. The gunners had great affection for their animals – as evidenced by the frontispiece of their Regimental History which shows a picture of a war mule and the inscription 'Our Trusty and Tireless Servant'.[11]

The Battery's guns, men and communications would all prove especially valuable in the coming days, and Hope-Thomson was indeed fortunate to have them added to his order of battle.

Badger Forward HQ

While the morning saw C Company fighting for its life on Hill 7378 and Holland's Company with its hands full at the roadblock, both Brigade and forward Battalion commanders were desperate for information on the enemy, in order to form plans for a possible counter-attack. To obtain a clearer picture of the battle around Sheldon's Corner, Hope-Thomson sent his second-in-command, Colonel Abbott, together with his intelligence officer, Captain 'Dicky' Richards, down to the 152 Battalion forward headquarters on Badger. Owing to the lack of motor transport, the pair started out to walk the nine miles, alone, in the morning heat. They arrived first at the HQ of 4/5 MLI at Kidney Camp and then, together with Trim in his very welcome command jeep, drove down the track towards Badger. They pulled into Hopkinson's forward headquarters at around 1030hrs, just after the final fateful message from Easton was received by a very concerned Lieutenant Colonel Hopkinson.

The commanders on Badger quickly realized that relief of C Company was now impossible. The Company had clearly been overrun, and no number of reinforcements, even if they had been available, would be able to get through in time to make a difference. The best that could be hoped for C Company now was that small parties of survivors might be able to slip through the Japanese cordon and make their way back to Badger.

With a relief mission no longer feasible, the commanders turned their thoughts to the possibility of mounting a counter-attack to push back the advancing Japanese. A plan was quickly devised that would see elements of 152 Battalion and 4/5 MLI attacking the Japanese from multiple directions. As the counter-attacking units were currently dispersed over a rather large area, it was decided that rather than bringing them all in and concentrating the force prior to the counter-attack, each of the units would make its own way towards the Japanese from its current location and then join up with the others just before commencing the attack.

The plan called for A Company, 4/5 MLI to push through the roadblock with support from 582 Mortar Battery, while A Company, 152 Battalion, in the hills east of Hill 7378, were to attack Hill 7378 from the east. At the same time, D Coy, 4/5 MLI was to move east towards Hill 7378 and conduct a 'demonstration', essentially a feigned attack with lots of noise and fire designed to distract the Japanese. This diversion would give the other units, moving silently to their forming-up points, valuable time to approach the Japanese positions. Warning Orders were sent to each of the Companies to begin preparations, with detailed orders and exact timings to follow.

On paper, the plan looked to be a classic pincer movement against the enemy forces near Hill 7378, with the preliminary diversion initiated by D Coy designed to confuse the Japanese as to the actual direction of attack. But while the plan might have sounded good in theory, in reality it stood little chance of success. The British were planning to send a mere two Companies that were already either engaged in hard fighting at the roadblock (A Coy, 4/5 MLI) or struggling through the jungle (A Coy, 152 Battalion) to attack a numerically superior enemy who had just occupied a series of fixed positions on a major hill feature. No reconnaissance had been undertaken to ascertain the present dispositions of the Japanese, and the British forces had no artillery or other fire support besides the 3-in mortars of the Mortar Battery.

While the Warning Order had been sent and some initial planning had commenced, the command team on Badger soon had second thoughts, as events on the ground quickly outpaced their planning. As we have seen, by 1325 hrs, A Company, 4/5 MLI was being pushed back from the roadblock position it had just cleared by very strong Japanese counter-attacks estimated to be at battalion strength – approximately three to four times the size of the lonely A Company. The diversionary D Company, 4/5 MLI was still not responding to radio calls, and even B Company, 152 Battalion, who so far had had a relatively quiet time on Gammon, were now reporting that the enemy was moving up to their flanks. The risk now was that the Japanese would form up in strength near Gammon, attempt a re-run of their assault on the isolated C Company and then soon destroy B Company as well.

Realizing that the pincer plan was a non-starter, it was quickly scrapped, and a new plan had to be devised. Rather than attempt a series of complex manoeuvres through the jungle by several Companies who were either isolated, out of communication or with no effective fire support, a decision was made to pull all remaining 152 Battalion and 4/5 MLI troops into a defensive box on Badger. The exception was to be B Company, 152 Battalion, who were to retain their current defensive position on Gammon. It was also decided that Lieutenant Colonel Trim, being the senior officer, would take command of the newly combined force.

With the decision made, signals were sent to the dispersed MLI Companies, who quickly hurried from their various positions back to Badger. Supply dumps across the battlefield were also destroyed to ensure that they did not fall into the enemy's hands. The Pioneer Platoon destroyed the V Force dumps at Blakes Camp as well as the remaining supplies at Kidney Camp which included 1,500 gallons of petrol and a large quantity of rations.

As troops started to arrive in the vicinity of Badger, Trim allocated areas of responsibility around the perimeter of the Box, and everyone started preparations for the defence. 'Everyone began to dig like hell. After that the scheme showed every man, including all officers, digging as fast as they could with bayonets, *dahs*[12] and even with their hands. The situation appeared to be very tense.'[13] While defensive positions were being dug, the wounded, including Easton and the remainder of his C Company comrades, were sent by truck back to Litan for medical treatment.

From a tactical perspective, the decision to concentrate the two Battalions was a sound one. Continued dispersal of individual Companies would not generate sufficient firepower to resist the numerically superior Japanese, but would risk them being picked off one by one. Communication between the dispersed units was also proving to be very difficult. A Company, 152 Battalion had been out of contact for the best part of twelve hours, and D Company, 4/5 MLI, which was located just a few miles away near Khangoil, had only been able to manage sporadic contact with their headquarters. Even Holland and his Company fighting the roadblock battle did not have effective radio communications with his HQ on Badger. He would be forced to rely on the old-fashioned expedient of runners, with Lance Naik Hari Kadam and two soldiers kept busy running the several miles between the two positions ferrying orders for the entirety of the morning and early afternoon.

At around 1635hrs Holland and his A Company finally arrived at Badger. 'A Company entered the box very tired but with their tails up! Casualties suffered had been 7 killed, 1 missing believed killed and 25 wounded.'[14]

As night fell, the steadily growing concentration of troops on Badger must have given Trim some relief, but he was not yet in the clear. Troop numbers were still low when compared to the number of enemy thought to be in the immediate vicinity of Sheldon's Corner. Almost as importantly, ammunition was running short, having been depleted by the intense action of Holland and his men. Trim knew that he was unable to get sufficient ammunition and supplies ferried to them along the jungle tracks, since the Brigade lacked sufficient available MT (motor transport). So that evening, he radioed higher Headquarters and arranged for an airdrop of key supplies to take place the next day at around midday.

* * *

By 1944 the use of airdrops to re-supply isolated British units in the jungle was becoming more and more common. Pioneered in 1943 to supply the long range 'Chindit' patrols who operated in Burma far behind enemy lines, airdropping supplies had become a fine art. With growing air superiority and the increased availability of transport aircraft, it was now becoming common to re-supply British units with ammunition, food and medicine from the air. It was this capability, air support and air supply, which gave the British the ability to stay put in a defensive box and fight off any Japanese attempt to surround them. No longer would the British be forced to break out to protect their lines of supply, as had occurred all too often in the early days of the war. Now the men could just hang on and fight, safe in the knowledge that crucial supplies could be sent to them by air. So important was this lifeline that when asked after the war, 'Who had won the battle for Imphal?' a common response from many 50 Parachute Brigade members was, 'The Dakota' – the ubiquitous Douglas C-47 transport plane that supplied Allied troops throughout the Burma theatre.[15]

* * *

At Badger Forward HQ, Trim and Hopkinson were on high alert, waiting expectantly for the Japanese attacks that they knew must come their way sooner or later. But that night was relatively quiet, with the exception of a single burst of heavy fire heard near Gammon around 2030 hrs and some sporadic shots in the far distance. Nothing followed the unexplained single heavy burst, and the defenders settled down to a nervous night, fully alert to the faint sounds of Japanese patrols moving around the very edges of their positions trying to find the boundaries and the gaps of the Badger defensive box. While faint, the tell-tale sounds of the Japanese scouting parties were persistent and betrayed their presence – which was brought to everyone's full attention by the loud detonation of a booby trap exploding forward of the Badger position. This trap was just one of several laid by the defenders, and it brought the enemy probes to an immediate halt.

Sangshak Defence Plan

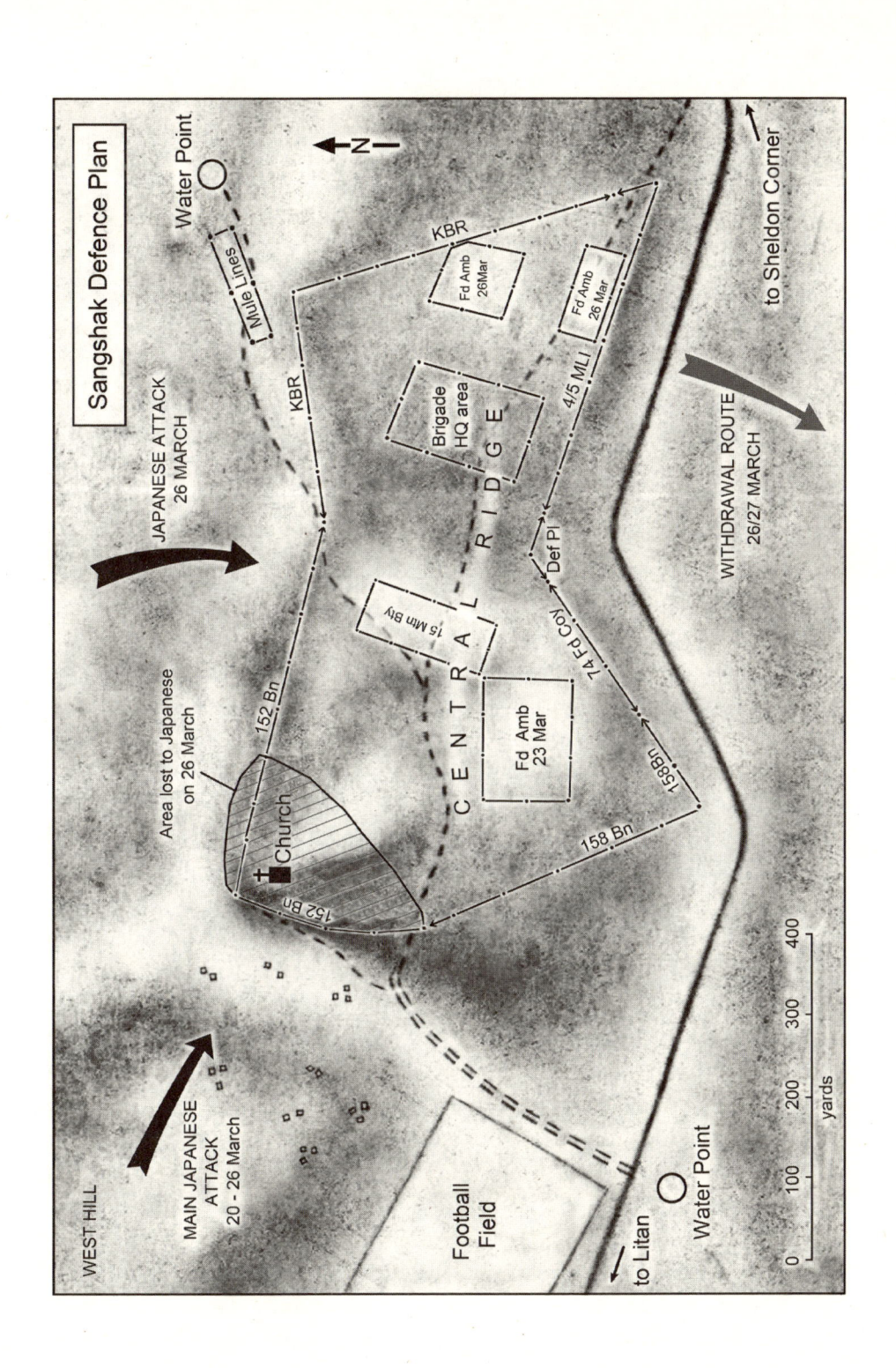

Chapter 6

21 March – Race to Sangshak

Headquarters– 50 Parachute Brigade

Just after midnight, the Brigade intelligence officer returned to the Brigade HQ position with orders from 23 Division. He told an anxious Hope-Thomson that 23 Division agreed with his plan to order the entire Brigade to concentrate rather than maintain their current dispersed dispositions. The 23 Division message further advised that Sangshak, a Naga village several miles south of Finches Corner, was the most likely defensive position – if sufficient water could be found.

The choice of Sangshak as the main defensive 'box' of the Brigade would become, after the war, a highly contentious one.[1] Sangshak is a curiously shaped position, comprising a typical Naga village dotted with many wooden huts ('*bashas*' as they were known to the British) for approximately 120 families, spread out over two main hill features – the so-called West Hill and the future main defensive position on East Hill. The entire area is at about 5,500ft above sea level, and its altitude gives it excellent views of the surrounding hills and country. It is, however, quite a compact village; East Hill was only about 800ft long by 600ft at its widest.

The two hills comprising the village proper were cut and divided by a deep gully with a track running between them, together with another track snaking off to the south along the contours of East Hill. While thick jungle came right up to the village edge to the north, the south-western edge of East Hill featured a deep cutting down to the large open 'football field' on the edge of the track. Seen from above, East Hill is shaped something like a giant pear laid lengthways east to west, with the fat end towards the east and the narrow end facing West Hill. The narrow end also looks as though someone has taken a big bite out of its south-western side – this being the cutting and football field.

The top of East Hill is relatively flat but slopes gently upwards from the west towards a middle ridge, before falling away again to the east. Seen from the west, most of East Hill is observable up to its centre ridge, the ground on the other side of the ridge being obscured. Dominating both hills, however, was the whitewashed American Baptist Church, perched at the highest point in the village on a little spur on the extreme north-western edge of East Hill.

Besides the compact physical layout of the village proper, Hope-Thomson's other key concern was water. While there were several water points around the village, as in most Naga villages none of them was on top of the hill itself or within the village proper. Rather, they were placed further down the slope – and outside the proposed defensive position. This layout suited village life but was to prove a major problem for the defending British forces.

Lieutenant Colonel Hopkinson in his post-operation report gave his reasons why he thought Sangshak was selected as the main defensive position:

> The question which at once arises is: why was Sangshak selected as the Brigade position? My personal opinion as to the factors which influenced the choice are as follows:
>
> 1. It commanded and was close to several important track junctions.
> 2. The Kali Bahadurs were already there and the position which they had dug could be incorporated in a Brigade position, and time was vital.
> 3. Lack of time to make a thorough reconnaissance of the whole area.[2]

While thorough reconnaissance of the whole area was not possible, upon receiving his orders, Brigadier Hope-Thomson, together with his tactical HQ and his engineering officer, Captain McLune, set off at first light towards Sangshak to reconnoitre the likely defensive position.

Hope-Thomson was well aware how fast the determined Japanese troops could move through the jungle. Accordingly, he also gave orders for non-essential troops, including his anti-tank platoon, to move back to Litan, and for all important documents to be burned! He also made the difficult decision to abandon Ukhrul, which the remainder of his MMG Company was currently defending. Uhkrul held extensive stocks of stores and ammunition, built up over time in readiness for the offensive that the British were planning to conduct later in 1944. It would be an important prize for the Japanese if captured. However, unable to carry these stores, the MMG Company reluctantly set fire to the lot, destroying it all before making their way down the track to marry up with the rest of the Brigade. Finally, Hope-Thomson dispatched Richards in the early morning to return to Badger and give instructions for the Sheldon's Corner outpost to withdraw to Finches Corner if the situation did not improve through the day.

152 Battalion – Badger and New Guinea

While Hope-Thomson was engaged in preparation for his reconnaissance of Sangshak, the early morning light at Badger saw British patrols stealthily creep out back towards the roadblock positions at New Guinea and C Company's position on Hill 7378. They had been sent out from Badger well before first light, tasked to collect intelligence on enemy strength and positions.

The patrols did not have to search long before spotting heavy concentrations of Japanese in both positions. In total, the patrols estimated that the enemy had around a battalion of troops on both Hill 7378 itself and further along the track junction near the site of the roadblock. At this time, the Japanese were busily engaged in collecting their dead, large numbers of corpses being brought out of the jungle and laid on either side of the track. It also became clear to the scouts that the Japanese were not statically fixed to Hill 7378 but rather had fanned out and were exploring the surrounding hills and country. Disturbed ground showed that they had visited the water point below the Badger hide sometime during the night, and small parties of the enemy were also observed moving down through the surrounding valleys.

Hopkinson relayed this information to the Brigadier on the radio just before he departed from Finches Corner for his reconnaissance. With information from his scouts fresh in his mind, Hopkinson reminded the Brigadier of the importance of the planned airdrop of water, noting that while the Badger position currently had sufficient water, they were unlikely to be able to access the water point for much longer without facing opposition from the Japanese. An airdrop was thus critical for the continued defence of Badger. Hope-Thomson in return told him somewhat cryptically to expect his Intelligence Officer at Badger later that morning 'with an important message'.

Even at this early stage, Hope-Thomson was rightly being circumspect about the information he relayed through the wired 'land-line' telephone system that connected Badger with Finches Corner. This instinct to maintain secrecy, or 'operational security' as it is known in the Army, would be shown to be well placed as, later in the day, it became obvious that the Japanese had tapped into the signal wires running between the various key positions and Brigade HQ. They were overheard talking on these wires, and Hopkinson thought it likely that they had also found the radio frequencies that the Battalion HQ on Badger was using to communicate with the forward units still defending Gammon.

As promised, Richards made his way back into the Badger defensive box at around 0900 hrs and gave Trim and Hopkinson the 'important message' they were waiting for. He told them of the preliminary plan for the Brigade to concentrate and form a Brigade defensive box, most likely at Finches Corner. Richards then asked Trim and Hopkinson if they thought they would be able to withdraw to the Finches Corner box within the next 24 hours.

Could they? The two Colonels replied immediately that they could not wait 24 hours even if they had wanted to. If they did, they would almost inevitably be cut off by the rapidly advancing Japanese and would have to fight their way out of an almost certain encirclement. Although only small numbers of Japanese were currently in the vicinity of Badger and Gammon, the morning scouting patrols had confirmed that much larger groups were nearby and, armed with their newly acquired intelligence of the Badger position, were certain to fall on their HQ soon. At the latest, the Japanese might wait until they brought up their artillery, but in any event, it was estimated that they would launch an attack within the next 24 hours.

Instead of waiting a whole day before withdrawing from Badger, Hopkinson and Trim suggested that they move their troops back to the Kidney Camp position in the middle of the night and then await further orders as to whether or not to move on to Finches Corner. Kidney Camp had obvious advantages – it was already well prepared, and its defensive positions were dug and ready for the troops to reoccupy them. Crucially, it also had a good supply of water. Richards said that he would relay the plan to the Brigade Commander, who would later confirm by wireless whether it was accepted or not. He said that he would also try to contact the remaining Companies of 4/5 MLI (D Company, at this time somewhere near Longshong and the long-lost A Company, 152 Battalion) and order them to move directly to Finches Corner rather than trying to return to Badger as originally planned.

* * *

The rest of the day saw the troops at Finches Corner engaged in reconnaissance, preparing orders and readying themselves to move. All knew that they were in a race with the Japanese and that victory would likely come to those who could move faster, dig quicker and prepare themselves better for the battle to come. Returning from his reconnaissance of Sangshak at around midday, Hope-Thomson radioed 23 Division Headquarters that the water supply at Sangshak was unlikely to be sufficient for a large force, including mules. He then spotted Richards, who had just finished his long round trip to Badger. After listening intently to the situational brief from Badger and the plan to withdraw to Kidney Camp, Hope-Thomson immediately gave orders approving Trim and Hopkinson's plan. They could commence moving at once.

Soon afterwards, 23 Division radioed through definite orders. The Brigade was to concentrate at and defend Sangshak. With the location of the Brigade box now settled, new orders were despatched for all units of the Brigade, minus the troops currently located at Badger, to move towards Sangshak as fast as possible. Fortunately, many of the troops had already spent the morning in preparations and were ready to move. As such, the first columns of soldiers almost immediately began to leave the Brigade position and make their way along the track toward Sangshak.

Almost simultaneously, shortly after midday, a Medium Machine Gun unit defending the 36-mile post, was engaged by a small enemy patrol. The Japanese had clearly been moving very, very fast, with their forward elements already probing the Brigade position and the Manipur Road.

This enemy patrol was the vanguard of a larger Japanese party tasked with cutting the vital main road between Imphal and Kohima. This road was critical to British plans in Manipur as it was the only effective means of land re-supply from the railhead at Dimapur to the main British base at Imphal. It was on this single narrow and winding road that all reinforcements of men, bombs and bullets arriving from India would need to travel. If it was seized and held by the enemy, then the British defending Imphal would be forced to rely upon re-supply by air only. And this is exactly what happened, when the Japanese seized the road in the days following this first encounter with the men of the MMG Platoon.

* * *

Back on Badger, but before receiving 23 Division's orders to consolidate at Sangshak, Hopkinson and Trim considered their options. They were quite certain that their proposal to move to Kidney would be approved by Hope-Thomson and that they would likely be ordered to withdraw sometime that evening. Their worry was that if the move was left too late, then the Japanese were almost certain to cut them off from behind, leading to a re-run of the roadblock battle but with the added complication of a large number of mules and heavy equipment moving back towards the main defensive position. It would be another roadblock battle but of epic proportions and to be avoided at all costs.

Major Smith, the Battery Commander of 582 Battery (the mortar battery), told Hopkinson that he would not be able to move his heavily laden mules at night. Even though the mules could not bray, their movement was nevertheless certain to be very noisy on the narrow and congested track, destroying any hope of secrecy. Since time was of the essence, and even before any orders were received from HQ, it was decided to send 582 Battery and their heavily laden war mules ahead of the main body during the afternoon towards Kidney Camp.

The Colonels then started planning the withdrawal of the remaining troops in detail. The plan called for troops to start leaving their current positions, in stages, from 0200hrs. Of primary importance was the need for secrecy, to ensure that the enemy had no inkling that the positions were being abandoned. To this end, troops were ordered to go about their duties normally, so as to give the impression to any watching Japanese that they were committed to defending Gammon and Badger. At the same time, they were to start secretly and quietly preparing for the move. All ammunition and equipment would need to be carried out on foot since no vehicles were available, meaning that large quantity of stores had to be left behind. Destroying stores noiselessly and without fire or explosives is difficult; thus large quantities of ammunition and other stores, carefully laid up over the previous week, were quietly buried in the hills.

At 1345 hrs orders were finally received from Hope-Thomson to start the withdrawal. At the same time a message was received from both the Division Commander and the Brigade Commander congratulating the Battalion 'for the fine defence put up by the Force'.[3]

By now, Hopkinson and Trim were also alive to the problem of Japanese tapping their phone lines, so orders for the withdrawal had to be sent in person to the men defending Gammon. This dangerous mission was entrusted to Lieutenant Alan Cowell, a young war service lieutenant from 152 Battalion, who set off with a small party through the jungle, now ever more infested with Japanese patrols. Fortunately, he got through, delivered his message and learned that the defenders on Gammon would start to leave their positions at 0300 hrs and then try to link up with the rear parties on Badger before withdrawing to Kidney Camp.

As light started to fade, preparations for the withdrawal continued silently, until suddenly the early evening quiet was broken by the sound of three Dakota re-supply planes making their way towards Badger. Hopkinson later conceded that he was not sure whether they had forgotten to cancel the drop in their haste to focus on the impending move, or whether they had deliberately decided to continue with the drop in the hope that it would deceive the Japanese into thinking that they intended to remain and defend the Badger/Gammon complex. It appears more likely that the planes had simply been forgotten, since the War Diaries show signallers from 4/5 MLI desperately trying to call off the drop as the aircraft drew near – but to no avail. So at around 1700hrs the planes let loose their cargoes of extra ammunition, food and water, which all softly floated down into the jungle under their parachutes. While this drop certainly convinced the Japanese that the British troops were committed to stay and fight, the additional supplies were of no use as the men were already overloaded with all the supplies and ammunition that they could carry. Thus, even more stores were collected only to be wastefully destroyed. The now plentiful supply of .303 ammunition was buried, the fuses for the 3-in mortars were burned and the shells themselves thrown down the side of a steep cliff into the jungle.

153 Battalion and the Race to Sangshak

153 Battalion endured a very long and bumpy day, driving almost non-stop from dawn to race back from Imphal to Sangshak. It was only very late in the day that they were finally dropped off at a riverbed some four miles short of Sangshak. With their motor transport immediately making its way back to Imphal, the Battalion was forced to make the rest of the climb up to Sangshak on foot:

> We then marched the two thousand feet and four miles to Sangshak. It was really quite a pull, and when on top we immediately had to start digging slit trenches. Scared by the influx of armed troops and the imminence of battle, the inhabitants of both villages [i.e. the villages on both West and East Hill] on our arrival left en bloc and took to the jungle. It was a shame – but then war is no respecter of persons. To the north of the village the ground, which fell precipitously away, was covered in jungle up to the village edge, while to the south the ground fell more gradually away but still steeply. We could see nothing, and the jungle surrounded us oppressively.[4]

They had arrived in the very nick of time. Two companies of Khali Bahadurs (the Nepali State Force unit) had been at Sangshak for a few weeks, but they only occupied a limited defensive position to the extreme east of the village, manning simple trenches that the local villagers had helped them dig. There was no way that the Khali Bahadurs would have been able to hold Sangshak alone if 153 Battalion had not arrived when they did.

Soon after 153 Battalion took up their positions, other units of the Brigade started to arrive at Sangshak. At around 1830 hrs, the remaining Brigade HQ troops from Finches Corner together with 15 Mountain Battery entered the position and were allocated sectors to defend. Almost immediately, troops started to dig slit trenches and gun positions, but the lack of picks, shovels and other stores made it impossible to prepare complex defences before nightfall. Most were forced to rely upon shallow shell scrapes and pits.

The newly arrived Gurkhas of 153 Battalion were allocated the perimeter and westernmost section of East Hill to defend. The men were stretched out over a long defensive line following the edge of East Hill overlooking the gully separating East and West Hills and looking towards the other half of the village on West Hill. They also had control of the strategically important church, located on the high ground in the extreme north-west of the sector. The church was a single-storey, whitewashed wooden affair with a thatched roof. Importantly, it also had a bell tower, which provided excellent observation onto both hills of the village and the surrounding country beyond. This church would prove to be a key site and the focus of a great deal of attention from both sides over the coming days.

Behind the screen provided by 153 Battalion, the mule lines for the Mountain Battery were placed at the base of the church plateau. Behind them, at the south-western corner of the hill, near the cutting which ran straight down towards the football field, were the doctors and men of the Battalion Field Ambulance who were busy setting up a temporary aid post. It is amazing to think how close to the perimeter the ambulance was located, but there was little choice. East Hill was quite small, and there was not the luxury of large open areas to spread out the men. The Brigade Regimental Medical Officer, Lieutenant Colonel Davis, was also allocated a small patch of ground for the construction of a rough field hospital. Places were set aside for the initial reception of wounded, an operating theatre and convalescents. His men started to dig trenches and dugouts for each of these important positions, but their work was interrupted by enemy fire throughout the night. The operating theatre dugout would only be finished later the next day.

East Hill was bisected east and west by a gentle central ridge, which provided a modicum of cover from attacks from West Hill to any troops placed on its far eastern side. Accordingly, Brigade headquarters, together with its vital signals section, started to set up a position and dig a command bunker for the signals equipment over the ridge on the eastern side of the hill.

As soon as the signallers set up their equipment, messages were relayed through to 23 Division providing SITREPS as to the arrival and disposition of the men. Requests were also put in for airdrops of ammunition and water. The Brigade reminded 23 Division about the very large supply dump left in enemy hands at Pushing and asked that it be bombed with incendiaries 'to set the whole lot ablaze' and deny the enemy any further use of it. This was arranged, and a flight of bombers set off from Imphal to Pushing to drop their incendiary charges.

The final but crucial British forces to arrive at Sangshak on the 21st were the guns, men and mules of 15 Mountain Battery. Traditionally, artillery units are provided with a generous area to disperse their guns, ammunition and equipment, but Sangshak did not permit Hope-Thomson that luxury. Instead, the only space that could be found was a very small sector on the forward western edge of the central ridge measuring about 100ft x 50ft. This is an extremely small area for a battery of four field guns, even the relatively compact mountain guns. The restricted space meant that the guns were lined up almost axle to axle, just a short distance behind their mules. 'There was no cover and very little elbow-room', notes the official history of the Indian Mountain Artillery.[5] While the gunners were busy assembling their guns and readying their ammunition, Lock also placed a forward observation post up on the church plateau which offered an excellent field of view over all the surrounding country.

Finally rounding out the defences at Sangshak were a small number of sappers from 711 Field Company, who took up a small section of the perimeter on the south side of East Hill overlooking the east-west track running between Sheldon's Corner and Litan. The sappers were the Brigade's specialist engineering troops who ordinarily would be tasked to conduct all kinds of minor engineering works such as clearing obstacles and mines or constructing defences. But at Sangshak the shortage of men meant that even specialist troops were required to man the defences.

The Box was now closed and defended from all directions. Hope-Thomson had succeeded in getting his men into position and into all-round defence before the Japanese arrived. This was nevertheless, a very thin line of troops, even for such a relatively small sector. Events would subsequently prove that the British forces had only arrived shortly before the advancing Japanese troops, who were swarming over the hills between Pushing and the Manipur Road.

With night starting to fall on the evening of the 20th, the Brigade signallers in their freshly prepared dugout noticed that their radio equipment was starting to fail. Their main radio, the No. 9 set, which was used for longer-range transmissions to Divisional HQ, was not working, and upon inspection it was found to be irreparable. Shortly afterwards, at about 1930hrs, the man-portable 48 sets, on which they relied for the bulk of communications with their constituent units, inexplicably started to fade out and would remain in this state until about 0630 hrs the next morning. This fading of signals occurred every night and may have been caused by atmospheric conditions in the high hills of Manipur. Nevertheless, while the fading in and out was not so serious as to halt all radio communications, this serious degradation of radio communications would prove to be a source of constant concern over the coming days.

As the signallers worked on their radio equipment, the men manning the perimeter on that first night were jittery. Shadows and flickers of movement were seen or imagined between the deserted huts and piles of brushwood that dotted the position, and sounds of furtive movement appeared to come from the jungle to the north. But mostly it was quiet, with the defenders being left to their own thoughts in the darkness.

Suddenly, late in the night, a short burst of enemy fire cracked towards the Gurkhas in their rifle pits. The men in the forward pits responded furiously, letting off streams of rounds from their rifles and Bren guns. As Neild describes it: 'That night, the 21st, we had a jitter-party. Even the best trained troops seem to have nerves the first night that they were in action in the jungle. Whether it was a wild pig or a Jap patrol we never discovered, but firing suddenly started and it was some time before it was stopped. During this time, several hundred rounds of ammunition had been fired off.'[6]

* * *

The men back on Gammon were also nervous, especially about keeping up the pretence of an active and vigorous defence while at the same time preparing for a secret withdrawal. Their preparations were interrupted at about 1900 hrs, however, by the sharp crack and whizz of firing near the listening post that B Company had placed forward of the main Company defensive position.

A listening post is just that, a small group of two or three soldiers placed well forward of the main position and tasked to detect signs of any approaching enemy. It is not manned or equipped to fight. So, when the B Company listening post was discovered and fired on by a team of about six Japanese infantrymen, the occupants quickly laid down a burst of fire to keep the enemy's heads down, before rapidly crawling back to the safety of the main Company position. This speedy withdrawal was entirely in accordance with standard operating procedures and battle drills. However, to their dismay, the soldiers were then ordered back to their positions at the listening post and to carry on looking for and reporting the enemy's movements. The Company was not ready to engage in a fixed fight, since they were wholly focussed on the upcoming withdrawal and still needed any early warning from the listening post.

Apart from the brief spat of fire exchanged between the competing listening posts, the British on Gammon also endured occasional bursts of fire sent in their general direction on and off throughout the evening. This shooting, whilst not accurate, was nonetheless disturbing and extremely distracting, slowing down their preparations for the move. But at 2245 hrs things changed, as the Japanese had now started to zero in on B Company. Fire intensified, and accurate and sustained machine gun fire was exchanged for about fifteen minutes. The Japanese had crawled close to the Company perimeter and started shooting into the position, supported by hollow thump of exploding grenades fired from dischargers. This probing attack was seen off, and it was thought that the Japanese force was about platoon-sized, just big enough to test B Company, draw their fire and fix their positions, in anticipation of a stronger attack later in the night. Amazingly, only one man from B Company was wounded in this exchange.

As the night wore on, the men on Gammon could clearly see the headlights of motor transport winking in the distance, snaking along the track from Pushing to the west and making their way towards them. This was a clear sign that despite the relatively light enemy action encountered so far, a much bigger group of Japanese would soon be expected in their sector.

Of more concern, however, were the unmistakable sounds of light machine gun and mortar fire commencing at around 2300 hrs a few miles to their rear in the direction of Sangshak – exactly where they were supposed to withdraw to! It must have seemed to B Company that rather than withdrawing from danger, they were instead headed towards it. With those sobering thoughts, the men of B Company prepared themselves for the move.

Chapter 7

22 March – Consolidating the Box

The British never expected such large numbers of Japanese to come through this sector near Ukhrul and Sangshak. Slim's original estimation was that any sizeable Japanese movements would almost certainly come from the south of Imphal, and that any incursions from the north would probably consist of nothing more than a raiding party of at most a single Regiment. When Mutaguchi's 33 Division started its march from the south towards Imphal on 5 March 1944, it seemed that Slim's prediction was right. He then immediately set about moving men and equipment to meet that threat on the south and south-east of the Imphal plain.

As we have seen, the British were largely taken by surprise when Mutaguchi's two northern Divisions, held quietly in reserve until 15 March, suddenly burst into Manipur through the jungle and descended on the isolated Parachute Brigade around Sheldon's Corner. In this regard, Mutaguchi's plan had succeeded. He had achieved surprise, gained the initiative and put the British on the back foot.

Unfortunately for the Japanese, however, their plan did not go exactly as envisaged, and a key reason was the relatively mundane issue of divisional boundaries. These are lines on a map separating the respective areas of operation of different divisions. It is imperative that each division stays within its own sectors and does not cross its boundary, otherwise there is a great risk of fratricide and general confusion. As planned, there was a clear divisional boundary between the Japanese 15 and 31 Divisions running in a rough line from the Chindwin River through the Ukhrul/Sangshak area; 31 Division was supposed to operate north of this boundary, while 15 Division would operate to the south.

What happened, however, was that the units of both Divisions closest to the boundary overlapped each other, with the consequence that Regiments from both divisions would end up fighting around Sheldon's Corner and Sangshak. It was this fact that led 50 Parachute Brigade to believe that they were facing such large numbers of enemy soldiers. What appeared to be a simple administrative or navigational error would eventually hold great consequences for the Japanese – a delay in their timetable that Mutaguchi could not well afford.

The blame for crossing the boundary falls most clearly on 31 Division. This Division, and its aggressive commander, Lieutenant General Sato, had been waiting impatiently on the banks of the Chindwin River for several days for the slower 15 Division to catch up after its long overland journey from Thailand. When the order to cross the river was given on 15 March, 31 Division wasted no time and moved rapidly westwards through the forested hills.

As we have seen, 31 Division's most southerly unit, 58 Regiment, inflicted a serious defeat on the paratroopers at Sheldon's Corner on 19/20 March. Not content with this victory, and chasing yet more glory, 58 Regiment's commander decided to veer off his planned route of advance northwards and pursue the retreating British forces south towards Sangshak. This was a serious incursion into the area of operation of 15 Division, whose men would only arrive in the vicinity of Sangshak on 24 March.

Analyzing 31 Division's movements and the decision to attack Sangshak, Japanese Operational Records noted after the war, 'Although Sangshak was outside its operational boundaries, the Unit believed it could quickly inflict an overwhelming defeat on the enemy and the decision was made to attack on the 22nd.'[1]

This decision would eventually have serious repercussions, not only for 58 Regiment, but for the entire Japanese plan to quickly overwhelm Manipur and the strategic town of Kohima.

Silence is golden – 152 Battalion withdraws to Kidney Camp

Neither Hopkinson nor his men were aware of 31 Division's boundary infraction. Nor would they have cared even if they had been. What they did know, however, was that more and more Japanese were surging towards them and that they needed to get out of Badger fast. Accordingly, at around 0200hrs and in accordance with their plan, the soldiers on Gammon and Badger started to slip out of their positions and make a quiet trek back down the track towards Kidney Camp. Hopkinson describes the move as follows:

> At 0200 hrs the withdrawal started and went according to plan, except that it took longer than we had anticipated to get along the jungle path. It was extremely dark in the jungle and the pathways very rough and hard going for heavily laden men. It was also difficult carrying the men on stretchers.[2]

22 March – Consolidating the Box 73

Hopkinson's understated account simplifies what was a meticulously planned and well executed withdrawal. It was important that the men departed in small groups rather than as a body, in order that noise be kept to a minimum. This also helped to minimize congestion on the narrow track. At exactly 0200 hrs, the headquarters of 152 Battalion commenced its withdrawal from Badger, moving quietly along jungle paths. D Company, 4/5 MLI set out thirty minutes later, and the rest of the units on Badger followed at fifteen-minute intervals. Finally, at around 0320 hrs, B Coy, 152 Battalion silently slipped out of the rear of Gammon and made its way via a series of separate tracks back down to the main path leading towards Kidney Camp. The withdrawal took several hours, with the last of the defenders from Sheldon's Corner arriving at Kidney around 1000 hrs on 22 March.

A stealthy withdrawal, with the enemy close by, is an extremely difficult military manoeuvre to execute successfully. For men fatigued by lack of sleep and having already fought several engagements with the enemy, the order to move out in the pitch dark through the enclosing jungle must have been very unwelcome indeed. They had to slip silently away from Sheldon's Corner while carrying as much of their ammunition and supplies as they could. Caring for the wounded was another challenge, and the already heavily laden men had to carry roughly constructed stretchers along the narrow track, taking care not to bump or drop their injured comrades. All the while, the retreating soldiers knew that the enemy, skilled night-fighters themselves, were out there somewhere looking for them. That the withdrawing Indian troops made it out undetected and with no additional casualties is a credit to both the plan and the discipline of the men who executed it.

From 0830 hrs to 1000 hrs groups of tired men slowly started to file back into their old positions at Kidney Camp. But there was to be no rest for them. Hopkinson knew the Japanese would soon discover that they had left Badger and would likely be making their way down the trails towards them. Anticipating the arrival of the Japanese, he immediately put the men to work digging and improving the defences at Kidney. He also detailed some men to look for food:

> The Battalion was searching for rations amongst our burnt dump – Major Higgins had destroyed it well, but we did manage to salvage enough to feed the men once. Everyone was very tired and rather wondering what had happened at Sangshak during the night and whether we could reach the remainder of the Brigade.[3]

Sangshak – Round One

Despite the rather limited engagement during the night, first light at Sangshak on 22 March revealed that one British soldier had been killed and another wounded. It was not an auspicious start. Realizing that reaching Sangshak did not guarantee safety, all units along the perimeter continued to dig into the hard earth and work to improve their defences. A complaint often heard from the survivors after the war was that the soil on East Hill in some places only extended down about 3ft or so until it was replaced by a layer of hard volcanic rock. This proved very difficult to penetrate with the meagre tools at their disposal, and it meant that many men had to fight crouched over or kneeling in relatively shallow trenches, often for hours and days at a time.

This was not Sangshak's only deficiency as a location in which to conduct an extended defence. As Hope-Thomson had identified during his initial reconnaissance, the other key constraint was the lack of drinking water. The nearest water points for the Brigade were one to the north-east, down the hill from the Khali Bahadur Company, and another to the south-west near the school and the football field. As neither of these was within the Brigade perimeter proper, and the south-west water point was near the Japanese line of advance from West Hill, fetching sufficient water would be a constant headache for Hope-Thomson and the Brigade throughout the siege.

In later years much criticism would be directed at Hope-Thomson's decision to crowd the Brigade into East Hill and leave West Hill undefended and free for the Japanese to occupy. But official records and personal recollections show that the Brigade commander was very much alive to this issue, and he spent the morning of 22 March actively considering how to defend West Hill. To Hope-Thomson, the immediate critical issues were his current strength and when the rest of his Brigade could arrive to bolster his defences. On the morning of 22 March, the only complete unit he had under command at Sangshak was 152 Battalion, and that was already under strength and holding an overly long perimeter along East Hill. Requiring it to defend West Hill as well would probably have been asking too much of the over-stretched Battalion. Hope-Thomson was also not sure exactly when 153 Battalion and 4/5 MLI would arrive at the village. If they arrived after dark, it would be difficult for them to prepare defences, as it was a problem to dig when under constant threat of an imminent Japanese attack.

So, balancing the few options available, Hope-Thomson decided to concentrate all his forces on East Hill. It is important to note that he did not merely 'circle the wagons', adopt a passive mindset and just 'wait for the inevitable'. Rather, within the limits of the resources available to him, he

22 March – Consolidating the Box   75

conducted a very active defence, using all of the men, weapons and tools at his disposal. To this end, he quickly ordered C Company, 4/5 MLI to move west of West Hill to act as a delaying force and screen the Brigade from any Japanese forces arriving from that direction. They were to hold their positions and delay the arrival of Japanese forces until 152 Battalion and the rest of 4/5 MLI could reach Sangshak. Official War Diary reports also show that throughout the siege, small patrols, listening posts and observation posts were regularly sent out from the main defensive position to gather information and harass the enemy. Again, this demonstrates that Hope-Thomson was determined to mount a very active defence, which was maintained throughout the siege of Sangshak.

Knowing that his relatively small force was very vulnerable on its own at Sangshak, at 1230 hrs he gave orders for the remaining troops at Kidney Camp to join the main Brigade defensive Box at Sangshak. Hopkinson called this an 'Emergency Operations' message, and it was sent 'in clear' (not coded). The message read, 'Rejoin me here at all costs. Way cleared.' The urgency was clear, and despite having just arrived at their old camp, the tired men at Kidney immediately repacked their equipment, took up their loads once more and headed off on the jungle paths and over the hills towards the Brigade Box.

Just as the men were about to move out of Kidney Camp, a patrol from 153 Battalion mounted on two 15cwt trucks[4] arrived at Kidney to inform Trim and Hopkinson exactly where the Brigade Box was located. The 153 Battalion men said the way was clear and then proceeded to load the wounded and the 3-inch mortars onto the trucks and ferry them back to Sangshak. Encouraged by the 'all clear' message from the patrol, the remainder of 152 Battalion and 4/5 MLI moved along the track with all haste towards the main Brigade Box.

* * *

While the rest of the Brigade units at Sangshak were busy digging in and setting up their defences, the 15 Mountain Battery Observation Post (OP) in the church tower had spotted a sizeable group of Japanese, estimated at up to several hundred, moving near the Brigade's recently vacated HQ positions at Finches Corner. The timing of the Brigade move had been fortuitous indeed!

After considering the report from the church OP, at around 1430 hrs Hope-Thomson ordered a small vehicle-mounted patrol under command of Captain Steele, 4/5 MLI, to try to scout around the edges of Finches Corner and report back on what the advancing Japanese were doing. Moving quickly towards the old HQ, Steele did more than merely observe; he set up a quick ambush and killed six Japanese soldiers, before retiring back to the main position. This was the type of quick, aggressive action that Steele would become known for over the coming days.

Besides the ambush, Steele's information about the disposition of the enemy concentrating at Finches Corner was also relayed to 15 Mountain Battery, who quickly prepared their guns and started firing at the concentrated groups of Japanese. The gunners reported a good day's shooting, and the high explosive rounds encouraged the Japanese to quickly take cover in the surrounding jungle. As they were clearly being observed by the British, the Japanese did not wait long near Finches Corner but rather turned their attention towards the sound of the guns. Leaving Finches Corner, columns of Japanese were now spotted heading back towards Sangshak.

The Japanese had once again advanced with their trademark lightning speed, being now both behind the Brigade and advancing from the east, as well as ahead of the Brigade and circling from the west. Despite the clear confirmation that there were Japanese in the immediate vicinity, the sight of a sizeable Japanese formation on the Manipur Road near Finches Corner must have come as something of a shock to Hope-Thomson. Just two days earlier, the Japanese were only just bumping up to the Brigade's easternmost defences at Hill 7378, whereas now they had already infiltrated *past* the Brigade and into positions to its west.

Critically, the enemy now held a portion of the main road between Imphal and Ukhrul, meaning that reinforcements and re-supply could no long reach the Brigade by road. With no other significant British units in this sector, the Brigade was at risk of being cut off.

It now became a race to see who would gain control of Sangshak first. Although the British were first to place troops in the village, it was by no means certain that they could hold it.

Fortunately, and after a tough slog up the jungle track, from about 1630 hrs the men from Kidney Camp started to trickle into the Brigade defensive position. Hope-Thomson must have been relieved to finally have his Brigade together in one location, knowing as he did that the Japanese were rapidly closing in. He recorded that when 152 Battalion and 4/5 MLI arrived at the Sangshak perimeter in the late afternoon they appeared extremely tired after their long march from Badger, heavily laden with equipment and ammunition. Then, as if to add insult to injury, the heavens suddenly opened and it began to rain heavily. As each of the tired, and now sodden, Battalions made their way into the village they were allocated a section of the perimeter and told to dig in.

As Trim moved his men into Sangshak he knew that there was no time for rest. He also noted that there was some initial confusion as to where his men should actually go. With his Companies filing into the perimeter at around 1800 hrs, a Khali Bahadur VCO (Viceroy Commissioned Officer – i.e. an Indian officer) came up to them and tried to direct the Battalion to an area which was just about big enough to hold a single platoon. This would not do, and after finding someone who was more senior and who was able to give him some sensible orders, 'a clearer picture emerged enabling me to locate a suitable defensive position for the Bn. D Coy re-joined me and was placed in reserve. Digging commenced immediately but was hampered by heavy rain and the ensuing thunderstorm.'

It was a very wet start but, urged on by their officers, within an hour all of Trim's Battalion was in position, with each of the Companies properly sited to provide mutual support. Besides the furious digging, the MLI troops also took time to employ their favourite tactic and placed grenades and mortar shells as booby traps to the front of their forward pits.

While 4/5 MLI were digging in to the south-east, Hopkinson's Battalion was allocated the north-west section of the perimeter, including the vitally important church. Lieutenant Bill Gollop, the A Company Lieutenant who had luckily declined breakfast with his unfortunate C Company comrades on the 20th, was ordered to occupy a defensive position just north of the church. He remembered that it was terribly exposed, clearly open to machine gun fire from both West Hill and the jungle to the north. He also noted that 'snipers had their pick', meaning that his men had to be careful to never show their heads above the edge of the pits.

The church itself was allocated to Alan Cowell and the fifteen men of his platoon. These men joined the OP team from 15 Mountain Battery at the church who were still on the lookout for more Japanese targets for their guns. While the building gave good views, and its walls gave a little protection, it was also a very obvious target, clearly visible and of vital tactical importance. The church was to be a focal point of both Japanese attacks and British counter-attacks over the coming days, and Cowell would find himself in the thick of it on several occasions.

As 153 Battalion arrived, the light was fading fast. The gloom intensified with the rain, and so Gollop, Cowell and their comrades had little opportunity to dig new defences. All they could do was locate and occupy the various slit trenches which had already been dug by previous occupants, or hide behind the cover provided by the church and other small structures which dotted this part of the hill. While clearly inadequate, the defenders would soon be grateful for even these makeshift defences. As night fell and the rain continued, the men of 153 Battalion hunkered low into their makeshift defences, waiting for the Japanese attack that they knew could not be far away.

* * *

About 500 yards in front of Gollop on West Hill, C Company, 4/5 MLI were hiding and waiting, silently occupying their temporary positions and ready to ambush any Japanese who moved into this sector. The ambushers spotted several small Japanese patrols lurking near the edges of West Hill, but these were discouraged from coming any closer by a short sharp fusillade from the MLI troops. Things changed, however, after dusk at about 1900 hrs. Under cover of darkness, a larger force from the Japanese 58th Regiment formed up to the west, ready for an assault eastward through the *bashas* and huts of West Hill and straight towards the MLI defenders.

There was nothing that C Company could do to hold back such a determined attack. With only light personal weapons, exposed above ground without the protection of weapons pits, all they could do was fire off a great deal of ammunition at the attackers, hoping to keep the enemy's heads down long enough to allow the defenders to escape and retreat to East Hill and the main defensive position.

As C Company pepper-potted their way rearwards, using the *bashas* for cover, their withdrawal was covered by fire from the invaluable mortars of 582 Battery. The hollow 'pop' as the mortar left the tube, followed shortly thereafter by the crump of the explosion to their rear, were comforting sounds to the MLI soldiers as they made their way back, giving them a precious opportunity to escape. But as they threaded their way through the forward line of 152 Battalion troops manning the perimeter, it must have been clear to them that the Japanese now completely dominated West Hill and that it would be next to impossible for the British to win it back.

Nightfall

The British and Japanese forces had run a very close race, but by nightfall on 22 March the result was clear: the British were firmly in command of the bigger and higher East Hill, while the Japanese dominated West Hill.

As the rain stopped and night closed in, the Japanese commenced their usual probing attacks on the Brigade perimeter. After they ejected the MLI screen from West Hill, fire from that sector slackened, only to be replaced at about 1930 hrs by the enemy's Medium Machine Guns (MMGs) set up in the jungle to the north and firing along fixed lines down the length of the central ridge. 'Fixed lines' refers to a machine gun being literally staked between two upright posts so that it fires a near-continuous stream of bullets along a narrow fixed path. This technique can be highly effective at denying a route to the enemy, effectively blocking any attempt at movement across the line of fire and almost certainly killing any man unfortunate enough to be in its path. Firing from the north, just to the side of the central ridge, this fire effectively cut the Brigade box in two, making any movement between the two sides of the central ridge particularly dangerous.

The Japanese also probed Trim's men down on the southern edge of the village. The fall of shot started at the B Company lines and then crept along the edge of the MLI perimeter. This was not the prelude to an attack but rather a ruse to induce the MLI defenders to reveal themselves. The Japanese were experts at using this type of tactic to get inexperienced men to reveal their position and strength. While the Mahrattas were certainly experienced, they still fell for this trick: 'At first the men fired rather wildly due no doubt to fatigue as much as anything else. However, after about three hours the firing was controlled and thereafter fire control was excellent.'[5] While the Japanese probes were testing the boundaries of their enemy, men from D Company, 4/5 MLI, who were held slightly rearwards and in reserve, ferried fresh ammunition to their comrades fighting in the front-line pits. To do so, the D Company men had to crouch and crawl between the pits, before dashing over open ground exposed to more and more Japanese fire. That they managed to do so without suffering a single casualty was a miracle.

But while the ammunition-carriers of D Company remained unscathed, the same could not be said for the defenders on the perimeter. Over the course of the evening, five men from the 4/5 MLI perimeter posts would be wounded and had to be carried or dragged back to the field hospital, which had been hastily set up near the Brigade HQ.

Medical

Fortunately for the wounded, 50 Parachute Brigade had a number of excellent medical teams attached to it, all of whom worked tirelessly to help care for the wounded and dying. Improvements in medical care and the availability of medical staff close to the fighting men were major changes that the British had instigated in 1943. These developments paid big dividends in reducing the rate of death and disability from both wounds and disease. The Japanese had nothing comparable, and even a minor wound to one of their men would often result in death.

Each of 50 Parachute Brigade's forward battalions had its own small Regimental Aid Post (RAP), usually located just to the rear of Battalion HQ. The RAPs were commanded by a doctor (holding the rank of Captain), with Captain A.G. Rangaraj commanding the 152 Battalion RAP and Captain Eric

Neild in charge of 153. Captain Rangaraj was a trailblazer, reportedly both the first Indian officer to join the Brigade and the first to make a parachute jump. Both Rangaraj and Neild would have long and successful military careers, with Rangaraj serving during the Korean War, and Neild, after a long and colourful career, eventually rising to the rank of Colonel.

The RAPs themselves were simple affairs but provided invaluable immediate care to wounded men soon after they were hit. Neild's post was small – comprising a little dugout and a clearing station, which he described as being no bigger than a badminton court. With space at a premium, he also had to share his RAP with the Battalion mortars.[6] Neild was assisted by a medical Havildar and several medical riflemen. These men were infantry soldiers trained in first aid who could provide immediate care to a wounded man before transporting him back to the Battalion RAP. This procedure usually involved placing the wounded on a carrying sheet, which was then lifted or dragged by several men. However, given the steep terrain at Sangshak, these medical riflemen would often be forced to lift the wounded and bring them, piggy-back style, to the aid post.

Initial care of the wounded at the forward RAP's was rudimentary but critical to keeping men alive. As Neild recounted, 'All night long the wounded passed through. There was little that could be done except to stop any bleeding, give morphia and then evacuate them in the lulls to the field ambulance.'[7]

Despite the evacuation routes to the Field Ambulance (the larger Brigade Field Hospital) often being cut and coming under sustained enemy fire, the stretcher-bearers continued to ferry the wounded from the forward battalions and RAPs to the Brigade Field Ambulance located near Brigade HQ. In total, one British officer, two British other ranks and twenty Indian/Gurkha other ranks were admitted to the Field Ambulance for treatment during the night of 22 March.

The Field Ambulance itself was located about 200 yards to the rear, on the far side of the central ridge and close to Brigade HQ. The work of the hospital staff in constructing the operating theatre dugout had paid off, and by evening the doctors had a relatively safe place in which to conduct resuscitation and operations. Lieutenant Colonel Bobby Davis, the chief medical officer of the Brigade, conducted most of the complex operations. He was assisted by Captain Pozner, the anaesthetist, and other members of the surgical team. They would work constantly throughout the remainder of the siege, irrespective of the chaos and carnage that was occurring all around them, saving many lives.

Chapter 8

23 March – The Onslaught Begins

Just after midnight, and through the early hours of 23 March, quiet returned to Sangshak. The jungle was silent, and the British and Indian soldiers crouching in their pits took turns to snatch a moment's rest between stints of guard duty. The Japanese were likewise quiet, and the only noises to be heard anywhere in the entire village were the soft sounds of the 50 Brigade signals section working on their fading wireless and trying hard to send situation reports back to 23 Division.

Hope-Thomson knew that this was only a brief lull. While he was not yet in danger of being surrounded, he knew that there was a sizeable enemy force heading for him, and unless some miracle made them decide to bypass his isolated Brigade, another clash was certain to come soon; thus his urging of his signallers to spare no effort in making contact with Division to see what support they could provide.

On West Hill, the newly ensconced Japanese were likewise taking a moment to rest and collect themselves before preparing for another push at the paratroopers to their front. The Indian troops were an irritant to them, but it was thought that speed and aggression was all that would be needed to break these stubborn defenders. So at 0130 hrs the Japanese assembled for a major assault, aiming to smash through the British perimeter and eject them from Sangshak altogether. The assaulting companies of 58 Regiment moved silently towards their forming-up points, directly opposite 153 Battalion's perimeter, and waited for the order to charge.

The type of assault that followed was to be replicated again and again over the next few days. Gone were the careful and tentative probing thrusts seen the day before. Instead, this was to be a fanatical Japanese frontal attack, what Allied soldiers often referred to as a '*banzai* charge' after the battle cry that the Japanese often yelled as they assaulted enemy positions. The charge was reminiscent of a First World War advance across no-man's-land, a rushing mass of fixed bayonets and drawn swords, accompanied by yelling and screaming designed to unnerve the defenders, break their will and send them fleeing screaming before the attackers.

While the *banzai* charges were legendary, and the Japanese soldiers were undoubtedly brave men, the attackers still had to deal with the twin challenges of unforgiving ground and a staunch and resolute opponent. Crucially, the Japanese were mostly attacking up hill. The Japanese infantrymen coming from the west first needed to descend the slope of West Hill, threading their way through the burnt-out or destroyed *bashas*. They would pick up speed as they hit the saddle between the two hills, before slowing almost to a walk as they made their way, leaning forward, up East Hill towards the plateau and the church beyond.

The terrain was not the only challenge facing the attackers. The Gurkhas of 153 Battalion were themselves very tough and resolute soldiers and would not leave their defensive pits unless bodily ejected from them. While the steel of the Japanese officers' swords glinted in the eerie light cast by the Very pistols' flares and the flickering fires of burning huts, the Gurkhas' curved kukri knives likewise shone, ready to slash at any Japanese who was able to make it past their rifle fire and into the forward pits.

Despite all their martial spirit and combat experience, the attacking Japanese quickly realized that they were facing a very different enemy from those they had met in the past. 'This was the first time we had fought with the British-Indian forces', recalled Captain Shosaku Kameyama, the adjutant of 58 Regiment's 3rd Battalion. '[This] was very different from our experience of fighting the Chinese army, which had inferior weapons to ours … Though we wanted to advance we could not even lift our heads because of the heavy fire which we had never before experienced.'[1]

Despite the terrain and the withering fire poured on them by the waiting defenders, the Japanese nevertheless conducted multiple attacks that night. They moved rapidly, skilfully using the available cover and trying their best not to be silhouetted against the fires of the burning *bashas* on West Hill. Three Companies of Japanese soldiers from the 3rd Battalion assaulted the perimeter but all were driven back after suffering horrendous casualties. The Japanese Battalion Commander was shot through the neck but, amazingly, he managed to stem the bleeding and continue to encourage his men forward, while a much-respected officer from 8 Company, Lieutenant Ban, was killed on the forward slopes of the British perimeter. Due to the intense defensive fire laid down by the Gurkhas, the Japanese reluctantly had to leave Ban's body where he had fallen. The loss of Ban would weigh heavily on the minds of the Japanese troops for days to come: 'Too shameful not to recover the bones of Lieutenant Ban' was how Kameyama would recall his feelings and the feelings of his comrades at the time.

The first night of *banzai* charges was furious and seemingly never-ending. Hopkinson noted that the Japanese attackers 'made no attempt at surprise, using lights to aid direction and shouting at each other … they set fire to the Naga village and the flames from the burning buildings lighted up the battlefield.'[2] The flames edged closer and closer, becoming so threatening that the British commanders almost decided to withdraw his troops eastwards from the perimeter as the fire leapt from hut to brush, to piles of rubbish and firewood, and almost to the edge of their forward defences. Fortunately, the wind changed, and with it the threat of being roasted alive receded. But the fires lit up the whole battlefield, silhouetting the attackers and casting long, flickering shadows all over the ground.

One British officer who had an unwelcome ringside seat in the unfolding battle was Captain Neild, terribly exposed in his RAP dugout towards the forward edge of the 153 Battalion line. Despite being fully occupied with tending the growing numbers of wounded men making their way to the RAP, Neild could nevertheless both see and hear the Japanese forming up for their attacks. He remembered clearly that these early attacks were supported by elements of the INA (JIFS). He recalled: 'Renegade Indian troops with them were shouting "cease fire" in English, Urdu and Gurkhali, while British officers were shouting even ruder things in reply. The night was brilliantly lit by Very lights, tracer and exploding Jap 2-inch mortar bombs which seemed to burn with a phosphorus glow.'[3]

The Gurkhas of 153 Battalion repelled the initial attacks and fought back fiercely. The attacks were also impeded by accurate British mortar fire, which was directed close to the front line of trenches, as well as by the steady stream of fire from the Lewis guns of the Medium Machine Gun Company. Exposed to this deadly hail, the assault was broken up, and many attacking Japanese soldiers fell in this first ferocious wave. Nevertheless, a few isolated groups of attackers succeeded in making their way into some empty trenches in front of the 4/5 MLI position, the momentum of the *banzai* charge having propelled a few courageous survivors into the forward trenches.

While the main weight of attacks that night fell on 153 Battalion, 4/5 MLI were not entirely spared, and a number of supporting attacks were also directed at their sector. Trim noted:

In this frenzy of activity the enemy attacked continuously during the night. I had no telephonic communications with Bde HQ and had to go to a gunner officer to use his. Both Mackay and I were subject to being hit by our own MMG fire while supervising the despatch of ammunition to Bde. The men were hungry and tired and as a result became trigger happy but we managed to calm them down. Heavy rain during the night helped us to assuage our thirst partially.[4]

In addition to the defending infantry, the gunners of 15 Mountain Battery received particular attention from the attacking Japanese that evening, since they must have recognized the critical importance of these guns to the British defence. No.1 Gun, under command of Havildar Mohan Lal, was the nearest to the jungle on the northern side of the perimeter, and it came under intense enemy fire as the Japanese tried to knock it out of action.

But the gunners fought back, courageously defending their guns, until the Japanese were forced to withdraw. The men manning the guns were relatively lucky in suffering only a single casualty during the attack: this was Naik Lal Chand, whose serious wounds necessitated him being dragged immediately to the Field Ambulance near HQ.

Chand was not the only wounded soldier needing attention that night. Despite it being the first night of serious contact, the doctors in the RAPs and Field Ambulance were already being swamped by wounded and injured soldiers. The grisly count would rise markedly over the coming days.

Unfortunately for the gunners of the Mountain Battery, Chand was not their only casualty that night. Shortly after the attack on the guns petered out, two of the Battery's cooks from the Punjabi Mussulman section were killed by mortar fire while trying to recover some of their cooking equipment. It is not known why the men felt they had to recover their pots and pans during such a serious engagement, but the incident also highlights the fact that all Indian units of this time invariably contained, besides the fighting men, a number of non-combatants who were also exposed to all of the trials of soldiering and the dangers of the battlefield.

* * *

After the first big wave of attacks, the Japanese thrusts towards the British perimeter slowed dramatically, before ceasing all together with the coming of dawn. Having failed to breach the British perimeter, the Japanese withdrew back to the far slope of West Hill or into the jungle just north of the village. They would use the day to bind their wounds, restock their ammunition and prepare for the next assault, which was sure to be ordered with the coming of night. Behind them they left a trail of their dead and dying, lying exposed on the hillside or in front of the Gurkhas' trenches.

Lieutenant General Renya Mutaguchi, the architect of the U-Go Campaign.

50 Parachute Brigade patch and 4/5 Mahratta Cap Badge.

The commanders. Brigadier Hope-Thomson (top) and Lieutenant Colonel Hopkinson (bottom) as a Brigadier in 1945.

Officers of 153 Parachute Battalion, January 1944. Captain Jimmy Roberts is front row, 4th from left and Jemadar Dudhjung Ghale is top row, 4th from left. Both were instrumental in the church counter-attack on 26 March. (*James McEmey*)

Gurkha Paratroopers. Note the distinctive padded helmets developed for use in India. (*AWM*)

A Gurkha Paratrooper explaining how to use a kukri. (*AWM*)

153 Battalion Officers, 1942. Lieutenant Seaman top row, 4th from right. Lieutenant Allen, the Intelligence officer who would later deliver the captured map top row, 6th from right. Captain Neild RAMC middle row, 4th from left. (*Gurkha Museum*)

A 153 Battalion Gurkha – probably Company Havildar Major Bhimbadur Thapa. Portrait by official war artist Harry Sheldon. (*Gurkha Museum*)

MLI Troops. At the centre is Havildar Sambhaji Bhuingde, who was awarded the Indian Distinguished Service Medal (IDSM) for actions at Sangshak.

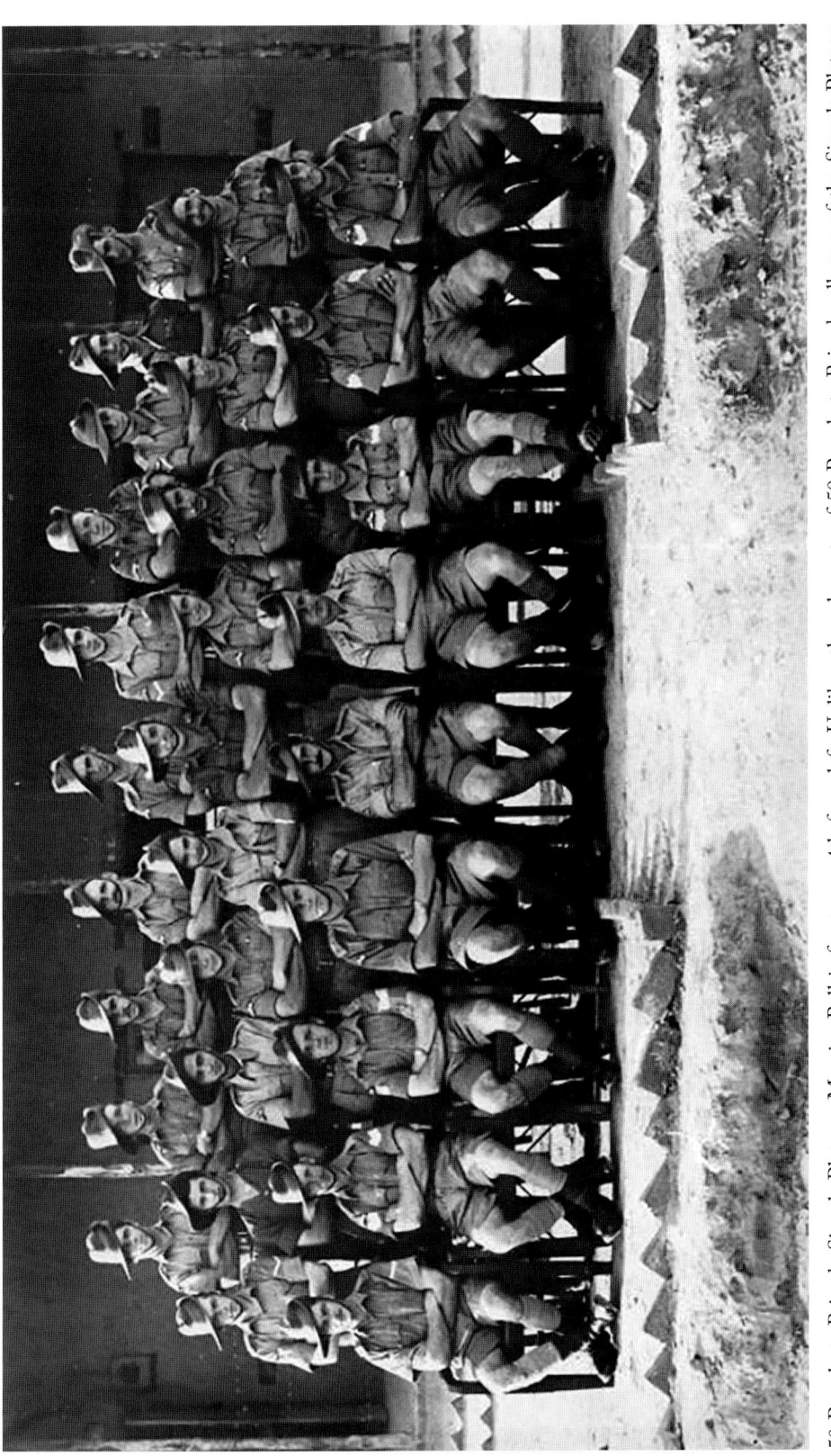

50 Parachute Brigade Signals Platoon. Maurice Bell is front row, 4th from left. Unlike other elements of 50 Parachute Brigade, all men of the Signals Platoon were British.

Uhkrul, 22 March 1944. Elements of 50 Parachute Brigade had just withdrawn when this photo was taken. Uhkrul was soon occupied by the Japanese. (*AWM*)

Manipur, May 1944. This country is typical of the mountainous terrain faced by 50 Parachute Brigade during its siege and withdrawal from Sangshak (*AWM*)

Hockings, Seaton and Hopkinson, a day before the battle.

Japanese soldiers manhandling a Type 41 75mm Mountain gun through the hills of Manipur during Operation U-Go.

Japanese 31 Division advancing through Manipur. All food, ammunition and supplies required by the Division had to be carried by the advancing troops.

Japanese soldiers attacking during Operation U-Go.

A 3.7-inch Mountain gun in action in 1944. (*IWM*)

The grenade was invaluable in close-quarter fighting. (*IWM*)

Airdrops over the jungle. Although up to 75 per cent of supplies missed their target, the drops of ammunition were vital to 50 Parachute Brigade's defence at Sangshak. (*AWM*)

A contemporary painting of the Battle of Sangshak by Sorensen. (*Author's collection*)

'Fight your way out' – the famous message of 26 March 1944.

Devastation. A Naga village near Kohima destroyed in the fighting in 1944. Sangshak would have looked very similar after a week of intense combat. (*IWM*)

Lieutenant Ronald Bolton.
(*Airborne Assault Museum*)

Lieutenant Robin Kynoch-Shand. The only British officer to be captured at Sangshak, he soon made a daring escape and endured a gruelling solo journey through the hills of Manipur back to Imphal.

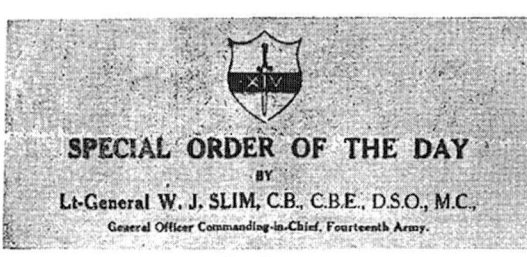

SPECIAL ORDER OF THE DAY
BY
Lt-General W. J. SLIM, C.B., C.B.E., D.S.O., M.C.
General Officer Commanding-in-Chief, Fourteenth Army.

—Addressed to The 50th Parachute Brigade

IN my last Order of the Day I told you that you had defeated the Jap armies opposing you and that it remained to destroy them. The extent to which you have done that is shown by the fifty thousand Japanese left dead on the soil of India and Northern Burma, the great quantities of guns and equipment you have captured, the prisoners you have taken, the advance you have made, and the flight of the remnants you are still pursuing. To the 15th Corps in the Arakan fell the unique honour of being the first British-Indian formation to hold, break and decisively hurl back a major Japanese offensive.

Theirs was an example of tenacity and courage which inspired the whole Army. The 4th Corps met the main weight of the Japanese Assam offensive, and, in one of the hardest fought and longest battles of the war, shattered it. 33rd Corps in their brilliant offensive from the North not only drove a large Japanese force from what should have been an impregnable position, but destroyed it. Together the 4th and 33rd Corps have swept the enemy out of India.

The troops of 202 and 404 L of C Areas, not only by their gallantry and steadfastness in action, but by their tireless devotion behind the immediate front, have made a contribution essential to victory. What you owe to our comrades in the Allied Air Forces I need not remind you. Our whole plan of battle was based on their support. There would have been no success had they failed us. Their share in our combined victory was magnificent and historic.

There is not a division or brigade in the Fourteenth Army which has not proved its superiority over the enemy and knows it. Your Parachute Brigade bore the first brunt of the enemy's powerful flanking attack, and by their staunchness gave the garrison of Imphal the vital time required to adjust their defences.

To the officers and men of the 50th Parachute Brigade I send my congratulations. The Fourteenth Army has inflicted on the Japanese the greatest defeat his Army has yet suffered. He is busily trying to build up again and reinforce his broken divisions. He will fight again and viciously, but we have paid him something of what we owe. There still remains the interest. He will get it.

Field
31 August '44.

Lieut-General.
General Officer Commanding-in-Chief.

Slim's Special Order of the Day.

Sangshak in 2022 with a new church in the distance. (*Findlay Kembar*)

Chapter 9

23 March – Of Plans and Captured Maps

Daybreak saw a marked reduction in enemy activity as the Japanese drew back to consolidate. As a heavy shower started to fall, the defenders looked out through the early morning gloom to see that the perimeter was littered with Japanese corpses. Taking care not to be hit by the ever-present Japanese snipers, men were sent forward to quickly search the bodies for useful intelligence.

Amazingly, a map was found on a dead Japanese officer which showed not only the complete order of battle of 15 and 31 Divisions but also their planned routes towards Imphal and Dimapur respectively. This was an incredible intelligence coup, and Hope-Thomson realized at once that the map must be sent back to headquarters at Imphal as soon as possible. Accordingly, he ordered a Brigade Intelligence officer, Captain Lester Allen, together with a single Indian escort, to slip out of the perimeter later in the evening and take the valuable map back to Imphal.

Subsequent histories of the Sangshak battle have spent a great deal of time discussing this map and pondering the 'might-have-beens' had it found its way into the hands of the senior British generals. That it existed and was recovered by the British paratroopers seems almost certain, since its existence has been reported by several commentators separately. Likewise, Allen, despite all the dangers, was able to make his way quite quickly to HQ in Imphal. What is not clear, however, is what then happened to the map.

Most previous general histories of the Imphal campaign or the Sangshak battle make no mention of the map, or if they do, dispute whether it was ever sent on to the generals directing the British defence. Seaman goes further and suggests some form of conspiracy – based on the fact that the map is not mentioned in any official record and, according to Seaman, that Allen was soon afterwards apparently 'banished' to an obscure staff job in India. But this is scant and unconvincing evidence of either a conspiracy or a cover-up. An equally likely explanation is that the map simply disappeared into the mountains of paper that accompany an army in the field, or may have been lost in subsequent fighting or discarded by people who did not realize its value.

There is no logical reason why HQ 23 Division would deliberately want to 'bury' such useful intelligence or 'banish' its bearer to obscurity.

On the other hand, a close inspection of the 23 Division War Diary for 23 March 1944 reveals the existence of a captured enemy map which indicates the routes of advance for several Japanese columns.[1] Rather than burying such a map, it appears that 23 Division immediately recognized its value and ordered British patrols to move up and watch these potential lines of advance. Without a surviving copy of the map it is not known whether the captured map mentioned in the 23 Division Diaries is definitely the same as the one found at Sangshak. But it appears likely that it was. The times of its discovery and its mention in the 23 Division War Diary are close to each other, and the coordinates of the likely enemy routes mentioned in the War Diary are located just to the south-west of Sangshak. Both of these facts suggest that that the map found by 50 Brigade and the one referred to by the 23 Division War Diary are one and the same. If so, this finally puts to bed the question of the captured Japanese map and lays to rest yet another conspiracy theory advanced by Seaman in his otherwise excellent treatment of the battle.

* * *

In any event, such debates and questions would only surface long after the war had ended. At the time, the Brigade was occupied with more pressing problems – the dead, the wounded, water and re-supply.

An immediate issue was the large number of enemy corpses littering the hillside in front of the Gurkhas. Taking great care, they started to search each of them for information. Besides the officer with the map, another Japanese officer was found on the forward edge of the position. After searching him for any intelligence material, he was wrapped neatly in a blanket with his sword and then buried as well as possible in the hard ground. It would only later be discovered that this was in fact Lieutenant Ban, the much-respected Company commander whose memory would be invoked numerous times over the coming days in order to inspire the flagging Japanese to mount yet further attacks.

While the large-scale assaults of the night had ended, enemy activity had not ceased altogether, and the men retrieving the bodies had to be careful. Sniping and desultory mortar fire continued through the day, hampering the efforts of the defenders to improve their positions, get food and water, or rest. The men were becoming increasingly tired, and whenever a man tried to snatch a moment of rest, a bullet would invariably zing across the position, suddenly jerking the exhausted soldier back to wide-eyed wakefulness.

While the clearance parties were recovering the dead and wounded, the Brigade Supply officer, Captain Roger Sylvester had a very lucky escape. He was in his trench when a mortar round fell just outside it, toppling the lip of the trench inwards and spraying soil all over him. As he shook himself clean, a single bullet shattered the stock of his rifle and ricocheted upwards to pierce the rim of his hat.[2] Sylvester dived back into the bottom of his trench as fast as he could, grasping his newly ventilated hat and reflecting that supply officers were not normally subjected to such intimate attention from the enemy.

* * *

Unfortunately, Sylvester's close call was not the Brigade's only encounter with Japanese snipers. They would prove to be a constant and deadly nuisance for the rest of the siege. Captain Hatton, an officer with the mortars of 582 Battery, complained with serious understatement that 'considerable trouble' was experienced throughout the day from them. The 'trouble' rose to such a level, however, that his mortars were being constantly harassed, and to continue firing he was forced to move the entire Mortar Battery to a new site just north of their initial position. They immediately commenced digging in at their new home, before once again opening fire.[3]

Even Brigade HQ in their relatively protected position often came under fire from the ever-resourceful snipers. Lieutenant Basil Seaton of 152 Battalion noted:

> It became customary for Brigade HQ officers to gather near the HQ at around 1pm for 'lunch'. There was little to eat but it was an opportunity to exchange information on the progress of the battle and generally update ourselves on what was happening. It was usually fairly quiet at this time with both sides preparing for the evening attacks. However, on one occasion, the peace was shattered by a stream of bullets and our very rapid dispersal. It still seems a miracle that no one was even wounded. Nobody could explain how the sniper had managed to infiltrate so far into our 'box' but his skill and bravery must have been of the highest order. As he must have foreseen, his own death came within seconds. We continued to meet for 'lunch' – but took much greater care. There were enough casualties without our adding to them in an irresponsible way.[4]

The morning also witnessed a slow but steady increase in British and Indian casualties. Besides the unfortunate Mountain Battery cooks and the men wounded during the night, 152 Battalion on the northern perimeter was now coming under sporadic sniping and rifle fire. Later that morning, Lieutenants Seaton and Patterson were both seriously wounded, as were a number of Indian other ranks.

Seaton was the acting second-in-command of A Company, 152 Battalion at the time and was sharing a trench with Bill Gollop. While they were in the process of digging and generally improving their trenches, Seaton was shot through the mouth, the bullet going straight in and out of his neck on the other side. It was a terrible wound, and it was amazing that he was still alive as he was carried directly to the Brigade Field Ambulance station. With the medical equipment available to them there was little that the doctors could do for him except to close his wounds, stop the bleeding and administer morphine. With his jaw and mouth shattered, Seaton was kept heavily sedated over the next few days and was all but oblivious to the battle raging around him – until he suddenly regained consciousness on the morning of 27 March.

* * *

Fatigue was now affecting almost every man in the Brigade. It was almost impossible to sleep at night due to the constant attacks, and daybreak brought little relief as the men were required to work constantly at improving their dugouts, fetch water or ammunition or labour in the numerous work parties needed to improve the Brigade's defences. Even when it was quiet, the constant threat of snipers and mortars kept them on edge. They were exhausted but they were unable to rest.

Hope-Thomson was likewise feeling the effects of exhaustion. The constant need to appear calm and give clear orders to his men, all the while worrying about his isolated Brigade and their precarious defences, must have added to his fatigue. Nevertheless, following his standard routine, at around 0800 hrs Hope-Thomson convened a conference at Brigade HQ to outline his priorities for the day.

The critical first task was to strengthen the Brigade's defences. When the Brigade had consolidated at Sangshak, most of these consisted of hastily dug pits and trenches, together with a few partially prepared trenches dug by previous occupants (49 Brigade and elements of 4/5 MLI). Hope-Thomson's units had also just been slotted into the perimeter in the order in which they arrived at Sangshak, with little time to consider carefully who was best placed to go where. As it was clear that the Japanese were not going to give up any time soon, improving defences was the top priority, and Hope-Thomson tasked the Brigade 2IC, Colonel Abbott, to review them and reorganize as required. He also gave orders to dismantle all *bashas* within the perimeter. This was to avoid giving obvious reference points for enemy mortar and artillery fire, as well as to deny possible cover to the enemy should they somehow make it inside the perimeter. The fires caused by the burning *bashas* from the night before were probably also in his mind.

The conference continued with the Battalion and sub-unit commanders reporting on the current strengths of their respective units, casualties and ammunition expenditure. Lieutenant Colonel Willis, the CO of 153 Battalion whose Gurkhas had borne the brunt of the previous night's fighting, then requested permission to mount a counter-attack and clear West Hill of the Japanese, who were thought to be re-forming on its far edge. The commanders discussed the proposal, but ultimately it was rejected as being too risky.

Most importantly, the water and supply situations were addressed. As revealed by Hope-Thomson's original reconnaissance, the water supply at Sangshak was limited at the best of times. But now, because of constant sniping by the Japanese, the water point closest to the village school and just outside at the south-western corner was effectively denied to the defenders. This left only one accessible water point for the entire Brigade. The men had tried to collect the early morning rainwater in tins and tarpaulins, but it was not enough. The water point near the 4/5 MLI line was inadequate to supply the whole Brigade, and there was also the question of how to water the many mules still within the perimeter.

A discussion was held about whether it would be better to just shoot the mules, but luckily for the poor beasts they were spared – not only because of sympathy for the gunners' 'faithful and tireless servants' but also because of the very practical problem of what to do with the carcases if they were killed. There was no way of either burying or burning forty-plus mule carcases within the perimeter, and so the animals were left to stand, increasingly thirsty, in their lines. Recognizing how short water was, the already limited supply was immediately rationed to one bottle per man per day.

The other major supply issue, even more critical to a continued defence than water, was ammunition. While the Brigade had brought up a good store when they occupied Sangshak, use of all types of ammunition was proving to be very high. As an example, the ammunition returns of 4/5 MLI show that during the previous 24 hours over 11,000 rounds of .303 and .45 ammunition had been expended (.303 for the rifles and Bren guns, .45 for the Thompson sub-machine guns) and over ninety-seven grenades had been used. The other Battalions had probably expended at least as much, and possibly more. In particular, 153 Battalion, who had borne the brunt of the previous night's fighting, had almost certainly fired at least the same number of rounds as 4/5 MLI, but in all likelihood very many more. This suggests that at least 33,000 rounds of small arms ammunition had been fired by the Brigade during the night of the 22/23 March, together with perhaps 200 grenades. Furthermore, the mortars and the mountain guns had also been in action throughout the night. Altogether, this was an enormous weight of ammunition expended in just one night, and a rate of fire that the Brigade would not be able to sustain without significant re-supply from 23 Division.

Clearly, an urgent re-supply by air was needed, and a request was sent to HQ 23 Division asking for an immediate airdrop of water, ammunition (both small arms and mortar and artillery) and food.

With the conference over, the Battalion officers moved cautiously back to their units to give orders to their subordinates. The day was then occupied in improving the position as best they could, a difficult task given the paucity of tools available and in particular, the lack of barbed wire. Survivors would frequently say that the absence of barbed wire was a crucial reason why the defence proved to be so difficult. But while the lack of wire certainly contributed to the defenders' difficulties, it is hard to see why some stressed it as a key concern, as opposed to the much more significant lack of all ammunition types, including grenades and shells for the guns and mortars. A robust defence can be maintained without barbed wire, but no defence at all can be maintained unless sufficient stocks of ammunition are available.

* * *

Hopkinson departed the Brigade O Group, carefully making his way back to his Battalion to begin the task of reorganizing its defences. Arriving back at Battalion HQ, Hopkinson noted:

> I now had a chance to examine the Battalion's position in detail and readjust lines of fire, siting of the LMGs, etc. We soon found that the reason for the slit trenches and weapons pits being so shallow was that in this sector about three feet down was a layer of hard rock which made digging any deeper impossible. There were no communication or crawl trenches dug to connect the various posts.[5]

This lack of connecting trenches was to prove especially dangerous to the officers and NCOs who had to move around the position checking on their men. Over the next few days, many officers and NCOs were killed or wounded making these highly dangerous, but necessary, visits. The lack of suitable crawl trenches would also impede the speedy re-supply of ammunition and evacuation of the wounded, both of which were time-dependent and could not

23 March – Of Plans and Captured Maps

wait until the conclusion of battle. Sometimes men would just have to make a dash for it – and hope for the best.

Despite the tough ground and the constant threat from enemy snipers, the men worked hard throughout the day, urgently attempting to improve their trenches. Where possible, logs were placed over the top of key positions and then covered with soil and brush, in an attempt both to provide overhead protection from grenades, mortars and artillery fire and to camouflage them from the eyes of the enemy.

Strengthening the dugouts of the Field Ambulance was another priority, as the doctors needed a relatively secure place to treat the wounded and carry out surgery. While a rough dugout had already been constructed as a field surgery, it was in urgent need of a solid roof in order to provide protection from the ever-present threat of mortar and artillery fire. With no spare men available to help, Captain Pozner, the anaesthetist, took it upon himself to collect logs and other material from around the deserted village to fashion a solid form of overhead protection. While building the roof, on more than one occasion Pozner came under accurate rifle and machine gun fire. Nevertheless, he struggled on and assembled protection over the surgery dugout. His efforts would prove to be invaluable, since they enabled surgery to proceed relatively undisturbed for the entirety of the siege, despite the battle often raging around them.[6] It was just as well that Pozner had taken up this task, since on 23 March alone a further thirty-five men were admitted to the hospital with wounds.

* * *

It was not all gloom and doom among the men defending East Hill, and some of the most satisfied soldiers defending Sangshak that day were the officers and men of the Mountain Battery. Throughout the day, Japanese targets continued to present themselves both in the vicinity of the village and on the track junctions leading to Sangshak and the surrounding area. These targets gave the gunners multiple opportunities to exercise their black arts and direct their deadly high-explosive shells at the enemy. Two observation posts (OPs) were established on the perimeter of the village to observe enemy troop concentration and to call in fire. When a target was located, the men in the OP would radio a call for fire to the gun line. After the first rounds crashed down near the startled Japanese, the OP would then continually relay adjustments to the gunners so that they could correct the guns' fire and walk subsequent rounds directly onto the enemy.

In the early part of the day the gunners had a free hand and received little harassment in return. The Japanese had yet to bring up their own artillery, and the guns were thus saved from any form of counter-battery fire. Nevertheless, the gunners' freedom was not to last; recognizing the danger from the British artillery, the Japanese tried to direct their machine gun fire at both the gunners and the OPs in an effort to disrupt their shooting.

One of the OPs was manned by a two-man team comprising Lieutenant Kidd and his all-important signaller. After calling in several fire missions, Kidd was subjected to a sustained and intense burst of LMG fire, which thankfully missed him. His signaller was not so lucky, however, and caught some shrapnel which wounded him slightly in the head. Although momentarily stunned, he quickly managed to shake it off. But the bad luck continued when a Japanese officer somehow managed to work his way close to the OP without being seen. Once in range, the officer lobbed a grenade at Kidd and his signaller.

Reacting quickly to the movement, Kidd spotted the officer and immediately shot him dead. But he was a second too late – the grenade had already left the officer's hand and it was arcing its way, seemingly in slow motion, towards Kidd. Incredibly, it then bounced off the unlucky signaller's head (he would have a terrible headache, having received both shrapnel and a grenade to the head within the space of a few minutes!) before landing with a thud squarely in Kidd's lap! The panic at this potentially mortal encounter quickly turned to relief as he realized that the grenade was a blind (dud). It was a very close call.

There was no time for the pair to congratulate themselves on their lucky escape, as almost immediately afterwards the OP started to take fire from a nearby Japanese 75mm mountain gun. The enemy had finally brought up their own artillery! While the 75mm mountain gun was inferior to the British guns in terms of range and capability, it was nevertheless a light-weight, manoeuvrable and incredibly versatile weapon which provided the bulk of the Japanese indirect fire assets at Sangshak.

The accurate attentions of the newly arrived 75mm guns made Kidd's OP untenable, and he quickly ordered his team to abandon it and start moving towards alternate accommodation from which to observe the Japanese. Kidd did, however, have the presence of mind to quickly search the dead Japanese officer lying outside his OP and sent the contents of the man's pockets back to the Brigade Intelligence section for analysis.

The other OP was manned by the Battery Commander, Major John Lock. He was having a much better day than the unfortunate Kidd; from his OP he spotted several concentrations of Japanese troops and was able to bring accurate and deadly fire down upon them. Later in the day, he had the guns load smoke rounds, ready to mark targets for the RAF re-supply planes circling nearby with their all-important parachute loads of ammunition, food and water.

23 March – Of Plans and Captured Maps

At 1630 hrs, a small complement of Dakotas flew over the Box bringing the badly needed water and ammunition. The defenders first heard the planes in the distance and then, a few minutes later, caught sight of them as they flew ever closer to the village. They watched as loaders in the rear of each plane hurriedly pushed boxes of supplies out of the side doors of the aircraft.

But to the dismay of the troops waiting below, almost all of the parachutes slowly floating to earth missed their mark. Instead of reaching the Brigade, the men watched incredulously as the white parachutes and their critical boxes of supplies floated away outside the perimeter, into the jungle and the grateful arms of the waiting Japanese.

The problem was that the planes had come in too high and fast – presumably for fear of being shot at. The result was that a large proportion, estimated at 75 per cent, of the crucial supplies fell outside the Brigade area, only to be quickly scooped up by the Japanese. Only one plane made a slow, deliberate and very low pass along the length of the position from west to east, making it possible to pinpoint the drop. Also, rather than dropping its load in a single run, this plane flew multiple low and slow runs over the Brigade, each time pushing out only a few pallets, in order to ensure that every one of them reached its intended target.

The efforts of this pilot made a critical difference to the fortunes of the besieged paratroopers, for without even this reduced re-supply of ammunition the men would not have been able to hold out for long. It was later learned that the pilot of this Dakota had worked with the Parachute Brigade in the past and was determined that his drop would get through. It did, and it made all the difference.

* * *

As the day waned, Hope-Thomson's attention focussed yet again on the evening's defence. The Box was now better dug in and much better defended than on the first day. But the men were tired, and there were still notable deficiencies in the perimeter. He was also increasingly concerned about a possible attack on the Khali Bahadur positions to the east of the box. His concern was such that he sent his trusted Intelligence Officer, Captain Richards, to the Khali Bahadur lines to act as a 'liaison officer' and forward observer for the 3-in mortars, which were placed on standby. It would prove to be a prescient decision, as just before dawn the next day, the Japanese mounted a raid against the Khali Bahadur Companies and the mule lines. It quickly fizzled out, since the defenders were on the alert and they were ably supported by accurate defensive fire from the mortars. Thwarted, the Japanese melted back into the jungle.

Apart from the dawn attack near the mule lines, the night had been relatively quiet. A patrol from 4/5 MLI, placed well forward of the main Battalion position on the south-eastern corner as early warning, suddenly found itself in an engagement with a small group of Japanese. It was over quickly, and the Japanese were easily beaten off. 'The men were very steady indeed and the Japs made no progress', was the confident verdict of the official 4/5 MLI War Diary.

Despite the lull in Japanese activity, the men were still on edge through the whole night. They were only able to snatch moments of sleep, and they remained on high alert, knowing that the Japanese were close by and could mount a rush at the perimeter at any time. Darkness brought its own worries, which played on the mind of even the stoutest of the defenders. Maurice Bell, from the Brigade signals section, described the anxiety felt by all the Brigade troops about the dangers of moving around the Box at night:

> The problem was that the Japs were clever at infiltrating and the 'front line' was never far away, wherever you were in the 'box'. It was good sense to avoid moving around after dusk, but sometimes, when a job overran the time estimated or where a problem had arisen which demanded my attention, there was no alternative. Each night a password was allocated and this, in theory, should have distinguished friend from foe. The problem was that whatever language was chosen for the password, it would be a foreign language for more than half the defending forces. Could the challenged person say the word quietly but clearly? Could the challenger recognize the word? It was always an enormous relief to reach HQ in one piece. [7]

Chapter 10

24 March – Wearing down the Box

Just before 0800 hrs, the Brigade's Battalion and Company commanders assembled at Brigade headquarters for their daily command conference. Hope-Thomson was convinced that the Brigade should not remain static but should, if at all possible, go onto the offensive and try to drive the Japanese off West Hill. To the assembled officers he laid out a plan that he had been considering. It was a relatively straightforward scheme which would see the entire 153 Battalion being used as the as the attacking force, supported by fire from the mountain battery and mortars. The remaining Battalions would continue to hold Sangshak and act as reserve.

Two matters, however, had to be resolved if the attack was to have any chance of success. The first was that the Brigade was still not sure exactly how many enemy soldiers were on West Hill and in the vicinity of Sangshak. The maps recovered from the slain Japanese officer suggested that elements of both the 31st and 15th Division were converging somewhere in the vicinity of Sangshak. The Brigade's own experience over the past few days had also clearly shown that there were large groups of enemy to the immediate west and east of their position. However, the exact strength of the Japanese facing them was unknown, and the only way to determine this was by patrols leaving the main Box and scouting the surrounding area for intelligence. Accordingly, small patrols consisting of three or four men were immediately ordered to set out towards Kidney Camp, Nungshing and Finches Corner/Mile 36 in order to determine the precise numbers of Japanese in the surrounding area.

The other key concern was supply. The ammunition state for 4/5 MLI showed that over the past 24 hours it had consumed over 3,700 rounds of .303, 53 grenades, 57 2-inch mortar bombs and 500 rounds for sub-machine guns. As 4/5 MLI held a relatively quiet sector during this period, it is probable that expenditure by 152 and 153 Battalions was at least double, very likely more than that. The mountain guns were likewise using ammunition at a rapid rate, and it took the best part of a single airdrop to fully re-supply these 3.7-inch guns for a single day of firing. The Brigade was simply unable to continue using up ammunition at such a prodigious rate without immediate re-supply. So once again, a signal was dispatched to 23 Division Headquarters for another urgent airdrop of ammunition, including the vitally important 3-in mortar rounds and shells for the mountain guns. Food, water and medical supplies were also requested.

The re-supply planes arrived quite quickly over the Sangshak area, since the main aerodromes at Imphal were only about 25 miles away as the crow flies. At approximately 0930 hrs the Dakotas began their approach, but as on the previous day the defenders were horrified to watch around two thirds of supplies again falling directly into Japanese hands. As before, only a single plane made slow, low and deliberate runs directly over the Box position and succeeded in posting its vital supplies directly into the laps of the desperate defenders.

* * *

Around noon, the gunners in the Church OP noticed a large formation of enemy troops apparently approaching them from the direction of Sheldon's Corner. This column was comprised of around twenty vehicles, 200–300 men and some elephants! It was thought that the elephants were probably hauling artillery pieces of some kind, most likely large ones. A group of this size moving up from Sheldon's Corner was particularly concerning to the Brigade Commander, since it showed the Japanese were bringing in both fresh troops and heavier weapons to blast the defenders out of their Sangshak village fortress. It also suggested that they were not going to bypass Sangshak but were getting ready for a decisive attack. In an attempt to disrupt and slow the advancing column, the gunners fired salvos of high explosive rounds at the advancing Japanese troops and also directed some fire at isolated pockets of the enemy that had been spotted in nearby villages. The gunners claimed success, reporting that they had not merely dispersed the advancing Japanese but had certainly inflicted significant casualties upon them.

As the afternoon wore on, the various patrols sent out in the morning started to return and reported a great deal of enemy movement in the surrounding area. Notably, the patrol sent towards Finches Corner confirmed that there was definite enemy movement near the Manipur Road and from the direction of Finches Corner. The intelligence gathered by the patrols confirmed that the enemy were now located in force both to the west and to the east of Sangshak, effectively cutting all road links and major tracks into Sangshak and making relief by nearby British force extremely unlikely.

The Brigadier was also very concerned about the presence of elephants and the heavy artillery that they were probably hauling. He spoke with Trim to see if 4/5 MLI were able to move quickly down the track towards them, set up an ambush and, if possible, destroy the elephants. But Trim said that he didn't have enough men to spare to send out on yet more patrols, let alone enough for a sizeable ambush party. As a compromise, efforts were made to contact Lieutenant Khurray, who was already leading a patrol down towards Kidney Camp, to see if he would be able to mount the ambush. But once again, radio communications proved erratic, and the commanders were unable to get through to Khurray. Reluctantly, it was acknowledged that it would be impossible to mount an ambush in time.

The failure to disrupt the advancing troops and elephants resulted in the enemy bringing up more of its 75mm mountain guns. By about 1400 hrs the new guns were in place, adding considerable firepower to the artillery brought up the day before. Quickly brought into action by their fast-moving crews, these guns commenced laying fire onto both B Company, 152 Battalion on the northern edge of the perimeter and Brigade HQ in their dugouts to the east of the central ridge. The signals section, too, was now in the line of fire, and the all-important aerials for the wireless sets were shredded by accurate shelling, temporarily halting all communications until they could be repaired.

* * *

The 75mm mountain gun was a mainstay artillery piece of the Japanese Army in this theatre. It was a relatively lightweight gun, at just under 500kg, and could be broken down into eleven main pieces for carriage by animals. At a pinch, it could even be man-packed, as had sometimes been necessary in the rugged terrain of New Guinea. Simple to operate, a good crew could reassemble the gun and bring it into action within ten minutes. While it was not the best type for firing at high trajectories (it did not use a variable set of charges but had a single fixed charge only), it was highly effective as a direct firing weapon in support of infantry. At Sangshak it would prove a formidable foe and a match for the guns of 15 Mountain Battery, firing high explosive, shrapnel and illumination rounds.

The increased fire from the 75mm guns was just the start of a savage series of attacks put in throughout mid-afternoon. Besides the B Company position being plastered by artillery shrapnel, the Japanese also mounted a major attack on 153 Battalion's A Company, which was holding the forwardmost point of the Box on the plateau, defending the all-important church.

Recognizing the seriousness of this new Japanese push, the Brigade called back to 23 Division Headquarters to request immediate close air support. They also requested an airdrop of new 300-watt chargers for the radio equipment. At 1600 hrs a flight of Hurricane fighter-bombers arrived from Imphal to strafe and bomb the attackers. But the planes found it difficult to distinguish friend from foe, given the closeness of the fighting and the covering of thick jungle. Some of the fighters swooped low and mistakenly strafed the defenders' trenches. Hopkinson himself dived to the ground just in time as a Hurricane swooped down and strafed the 152 Battalion HQ, riddling the trenches near him with long lines of machine gun fire!

The close air support had its desired effect, however, and the Japanese attacks faltered, before ceasing altogether. After the Japanese had withdrawn, the defenders cautiously looked out from their trenches to see ten or twenty Japanese bodies lying to the front of A Company, among them a wounded officer. Carefully, the Indian soldiers of 152 Battalion approached the wounded man, before dragging him inside the position and then on to the Field Ambulance to the rear. But their efforts to save him were in vain, and the officer soon died of his wounds. On the British side, the morning saw 152 Battalion suffering a further four men killed and another six wounded. Major Ball, who was commanding the MMG Company, was also killed, adding to the already very heavy casualty rate among the British officers.

* * *

Logistics continued to worry the senior officers in the Box. Water was critically low, but thankfully there was a brief downpour of heavy rain, which was quickly collected in every available mess tin, cup and tarpaulin. It went a little way towards assuaging the thirst of the men, but it also turned the floors of the defensive pits to mud.

Another recurring logistical headache was the large number of mules still standing nervously just outside the Khali Bahadur lines on the north-eastern slope of East Hill. While most Brigade mules had been sent out of the position to Litan before 22 March, the Brigade still had a large number belonging to both the Jungle Mortar and Mountain Gun batteries. With water so critically short for the men, there was precious little for the poor mules. There was also very little feed left for them. Inevitably, the question was raised again, 'What to do about the mules?' But the situation had not changed, and the Brigadier knew that shooting them would mean the mountain guns and mortars becoming immobile.

Eventually, however, it was decided that the animals had to go, and so with heavy hearts a party from Brigade Headquarters was sent down to the mule lines to drive them out of the position. The mules were untied and chased into the jungle, where presumably at least some of them were captured by the Japanese to act as carriers. It is quite likely, however, given the perilous state of the Japanese supplies, that any captured mule would have been quickly slaughtered and put into the pot.

While supplying the living and caring for the wounded stretched the Brigade, dealing with the dead was also an increasing challenge. The growing numbers of bloated and decomposing Japanese bodies lying just outside the perimeter would have to be left where they were. Sometime a body was spirited away by a brave and ghostlike Japanese rescuer, but most were left where they lay in the mud and the wreckage of the burnt-out village.

The Brigade did try to bury its own dead, but the hard ground made digging sufficiently deep graves difficult. Also, the incessant shelling from the 75mm guns often disinterred the recently buried. 'Conditions were becoming appalling', remarked Hopkinson, describing the growing piles of corpses both within and just outside the Box. The smell was revolting, too, and one can only imagine the effect seeing so many of their comrades lying dead around their fighting trenches and pits had on the defenders' morale.

Nevertheless, the men of 50 Parachute Brigade were still holding on surprisingly well. Despite the many casualties, they kept up their grim defence, not having the luxury of time to reflect on what had happened to their comrades or on the carnage surrounding them. Maurice Bell from the Signals section recalled the effect of the battle and how by this stage the survivors had no choice but to press on:

> I had a personal slit trench near the Signals Office in the Brigade HQ area. It was shallow but long enough for me to lie down and grab a couple of hours sleep whenever operations allowed. It also stored my scanty personal kit. Two or three days after the start of the battle I found that someone had installed a mortar alongside the trench. This seemed unsociable, to say the least, but I was much too busy to argue. However, the matter was quickly resolved by a direct hit from the Japanese artillery. And I was left to pick pieces of dead Gurkhas out of my bedding roll and kit. I don't remember any qualms, or even distaste, at having to do this though I now feel physically sick at the thought. By that stage of the fighting I must have been inured to the sight of shattered bodies and human blood.[1]

* * *

At 1700 hrs another British Hurricane circled over the Sangshak Box and proceeded to drop a written message attached to a long streamer into the defensive position. This type of streamer had been used since the First World

War to drop messages to troops when radio communications had failed. Given the exceedingly erratic nature of communications between 50 Brigade and 23 Division, the Division must have felt that an old-fashioned written note was in order. The streamer, however, contained a very simple message which told the defenders that 'The Sangshak position was vital to the main plan and arrangements for relief of the Brigade were in progress. However, the relief could not be carried out for some time.'

As fate would have it, shortly after the streamer message was successfully delivered, wireless transmission resumed, and the Commander of 23 Division was able to send through the following message to Hope-Thomson:

> Well done indeed, you are meeting the Jap main northern thrust (.) of greatest importance you hold your positions (.) will give you maximum air support (.) convey to all ranks my greatest appreciation of what already achieved and confident they will deal equally thoroughly with any further attacks.[2]

The congratulations may have been appreciated, but of more immediate interest to Hope-Thomson was the promise, however tentative, of reinforcements.

It was strange for 23 Division to tell Hope-Thomson that reinforcements were coming, when they knew full well that there were hardly any men to spare in that part of Manipur. The regional capital of Imphal was already being threatened from the south and south-east by a determined thrust from the 33rd Division, the largest and best-equipped of Japanese Divisions assigned to U-Go. To meet this threat, the British had hurriedly pulled in all available fighting units from the Ukhrul sector, including 49 Brigade, which was 4/5 MLI's parent Brigade and the previous occupant of Sheldon's Corner and Sangshak.

So acute was the lack of troops to defend Imphal that the British commanders were at that time desperately arranging to fly an entire division back from the Arakan in Burma. The truth was that there were precious few men left to reinforce let alone relieve 50 Brigade. So promises of relief could be seen at best as providing the beleaguered paratroopers with false hope; at worst, they were an outright lie.

However, and unknown to Hope-Thomson, 23 Division had in fact being making attempts to have what few troops were left in the area try to link up with 50 Brigade and eventually provide some support. From 21 March, orders were given to the commanding officer of 2/1 Punjab Rifles, presently located at Litan defending that the 'Gnat' Box, to patrol out to Sangshak.[3]

2/1 Punjab Rifles were an extremely experienced Battalion, having recently returned to India after fighting a series of very hard actions in Burma. They had been sent to Litan to bolster the defence of the important supply point, at that time defended by the Supply Company of 50 Parachute Brigade, a small number of engineers and, importantly, a troop of three Stuart Light Tanks. The Punjab Rifles were to strengthen the defences at Litan, and their CO was placed in overall command of all troops there. Furthermore, immediately after occupying their new positions at Litan on 21 March, 2/1 Punjab were given orders to send patrols to Sangshak and link up with the paratroopers.

As it was already late afternoon, the plan called for the patrol to follow the general direction of the Manipur Road towards Finches Corner, clearing the way for a larger follow-on support column. The patrol would then find a place to lie up for the night just short of Hope-Thomson's old HQ. There they hoped to remain undetected until morning, after which they would lead the support column, undertake a dash towards Sangshak and make contact with the paratroopers.

Unfortunately, the support column never made it to Finches Corner, being engaged in a sharp action with the enemy just short of the 36-mile post. Disengaging, the Punjab Rifles pulled back to the safety of the Litan Box just before nightfall. The first attempt at contact with the men at Sangshak had failed, and the Paratroopers were not even aware that an attempt had been made.

Over the next few days, 2/1 Punjab made several more attempts to link up with the Paratroopers, using a variety of jungle paths and circuitous approaches. But in the face of increasing enemy presence in and all around Sangshak it soon became clear to the Punjabi soldiers that it was impossible to get through. Finally, after a major attack on Litan on 25 March, the Gnat Box was ordered to be abandoned. The Punjabis, together with about 100 support and transport troops from 50 Brigade, abandoned the Box and made their way back to Imphal. With this, the only troops who tried to relieve Sangshak during the siege had gone.

* * *

Temporarily halted by the threat of the Hurricanes overhead, as soon as they flew away, the Japanese emerged from their hiding places and recommenced the bombardment of 50 Parachute Brigade. The Japanese on West Hill, supported by the recently arrived 75mm mountain guns, resumed firing at the men of 153 Battalion. This continued for some time, forcing the defenders to stay low in their trenches. Under cover of this intense fire, another group of Japanese crept forward before mounting yet another human-wave attack directly at the waiting troops on East Hill.

The Indian troops of 152 Battalion met the onrush with bursts from their Bren guns and well-aimed fire from their Lee Enfields. The Brigade then supported the defence with a furious barrage from both the Brigade mortars and the guns of the Mountain Battery. The whizz of the falling shells and the crump of the mortars sounded moments before the shock wave and shrapnel of the high explosive rounds scattered the attacking Japanese troops. The Japanese tried to reorganize and continue moving forward, but their momentum was lost, broken by the weight of accurate artillery fire. They had no choice but to flee, yet again leaving many of their fallen comrades.

With the charge broken, the gunners turned their attention to Japanese troops seen forming up in the nearby village of Lungshang, desperately trying to disrupt any attempts by the enemy to bring up fresh troops or supplies.

The Japanese also conducted small attacks on both the 4/5 MLI and 153 Battalion positions, but these were mere demonstrations, ruses designed to distract the defenders from the main focus of their attacks – the church area and 152 Battalion. A few quick rushes were put in – fast charges of flashing swords, grenades, bayonets and rifle fire, but these were easily repulsed. The defenders were holding fast.

With the daytime attacks temporarily halted, both sides settled back into the acknowledged routine of an uneasy face-off. Just before last light, the final patrols that had been sent out to gather intelligence slipped back into Sangshak. Lieutenant Khurray reported that his MLI patrol to Kidney Camp had taken fire from somewhere just west of the old camp. In the exchange his patrol had suffered some minor casualties, which forced him to head back to Sangshak with no clearer picture of enemy numbers in that area. The other patrols also returned cautiously to the Brigade perimeter, each of them carefully signalling to their comrades manning the forward defensive pits, anxious not be accidentally shot by a trigger-happy sentry. In the end, all the patrols made it back safely to the village, except for one sent to scout out the Finches Corner position. This patrol was never heard of again.

* * *

At the end of another long day, Bobby Davis, the Senior Medical Officer, briefly paused from his work to survey his Field Ambulance. The doctors and medical orderlies had been working non-stop both to treat the newly wounded and to provide care to those who had been brought in over the preceding days. Spare room was increasingly hard to find in the already overcrowded hospital, with the Field Ambulance now holding more than sixty wounded men.[4] This was in addition to the numerous officers and soldiers who, despite having been treated, had later died of their wounds. Without proper stretchers or a place to recover, many of the wounded were merely patched up as best as possible, sedated and then deposited into a nearby trench or shell scrape while the battle continued to rage around them. Although medical supplies were still adequate, space to treat any further wounded men was at a premium. Yet despite all of the difficulties and the fatigue from near-constant work, including the need to carry out a number of major surgical operations during the day, Davis was quietly pleased that the morale of the Field Ambulance staff remained surprisingly high.

But Davis' optimism was to be severely challenged as evening set in and the heavens opened. A massive downpour continued to pelt the position throughout the night. Manipur is often described as one of the wettest places on earth, and although the monsoon was still a month away, the constant rain soon turned the battlefield into a muddy and slippery mess. Trenches and shell holes were filled with water, adding to the misery of the defenders. Most keenly affected were the men of the Field Ambulance and their patients. 'Water seeped everywhere', recalled Captain Tom Monaghan, the Adjutant of 152 Battalion. 'The wounded and dying slid into the mud, and the floors of the operating dugout became a treacherous maw into which precious surgical instruments and dressings were washed and finally disappeared.'[5] Davis and his doctors hurriedly retrieved their instruments from the mud, while the other ambulance staff went from shell scrape to shell scrape attending to the wounded, careful to ensure that after surviving the fight they did not drown in their shallow trenches. Parachute silk from the airdrops was quickly repurposed as temporary cover for the wounded in their trenches, or used as makeshift blankets.

But despite the rains and the mounting losses suffered in their daytime assaults, the Japanese never let up the pressure on 50 Parachute Brigade. Perhaps sensing that the rain and the gloom would make it harder for the defenders to see them, the Japanese once again renewed their assault on the 152 Battalion perimeter. From last light until midnight they undertook four strong strikes directly at the church position, with 5 Platoon, commanded by Lieutenant Cowell, being the focal point of their attack.

Cowell and his Platoon Havildar, Mohd Ali, were subjected to wave after wave of screaming Japanese rushing at them with fixed bayonets and supported by direct fire from the newly arrived 75mm guns. They made several desperate assaults direct from West Hill, charging down the saddle and up the forward ridge towards the plateau. After the initial charges failed, a section of Japanese finally penetrated the 5 Platoon position. However, Havildar Ali remained in his trench, firing at the newly arrived attackers and preventing the position from being overrun. The Japanese continued the fight, flinging grenades and making short rushes, working around the edges of the Platoon as they tried to cut it off from the main position.

That 5 Platoon, terribly exposed on the forward edge of the plateau, was able to hang on despite repeated attacks, is testament to the steadfastness of both Cowell and his Platoon Havildar. Cowell is reported to have been very steady throughout the engagement and 'inspired such confidence that the position held despite strong enemy attacks'.[6]

Cowell's resolute Platoon Sergeant made all the difference; Havildar Ali was critical in both holding the Platoon together and saving Cowell's life. Understanding the need to maintain contact with Company HQ, Ali left the relative safety of his trench and made the dangerous journey back to Company Headquarters to request assistance. Message delivered, he crawled back towards his trench, again under heavy enemy fire, to find that the Japanese had fixed the position of his Platoon commander and were attacking his trench from *inside* the perimeter. Havildar Ali immediately fired bursts at them with his Sten gun, attempting to distract them and break up their attack. He kept crawling towards Cowell, firing a burst, then moving forward, then firing another burst, until the Japanese had had enough and broke off their attack. For this brave action, as well as his continued devotion and inspiration to his Platoon over the next few days, he would eventually be awarded the Military Medal – the equivalent of the Military Cross for enlisted men.[7]

While the church was being attacked, the medium machine gunners, who provided constant and vital fire support to the men holding the perimeter, were again being severely hammered by the Japanese and suffered further casualties. As it was impossible to dig deep into the hard soil, the MMG gunners were particularly exposed, since they needed to fire their weapons from a sitting position with much of their heads and bodies showing over the rim of their shallow pits. Captain Gaydon, the 2IC of the MMG Company, was killed, and command devolved yet again down the order of succession, this time to Captain Lewis.

4/5 MLI's C Company was also raided twice during the night, but once again these were half-hearted affairs which quickly faltered. As the Japanese withdrew, the British 3-inch mortars were called in on the retreating raiders. The heavy crumps and explosions of the mortars were soon replaced by the sounds of groaning from out from beyond the tree line. Trim sent out clearance patrols, but they failed to find any bodies, the Japanese having likely taken their wounded comrades with them as they retreated.

24 March – Wearing down the Box   105

Such raids as those on the MLI and Khali Bahadur positions were, however, relatively minor affairs; the Japanese had obviously fixed their main attention firmly on the church. They knew the building was important and they were determined to gain the advantage that the high ground would afford its possessor. Despite the numerous casualties that they had suffered, their intense focus paid off, and just before midnight a small group of Japanese snipers finally managed to gain a tentative foothold inside the church building itself.

Cowell knew that he had to evict these snipers as soon as possible, since their presence endangered not only his Platoon but the entire Brigade. So, before the snipers had time to properly establish themselves, Cowell mounted an immediate counter-attack. Hand grenades were his close-quarter weapon of choice, and flinging them in front of him, Cowell fought his way back into the church and evicted the snipers in desperate hand-to-hand fighting. However, just as he succeeded in driving the Japanese out of the church, Cowell was shot in the shoulder. It was a serious wound, immediately rendering his arm almost useless. Nevertheless, after having the arm bandaged, he continued to command his Platoon until, during a lull in the fighting, he was relieved later that night.

Cowell's quick thinking and aggressive action allowed the Brigade to retain possession of the Church, the lynchpin of the defence for the entire Brigade. Cowell would eventually receive the Military Cross for this action – one of the very few awarded to the hard-pressed 152 Battalion. The citation describes his actions and ends with the words, 'This officer, by sheer courage and personal leadership, was directly responsible for holding this forward position despite the attacks by superior enemy forces.'[8]

Through dogged defence, 5 Platoon and 152 Battalion had beaten off these determined attacks, and in the hours after midnight the Japanese retreated to their start lines past West Hill. The British and Indian troops had fought magnificently and had held on, but fatigue was taking its toll. Most of the men had not slept for several days and had had precious little food or water to sustain them, besides what rainwater they could catch in their cups and tarpaulins. Ammunition, particularly grenades, was running terribly low. If attacks continued with the same frequency and ferocity, the defenders would be hard pressed to continue their defence of the Box.

Chapter 11

25 March – The Church at Dawn

The Church

Dawn found Lieutenant Gollop and his remaining fifteen men holding the forward line closest to the edge of the plateau. Incredibly, and despite their furious attempts during the night, the Japanese had not yet been able to reclaim the church. Perhaps they had given up or withdrawn to rest and refit after their evening exertions. Whatever the reason, 50 Brigade decided to make the best of their good fortune and ordered Gollop's Platoon to move forward and reoccupy the abandoned church.

But the Japanese had not withdrawn, and almost immediately after taking up their new positions, Gollop's men were rushed by the enemy, once more attempting a furious assault on the church area. Several of Gollop's men were hit in the opening fusillade, and that was when he 'decided it was time to do something positive'.[1] He recalled:

> I moved around to the Havildar's position from where I could see a machine gun firing into our main body. Having concluded that a direct attack by the few men I had left would be ineffective, I decided that my Havildar, Khan Zaman, [and I] would go and get it. I can still see the look on his face when I told him to go first! We had only gone a little way down the bank when he motioned me down. And I heard the grenade as I hit the ground. He rolled down the rest of the bank and I never saw him again. I had six bits of grenade in my leg but the one I was most worried about was in my top lip. There was blood all over the place and I thought that half my face had been blown away.[2]

Dazed and confused, Gollop crawled forward towards the machine gun with only a grenade as a weapon. He dropped into another trench and then looked up at what he thought was a Gurkha waving to him from across the track. He was promptly shot at again, but thankfully it missed. Still convinced that the Japanese soldier ahead of him was a friendly Gurkha, the dazed Gollop waved at him, only to be shot at once more, and this time hit through the neck! He immediately passed out, but when he came to he somehow managed to crawl out of the trench; this time, he was found by a genuine Gurkha, who put him over his shoulder and carried him back to the Field Ambulance. The doctors got to work on him right away, heavily sedating him while they operated. This was all that Gollop recalled until he came to with a start to find himself lying in a trench, with several other wounded men around him, some time on the evening of the 26th.

* * *

Watching the furious battle around the church position, Hope-Thomson concluded that the church could no longer be held. He was convinced that the Japanese would probably break through to the building sooner or later and so, at 0800 hrs, he decided that the best option was to destroy it. This would ensure that the Japanese could not use its strong walls as cover.

Hope-Thomson consulted with Captain McLune, the officer commanding the small attachment of sappers from 411 (P) Field Squadron, to see whether the church could in fact be demolished. McClune sent forward several of his sappers to inspect the building, but after an exhausting crawl up to it and back again, the tired sappers reported that the structure was far too solid to be destroyed with the meagre amount of explosive that they had at their disposal.

With destruction out of the question and fewer able-bodied men left to defend it, the decision was made to evacuate the church, leaving behind only a small listening post, while 152 Battalion would then shorten its perimeter to just behind the area. Orders were passed to the forward line of troops, and the soldiers still manning the church reluctantly gave up the position that they had fought so hard to retain. But before they left, they demolished the piles of firewood stacked around the church so they could not be used as cover by the Japanese when they made their inevitable return. It is reported that the thatched roof of the church was also set alight to deny it to the Japanese snipers, who would most likely try to use it for cover and as a perch from which to shoot down at the paratroopers below them.

Soon after the order to abandon the church was given, a message was sent from the gunners to the Brigade Commander informing him that one of the OPs had spotted 200–300 Japanese troops massing in the nearby village of Sanjing; these would most likely be used to reinforce the troops attacking Sangshak. Major Lock, the OC of the Mountain Guns, spotted flashes from a 75mm gun firing from about 3,000 yards away. He immediately gave orders for his No. 2 gun to respond, eventually silencing the enemy artillery piece with a salvo of high explosive 3.7-inch shells. Lock was pleased with this excellent piece of gunnery, but unfortunately, not everything went his way that morning; he caught a small piece of stray shrapnel to the face causing a nasty-looking wound. Luckily, it was not serious, and after being dressed at the Field Ambulance he quickly returned to his men and the guns.

* * *

Down on the southern perimeter, Trim returned to his Battalion after morning orders to find that a persistent Japanese sniper had established himself with clear lines of fire somewhere near the MLI water point and just in front of his A Company. One Indian soldier had already been killed that morning while trying to get water. Besides the tragic loss of life, the sniper had now effectively cut off the Brigade from this all-important water source.

With all of the external water points now under direct observation or fire by the enemy, the Brigade was reduced to relying on a small seepage well inside the perimeter near the Field Ambulance. This was plainly insufficient for a force of 2,000 men, many of them already dehydrated, despite the drenching downpour of the night before. What little water could be spared was mainly given to the wounded. Even that was not enough, and the Field Ambulance was forced to use blood plasma to make up plaster for the casts needed to immobilize the many shattered bones. Desperate times called for the daily water ration to be cut once more, this time to half a bottle of water per man. Hope-Thomson knew that unless supplies could reach them soon, even this reduced ration would need to be cut again.

Besides food and water, ammunition of all types was desperately low. Most worrying to Hopkinson was the lack of grenades, which he viewed as 'possibly the most useful weapon for breaking up night attacks at close quarters'.[3] Besides grenades, a lack of 3-inch mortar and artillery rounds was also being felt, requiring the gunners to be very careful with their shooting despite the 'target-rich environment' surrounding them at Sangshak.

Obviously, airdrops were the only answer to the Brigade's supply troubles, and once again a signal was sent out to 23 Division for an emergency drop of ammunition, food and water. In reply, the Brigade was told to look out for re-supply aircraft just before dusk.

* * *

The Mahrattas of 4/5 MLI received some welcome news when, at around 1000 hrs, the lost patrol sent to Finches Corner on the morning of the 24th found its way back into the Brigade area. They had been delayed by the numerous Japanese patrols and columns now making their way over the hills surrounding Sangshak. They did manage to discover, however, that the enemy appeared to have established an administrative position near Mile 36 and that there was a considerable number of enemy troops in the vicinity of that road marker. This vital information was reported up to 23 Division HQ.

Buoyed by this success, Trim decided to send out another small patrol, again under command of Lieutenant Khurray, towards Kidney Camp. They were to try and locate the Japanese coming from that direction, particularly the elephants and motor transport spotted the day before. The intent was to find these formations and then call for artillery fire to break them up before they reached Sangshak. The small patrol of four men quickly assembled their equipment, then slipped quietly out of the position and into the jungle towards Kidney Camp.

* * *

Having failed in their night attacks, the Japanese were heard throughout the day digging in amidst the destroyed *bashas* of West Hill and to the south-west somewhere in the jungle across the Sangshak road. There were no further infantry attacks, and the battleground was ceded to the artillery engaging in a long-range duel between the Mountain gunners and the Japanese artillerymen. Salvos lobbed from the Indian 3.7-inch guns delivered a rain of deadly high explosive onto the 75mm Japanese pieces, only to be answered in kind by the 75s firing on a direct line back at the gunners' exposed position just forward of the central ridge. After several exchanges, one 75mm gun sustained a direct hit, immediately knocking it out of action and scattering its crew. But its place was soon taken by another 75mm firing from the small village of Koushou, located on a small hill about a mile south of Sangshak as the crow flies.

The loss of the 75mm was a blow to the Japanese, but the British artillery did not have things all their own way. Operating near the Brigade Headquarters, the mortars of 582 Battery sustained a direct hit from a 75mm shell which tore through a detachment, destroying a mortar tube, killing one gunner outright and badly burning three more. A significant part of the Mortar Battery had been taken out of the battle by a single shell, resulting in yet more men being sent to the already overcrowded Field Ambulance.

* * *

The additional craters from the incoming 75mm shells went almost unnoticed in the already ravaged and desolate landscape of the village. After several days of fighting it was a scarred and cratered place, littered with decomposing Japanese bodies strewn along the forward slope of the position or lying twisted between the shells of burnt-out huts. The hill was also covered with rubbish, human excrement and all of the detritus of battle – piles of brass shell casings, broken ammo crates, empty ration tins, scraps of clothing and bloodied bandages. The survivors recalled the ever-present stench of the battlefield, a mixture of mud, blood, excrement and rotting corpses.

But despite the mess and the smell, the thirsty and exhausted men of the Brigade tried to snatch moments of sleep throughout the day, knowing full well that the Japanese were likely to resume their assault as soon as night fell. But sleep was hard to find, interrupted as it was by constant rounds of guard duty or the sudden unexpected crack of a sniper round whizzing past their heads.

Later in the afternoon, an NCO from Khurray's patrol made his way back into the MLI position to report that Khurray and another soldier had been wounded and were lying about 200 yards outside the perimeter. Under cover of the Battalion's 2-inch mortars, a small sortie was made from the MLI position to rescue them. The unhurt NCO reported to Trim that the patrol had slipped unnoticed down the track towards Kidney Camp, where they had spotted a large group of Japanese, perhaps at battalion strength. No vehicles or elephants were seen, but the presence of such a large number of fresh troops was very worrying. Silently, the patrol immediately crept back along the track towards Sangshak, but with the village and defensive positions already in sight they had the misfortune to be bumped by a Japanese section overlooking the water point. A short exchange of fire followed, killing one of the Indian patrol members outright. Escaping back towards the Brigade, both Khurray and another soldier were hit just as they approached the outskirts of the position.

Here they waited until the relief party from the MLI could get to them and escort them back to the Field Ambulance station. When they arrived there the wounded men saw that the Field Ambulance was now overflowing with casualties. There simply was not enough room to house them all. Over the course of the day, seventy-two men were admitted, including three suffering from phosphorus burns, the result of an enemy mortar attack. White phosphorus is a particularly nasty material, a chemical which burns fiercely and continues to do so for an extended period while in the presence of oxygen. The doctors tried their best to remove the droplets of phosphorus from the wounds and to stop the burning. However, knowing that the enemy would probably fire more of this type of ordnance, the Field Ambulance put in an emergency request for an airdrop of copper sulphate, a chemical widely used at the time to treat such burns.

* * *

Just before dusk, the defenders were greeted by the welcome sight of twelve Hurricane fighter-bombers descending on Sangshak to strafe enemy positions and troop concentrations. This was followed by another supply drop from the slower-moving Dakotas. But while the Hurricanes skilfully brought fire directly onto the enemy positions, the Dakota pilots had still not improved their aim from the days before. Infuriatingly, most of the badly needed supplies once again drifted down just outside of the perimeter and into the hands of the Japanese. Among the ammunition and food collected by the Japanese was the Brigade's rum ration – most likely added at the last minute by a thoughtful loader in the hope that it might help to lift the Brigade's flagging spirits. While the rum did not find its intended recipients, the Japanese were very happy to receive this unexpected gift; reports over the following days noted that the IJA troops appeared to have had more than their share of the rum ration, some sounding riotously drunk.

As the planes flew off into the distance, the quiet of night quickly descended over the Brigade. Then, suddenly, the Japanese broke the still evening air by launching another assault against both A Company on the plateau and the Khali Bahadur Regiment soldiers defending the east of the Box. A bombardment of 75mm artillery fire preceded each assault, followed by a wave of infantry once more running at the Brigade position supported by both MMG and LMG fire. The assaults were quickly repulsed, but these constant attacks were taking their toll. The defending men were becoming increasingly exhausted, some reportedly falling asleep in mid-sentence and physically unable to stay awake except when actually being attacked. They were also hungry, and their mouths were dry from the acute lack of water. The foetid smell of rapidly decomposing human and animal corpses only added to the increasing feeling of gloom that was settling over the Brigade.

* * *

The officers were no less exhausted than their men, none more so that the Brigade Commander himself. The days of constant action and anxiety, the desperate lack of sleep while constantly needing to be seen to be 'in control' – all this was taking an increasingly heavy toll on Hope-Thomson. Even during lulls in the fighting he was unable to sleep, and he was on the brink of a nervous collapse. Then, sometime on the 25th, he snapped, breaking down and becoming temporarily unable to function. As he would say to the historian Louis Allen after the war, 'From the 25th my recollections became confused and hazy, for obvious reasons.'[4] In a later letter he wrote:

> Nor have I ever sought to deny or conceal the fact that for a very brief period during the last two days of the continuous eight-day battle I did suffer a short collapse from exhaustion, which collapse was witnessed by, and at the time known to, one other officer. On quickly recovering, I resumed my duties and continued them until the evacuation of Sangshak, not cowering in my trench as stated by others after the war.[5]

At least partially recognizing his own declining state, Hope-Thomson sought out the Senior Medical Officer, Lieutenant Colonel Davis, for help. Davis noted his extreme fatigue and gave the Brigadier a 'pill' of some sort, presumably to calm him and put him to sleep.[6] But there was no time for rest, either for Hope-Thomson or for his hard-pressed Brigade. So the plainly debilitated commander was forced to carry on as best he could, despite the fact that he was clearly nearing the end of his reserves.

Hope-Thomson's nervous collapse at this stage of the battle and his increasingly weak grip on the situation over the next few days would generate decades of bitter controversy. During the battle itself, few men in the Brigade besides Davis and perhaps some in the immediate Headquarters staff even suspected that Hope-Thomson was unravelling. He continued to conduct briefings, issue orders and visit the men in the forward sectors of the position, just as he had done throughout the siege. When it was later revealed, well after the battle had concluded, that he was at this time suffering from nervous shock, many of his men did not believe it. They had seen Hope-Thomson with their own eyes moving around the Brigade and continuing to give orders. To them it just wasn't believable that he had collapsed, and any suggestion that he had done so was both an outrageous slur on their commander's honour and yet more evidence of a conspiracy by 'higher command' trying to make Hope-Thomson into a scapegoat for their own failings in not being able to anticipate the Japanese surprise attacks through Manipur.

But the fact is that Hope-Thomson did suffer a collapse and was becoming increasingly unable to cope. For all men, no matter how well-trained or brave, there arrives a point when the 'bank account of courage' becomes dangerously overdrawn. Hope-Thomson had now reached that point. Nevertheless, at a time when mental illness was looked at less sympathetically than it is now, everyone who knew of Hope-Thomson's predicament, including the Brigadier himself, tried their best to disguise it and shield the men from any knowledge that their commander was suffering. He would just have to take his 'medicine' from the sympathetic doctor and soldier on as best he could. That he did so, even in a seriously diminished manner, is testament to Hope-Thomson's strength of character and overwhelming commitment to his men.

* * *

As evening fell, Hope-Thomson had recovered sufficiently to hold his evening command conference. He warned Trim that his Battalion, having lost the fewest men up to that point, would need to designate a few platoons to act as Brigade reserves should the need arise. But besides this minor reallocation of troops, there was little else that the Brigade HQ could do to influence the battle. As Hopkinson noted, by this time 'it had developed into a soldiers' [battle] with platoons and sections fighting desperately to hold existing positions. Each evening we wondered how many of us would be left to attend the next conference.'[7]

The conference ended and the officers dispersed. Arriving back at his Battalion, Trim warned Captain Steele to prepare his D Company men to act as the Brigade reserve. Hopkinson, however, as soon as he neared his Battalion HQ, was greeted with a burst of 75mm artillery fire which registered five direct hits on his currently unoccupied command post. Hopkinson dived into a nearby pit to escape the fire and was fortunate not to be hit. The shells had missed all his men, but the command post was terribly torn up by shrapnel and all their meagre possessions were destroyed.

* * *

Another brief attack was beaten off at around 2130 hrs. While the defenders were plainly exhausted, the Japanese, too, were almost at the end of their strength, worn down by days of repeated *banzai* charges, counter-attacks, artillery fire and insufficient food and water.

The attackers' tactic of persistent charges directly into the fire of the waiting defenders had also taken its toll, and casualties were mounting. Unlike 50 Parachute Brigade with its excellent RAP and Field Ambulance, little could be done for any Japanese soldier wounded in the fighting. Susumi Nishida, a platoon commander in the 11th Company recalled:

I was again crawling near the enemy position to see what was going on. I then heard some groans about ten metres ahead. Someone was calling, 'Tachibana, Tachibana'. I suddenly remembered that there had been a Private named Tachibana in my platoon when I was in 6th Company. The man groaning must also have been a former platoon member. I cautiously crawled along in the shade of the shrubs and found Corporal Masaharu Okazaki, who I heard had been shot during the previous day's escape. He had been shot right through the stomach. I was surprised he was still alive with such a deep wound. As I pulled him down into the shade, he pleaded for some water. It is common knowledge that water cannot be given to one with stomach wounds. He then said to me, 'Sir Commander I know that Okazaki will not survive. Therefore, please give me just one mouthful of water.' I was also wondering whether I should give him some water as he was near death. I made up my mind and brought to his mouth a full flask lid of water. He looked me straight in the face and said clearly, 'I never dreamed that I should have the honour to be given my last drink of water by you, Sir Commander', a bit tongue in cheek with a big smile. Okazaki had a reputation within the Company as a man of great courage at the time of the Chinese front. And now, to be able to die with a smile on one's face! I have the greatest respect for Okazaki's fortitude.[8]

The living, too, were facing increasing hardship because of the lack of food and water. A large part of the supplies they had carried from the Chindwin had already been consumed, and it was noted that most of the cattle which were supposed to sustain the Division had already died, escaped or fallen into ravines during the approach march. If not for the fortuitous re-supply unwittingly dropped by Allied aircraft, it is unlikely that the Japanese would have been able to sustain the ferocious pace of their attacks against Sangshak. Besides the lack of food, many of the men were starting to feel the effects of dysentery, no doubt brought on by drinking unclean water and living in filthy conditions. That the Japanese soldiers continued to fight, day after day, poorly supplied and in such appalling conditions, says much about the strength and tenacity of the individual Japanese infantryman.

But the Japanese were about to get some good news. Unlike the British, who had no hope of reinforcement or relief, elements of the Japanese 15th Division, were starting to arrive in the Ukhrul/Sangshak area. As the 15 Division's 60th Regiment approached Sangshak, its commander, Lieutenant Colonel Matsumura, ordered one of its battalions to prepare for a dawn attack on the 26th. The fresh troops of Matsumura's 3rd Battalion silently took up positions during the night, ready for a final push against exhausted paratroopers.

Chapter 12

26 March – 'A terrible day, never to be forgotten'

'A terrible day, never to be forgotten by anyone who survived it', was how Hope-Thomson described the fighting on 26 March.[1] Despite a previous week of brutal and incessant combat, the fighting rose to a new level of vicious desperation on the 26th as both sides took, lost, then retook the vital church position on the high plateau.

The early hours of the 26th saw a lull in Japanese attacks as they prepared themselves for an all-out effort to sweep away the defenders and take Sangshak. But the Indian and Gurkha soldiers crouched in their shallow trenches could hardly sleep for the whizzing of stray mortar rounds. Although most fell long, mainly on the Khali Bahadur Regiment manning the far eastern portion of the Box, the constant sound of far-off explosions kept nerves on edge.

Unknown to the British troops, the Japanese attackers from 58 Regiment were also nearing the end of their strength. After five days of continual assaults, and suffering horrific casualties, the original Japanese attackers were nearly spent. The Commander of the 11th Company, Nishida, was almost overcome by grief at the sight of so many of his comrades lying dead on the forward slopes of the British position. In accordance with standard Japanese procedure, the wounded were not to be moved until the enemy position was cleared; thus men continued to lie where they fell, in pain and with little hope of rescue. What effect this had on the morale of the living can only be imagined, and Nishida, against orders and unable to bear the sight of so many of his wounded comrades exposed to British fire, had them pulled back and moved into safety.

Nevertheless, the pressure was becoming unbearable. Overcome and seeing no way out, Nishida informed his men that he intended to kill himself with a grenade. This startling proposal was not strange from a Japanese perspective; indeed, it was a common way in which many Japanese soldiers, when faced with either debilitating wounds or the prospect of imminent defeat (surrender never being an option), chose to end their lives. But several of his men begged him to carry on. They encouraged him to attack again saying, 'Commander, why not give it one more try?'

His soldiers' encouragement rallied Nishida to make one more effort. In the early morning darkness, at around 0400 hrs, he assembled the remaining men of the 6th and 11th Companies, about 150 in total, for a renewed push towards the church. Once more they lined up grimly at their start positions to the west of Sangshak. The officers drew their swords and the men fixed bayonets to their rifles. They moved slowly through the burnt-out *bashas* of West Hill until, at the forward edge of the dip, they started to run, charging back up East Hill towards the waiting Indian soldiers in their forward pits. Fire from the defenders' rifles whipped through the attackers, and the concussive thuds of exploding grenades shook the charging Japanese. But this time, the *banzai* charge succeeded. Despite the valiant efforts of the defenders, they could not hold, and the rushing Japanese were soon among them, firing, bayoneting and forcing the defenders back out of their pits. Nishida and his triumphant men quickly occupied the recently vacated pits and trenches. The Japanese were finally masters of the plateau!

It had been a long and desperate fight, but by 0630 hrs the Japanese were in control of both the forward edge of the plateau and the church building itself. The men of 152 Battalion's A Company had been either killed or forced back off the plateau. A Company's commander, Major Gillet, had been badly wounded in the assault and was evacuated from the church position with the remainder of his men back to the positions of B Company, who were holding a defensive line east of the church and across the entrance to the plateau. Under sustained fire, Gillet was dragged back to the Field Ambulance and added to the growing number of casualties being tended by the medical staff.

The loss of the church was a serious blow to the Brigade, and Hope-Thomson, now somewhat recovered from his earlier collapse, crawled forward to observe the fighting at first-hand. Seeing that A Company had been completely run out of its position, he realized that the fight had now reached its most critical stage. Speaking to the remaining B Company officers, who now commanded his most forward line of troops, Hope-Thomson told them that the position 'must be held at all costs'. He knew only too well that if the Japanese succeeded in reinforcing their toehold in the church, his defence of Sangshak would no longer be tenable. With the church in their hands the Japanese would be able to command all of the ground between them and the central ridge, picking off the remaining parachute troops and the mountain guns at their leisure. It would then only be a matter of time before they destroyed the remnants of the Brigade piecemeal, trapped as they would be in the rapidly shrinking defensive square east of the central ridge. Knowing this, Hope-Thomson resolved that the Japanese had to be removed from the church quickly, despite the heavy losses this would probably entail.

What followed was a series of short and extremely vicious counter-attacks attempting to dislodge the newly installed Japanese defenders.

A counter-attack often enjoys its best chance of success if put in immediately after the enemy's assault and before they have time to consolidate their new position. Accordingly, 152 Battalion mounted the first counter-attack almost immediately after receiving Hope-Thomson's orders. The Brigadier watched as the men moved forward, in turn crawling, then rushing, in and out of the weapon pits and between the remnants of the destroyed *bashas* and strewn piles of firewood. Met by a hail of rifle fire and a barrage of thrown grenades, the 152 Battalion soldiers quickly lost momentum as casualties mounted. The attack stalled, then stopped entirely, having made no significant headway. The few men who remained, most of whom were wounded, were forced to pull back.

At this stage, Hope-Thomson had few reserves available, but he did have one *relatively* fresh platoon back at his HQ – his Brigade Defence Platoon commanded by Lieutenant Robin de la Haye. All accounts of de la Haye describe him as a particularly cool and suave customer. He also went by the unusual nickname of 'The Red Shadow' on account of his apparent penchant for occasionally wearing red pyjamas under his battledress. Just before he was ordered forward to relieve the church position, Neild recounted:

> That morning, the debonair Robin de la Haye, another to have his Oxford career broken, had been seen to be adjusting his gaiters and smoothing his hair. 'What are you going to do, Robin?' someone asked. 'Oh, I believe it is a counter-attack' came the cool reply. Five minutes later he was dead.[2]

Hopkinson recalled that de la Haye's attack 'was met by a withering fire of Japanese LMGs, mortars etc. from the edges of the surrounding jungle as they tried to fight their way up to the church. The platoon was overwhelmed and de la Haye killed.'[3]

There was no time to mourn the loss of de la Haye, and soon it was Hopkinson's turn to go forward. He and his second-in-command, Major Stewart, gathered up any spare men they could find, at this stage mainly runners, signallers and orderlies – indeed, any Gurkha who could still hold a rifle or fling a grenade. Leading this scratch team, Hopkinson charged at the Japanese pits. The Brigadier looked on as 'Hoppy', throwing grenades at the enemy, almost pushed into the enemy positions, until he, too, was wounded, catching numerous grenade fragments in his leg. 'It was very much a forlorn hope', said Hopkinson. 'After fierce fighting we got back into some of our old positions but were caught by a counter-attack from the flank and, largely owing to our lack of grenades, could not hold them.'[4] This attack, too, faltered, then failed.

Luckily for Hopkinson, he was dragged out by the Quartermaster and evacuated to the Field Ambulance. The grenade fragments in his leg and foot caused him much grief over the coming days, and he would soon live up to his nickname, as he was only able to move around slowly and painfully, 'hopping' on his remaining good leg.

On the gun line

While the fight was swinging back and forth on the forward edge of the plateau, the Japanese had also hooked around through the jungle on the north side of the Box and directly threatened both the mountain guns and the Mortar Battery. As they emerged from the jungle, the Japanese threw multiple grenades into the No. 1 Gun position right on the very edge of the jungle. These killed two gunners outright and wounded their troop commander, Lieutenant Malhotra.[5] Japanese infantry then seized the opportunity to rush at the stricken gunners. They ran right over and through the rest of the No. 1 Gun crew, who were forced to flee towards their comrades manning No. 2 Gun directly to their south.

By now the Japanese had their blood up and quickly re-formed for a follow-on attack to storm No. 2 Gun, the next in line. But the gun crew of No. 2 Gun were ready for them. Under command of their steadfast leader, Havildar Sarwan Das, a Punjabi Brahmin, the crew together with some men from No. 3 Gun and a scratch team from 152 Battalion managed to hold the line and repel the attackers. The Japanese drew back to the pits of No 1 Gun, where they proceeded to trade pot shots with the crew of No. 2 Gun.

The loss of even one gun was critical to the Brigade, as without the heavy fire that it could bring to bear, the fighting power of the Brigade was seriously diminished, as was its ability to disrupt and break up major Japanese attacks.

The loss of a gun was also a major stain on the honour of all the gunners and particularly their commander, Major Lock. By tradition, the guns of an artillery regiment were the 'colours'[6] of the unit, and their loss was the equivalent to an infantry regiment losing its flag to the enemy – unthinkable and to be avenged at all costs.

When No. 1 Gun was taken, the Battery Commander, Major Lock was in the Field Ambulance having the wounds he had received to his face the previous day re-dressed. However, upon hearing that the guns had been threatened he immediately discharged himself and went forward, over the central ridge and straight towards his men. Reaching the Battery lines, Lock moved carefully around his gun positions, encouraging his gunners to keep up their defence, and directed fire at the stubborn Japanese now holding his No. 1 Gun.

Accounts of what happened next are mixed. Some say that Lock and Smith (the Mortar Battery Commander) went forward with revolvers to try to winkle out the recently installed Japanese. Others say that they saw Lock entering one pit and bayoneting a Japanese soldier, before moving forward to clear the No. 1 Gun position. Whatever weapon he was holding, the accounts are unanimous that, despite a valiant effort, both Lock and Smith were hit by Japanese fire and killed as they tried to recapture the lost gun.

The loss of Lock was a terrible blow to the gunners. A footnote in the Mountain Battery's official war diary gives a rare glimpse of the feelings shared by the men of the Battery at this time. Rather than the usual dry recitation of dates, times and events, the author of this entry describes the mood of the Battery after enduring the defence of Sangshak and the loss of their OC:

> Those who returned came in with their tails up ready for another crack at the Japs. But every man in the Battery feels the implacable loss of Major Lock who, commanding the Battery for the last 2¾ years, had become inseparable from it and his men. They had the utmost faith in him as was shown by the spirit of the gunners at Sangshak, a spirit of an example of unity between Brahmins and Musalmen [sic] that was the direct result of Major Lock's influence, which has strengthened considerably the reputation of the Battery.[7]

But despite Lock's example and the bravery of his men, the Japanese still retained control of one of their guns.

* * *

Back on the plateau, the situation was becoming reminiscent of a First World War battle. Men charged in waves at each other, trying to dislodge the enemy from trenches with bayonets and grenades, only to be met by withering rifle and LMG fire; or if they somehow found their way into the forward trenches they engaged in desperate hand-to-hand fighting. Neither side was prepared to give way, and it was becoming an terrible battle of attrition, witnessed silently by the growing piles of corpses and wounded men.

The paratroopers tried attack after attack to dislodge the Japanese, but each one failed. Hope-Thomson then called up Captain Steele and the two platoons of MLI troops who had been placed on standby after the morning's command conference. In comparison to the seriously depleted 152 Battalion they were relatively fresh, and Hope-Thomson hoped that they could break the deadlock. One platoon of Mahrattas was sent on a flanking attack to the left of the plateau but it was beaten back, so the other platoon tried a flank attack to the right of the plateau. Again, the attack was repulsed.

The situation was now desperate. Each counter-attack had failed, and Lieutenant Nishida's men were still firmly lodged in the church area. The supply of grenades, the most useful weapon in the hand-to-hand fighting to take the pits, was almost exhausted. Of the few grenades remaining, many were found to be faulty, rolling uselessly into the enemy pits and failing to explode.

At 0900 hrs it was 153 Battalion's turn to try to take the church. The first platoon ran forward in a bayonet charge but failed, their assault halted as much by the churned and broken ground as the heavy enemy fire. They fell back, withdrawing through the gun lines – itself a fraught area, given that the Japanese were now firmly ensconced in the No. 1 Gun pits on the edge of the perimeter.

* * *

You get a sense of the desperation overtaking Hope-Thomson from the commands he issued at this time. Not yet fully recovered from his breakdown, and faced with the prospect of the total collapse of his forward positions, Hope-Thomson saw no option other than to withdraw his remaining men eastwards. Crawling back to his headquarters, he called for Trim to come to the command post. The latter's MLI troops would be needed to assist in bringing the mortars back to a position behind the Brigade Headquarters and then in evacuating the Field Ambulance to a position just north of the 4/5 MLI positions.

Hope-Thomson then called to the remaining men of A Company, 152 Battalion and ordered them to pull back and form up behind Brigade HQ. It was apparent that he was now pulling back all of his forces to the east side of the central ridge and readying himself for a 'last ditch' stand.

Having given his orders for the reorganization of the Brigade position, Hope-Thomson then sent a radio message to HQ 23 Division. He noted the very heavy casualties sustained by 152 Battalion and said that if 'strong enemy attacks were sustained on the vital plateau position it was unlikely that it could hold out for another two hours'. He was clearly becoming desperate.

Just over an hour later, the situation still looked bleak. With no way to get the guns rearward, Lieutenant Kidd, now commanding what was left of the mountain gun battery, was ordered to destroy his guns in place. With what must have been a very heavy heart, Kidd started by removing the sights, valuable equipment that had to be salvaged if possible. He was about to make the dangerous journey back to Brigade Headquarters when the Japanese launched another attack towards the gun positions, coming in from the north.

In hard hand-to-hand fighting this attack was repulsed, in no small part due to the efforts of two key Battery NCOs – Havildar Sarwan Das, the 'Number 1'(Commanding NCO) of No. 2 Gun, aided by Havildar Mohan Lal, the Number 1 of the recently lost No. 1 Gun. Under their steady leadership, the Japanese were flung back, and the gunners held onto their guns.

As this stage, the Gurkhas of 153 Battalion were either pressed up against the forward edge of what remained of the gun line, or even slightly behind it. When the Japanese next attacked, the gunners formed more or less the extreme forward edge of the Brigade perimeter. So while Havildar Sarwan Das continued to encourage his men to stick to their positions and keep fighting, Havildar Mohan Lal unexpectedly found himself in a pit with a wounded British officer from 153 Battalion. This officer was trying to fling grenades at the Japanese who were picking their way forward between the pits and shell scrapes, but his efforts were largely ineffective because of his wounds. Havildar Lal took up the grenades and threw them at the advancing Japanese. Apparently, one expertly lobbed grenade dislodged a Japanese flag that had been planted at the edge of the gun position nearest the jungle, presumably as a marker for follow-on troops. Whatever its purpose, its destruction was much appreciated by all the Indian troops near the gun line and gave their morale a very welcome boost. Havildar Lal then rallied several of the nearby 153 Battalion riflemen around him and made a series of successful local counter-attacks, killing the closest Japanese and pushing them all back slightly. Despite being previously unknown to the Gurkhas of 153 Battalion, Havildar Lal was able to inspire them to continue resisting and to take the fight to the enemy. For their steadfast courage that day in defence of the guns, and for organizing the local counter-attacks, both Havildar Das and Lal would later be awarded the Indian Distinguished Service Medal.[8]

It is not known if it was the example of these brave gunners that inspired the infantry, or whether it was the Japanese who started to run out of steam, but by late morning the fortunes of the beleaguered paratroopers started to turn. Some much-needed hand grenades were scrounged from 4/5 MLI and passed up to 153 Battalion, who were just then readying themselves for yet another counter-attack.

By now it was clear that the platoon-sized bayonet charges and grenade bombing runs that had characterized the morning's fighting simply would not work. If they were going to succeed, the Brigade needed to try something much more substantial to overwhelm the Japanese and force them off the plateau. Accordingly, the Brigadier decided that the only option was to put in a full Company-sized attack.

But by this stage of the siege the Brigade did not have a Company to spare. So, to assemble the number of men required, at least a hundred, the decision was made to pull the whole of Major Jimmy Roberts'[9] A Company, 153 Battalion out of its position defending the perimeter of the village and use them to mount the attack. This was a dangerous gamble as it meant that their section of the perimeter would be left temporarily undefended, a potential gap for the Japanese to pour through if they twigged to what was happening.

Fortunately, the gamble paid off, and the rush of an overwhelming number of comparatively fresh troops helped drive the Japanese out of their trenches and off East Hill altogether. It was not an easy attack, however, and the Gurkhas paid for every yard of their advance. In the centre of the attack, Jemadar Ghale, leading No. 2 Platoon, found that the ground was heavily cratered and cut up, making it difficult to run at the enemy. Every time he tried to push his men forward, they would be met by heavy LMG and rifle fire, forcing them to duck into shell scrapes or craters and quickly return fire, before once again picking their way forward. Ghale himself was hit early in the first charge but somehow found the strength to keep moving forward, constantly encouraging his men. The stop-start nature of the Gurkhas' advance – they could only move forward several yards at a time – offered the enemy many targets. Ghale continued to push his men forward even though they were terribly exposed and taking heavy casualties. In another rush, Ghale was hit once more, but in spite of this he and his remaining men made a final rush into the Japanese pits, silencing the remaining enemy troops inside.

The assault had been a success but it came at a great cost to the Gurkhas. Out of Ghale's original thirty men, twenty-six were killed or wounded in the counter-attack, including Ghale himself. For his bravery and example, Jemadar Ghale received the Military Cross.[10]

All through this attack, the gunners of the Mountain Battery again helped their infantry comrades, ferrying grenades, ammunition and water to the men fighting to their front. Havildar Lal even left the gun line and joined the attacking riflemen. As he moved forward he came upon a wounded gunner from No. 1 Gun, immediately took hold of the wounded man and dragged him back to safety.

After several hours of bitter fighting, Nishida and his men were no longer able to resist the attacking Gurkhas of A Company charging at them with bayonet, Sten gun or flashing *kukri*. They had been killed off one by one by the successive waves of British counter-attacks, and the few remaining men were now dangerously low on ammunition and barely hanging on. In the face

26 March – 'A terrible day, never to be forgotten'   123

of the charging Gurkhas, and suffering from a terrible neck wound, Nishida ordered his remaining men to reluctantly retreat back the way they had come, eventually returning to their start positions west of West Hill. It had been a bloody day for the Japanese, and by nightfall Nishida only had around twenty men left from his original force – the same men who had encouraged him to attack just few hours before.

* * *

By 1000 hrs the British line around the front of the church was finally restored, and Japanese attacks ceased for the rest of the day. The mountain gunners then had a spot of luck. Major Holland from 4/5 MLI reported that he had located a Japanese gun position and asked the gunners to send their OP team down to his position to have a look. Kidd crawled to the MLI lines and confirmed Holland's sighting – enemy 75mm guns. The remaining mountain guns were then hastily brought back into action. The dismantled sights were refitted, and the gunners soon started sending well-aimed rounds crashing onto the enemy gun position. A furious barrage of about seventy high explosive rounds was fired by the mountain gun battery, and explosions at the other end indicated that at least one of enemy guns had been silenced.

With the church back under the Brigade's control, and the Japanese having withdrawn, the Brigade was secure for another day. But despite the reprieve, Hope-Thomson knew that time was against him, as both men and ammunition were in critically short supply. He dictated to the signallers in their dugout a message, which they sent in code back to HQ 23 Division, saying that the Brigade could not hope to hold out for another 24 hours. It read: 'The Brigade could only hold out today with luck. It [is] imperative that help should arrive before night.' A response arrived from 23 Division at 1225 hrs ordering them 'to hold at all costs'.

The order to hold at all costs must have been a blow to Hope-Thomson. It was also unrealistic, given that 23 Division must have realized the desperate straits the beleaguered paratroopers were in. Air reconnaissance that morning had revealed a position wreathed in flames and smoke and surrounded by the Japanese. 23 Division also knew that with the failure of the 2/1 Punjab troops to break in from Litan, there was no prospect of any relief from nearby British units; the only real assistance that higher HQ could provide was regular close air support. Given this, the 'hold at all costs' order was alarming, impractical and unrealistic.

The Brigade commander recalled his feelings at this time, saying that '[we] had all passed the point at which fear or the prospect of death seemed matters of any importance'.[11] He was clearly exhausted and still in a fragile mental state. All the men were suffering from exhaustion, reduced to a zombie-like state by days of constant combat and lack of sleep. But Hope-Thomson seemed to be particularly affected, weighed down by the crushing responsibility of command and the clear evidence that his once fine unit was being shattered all around him.

In any event, he continued to direct the battle as best he could and to issue orders for a 'last ditch' defence line to be established just west of the Brigade HQ. The two remaining mountain guns were dragged by the weary gunners to just outside the Brigade HQ and had their barrels lowered to the horizontal so that they could fire over 'open sights' directly at the charging enemy, who were certain to come after nightfall. Ammunition for the guns, however, was nearly exhausted, so the gunners would not be able to provide final protective fire for very long. A company of 4/5 MLI was sent forward to strengthen the 153 Battalion line, and the Field Ambulance was moved to just outside the MLI lines. Wounded men were hastily moved from their resting positions near the Field Ambulance. Teams of medical orderlies picked up the wounded and deposited them into the shell scrapes and weapon pits of the recently departed MLI infantrymen in an attempt to provide them with some protection from the coming final battle that all knew would soon be upon them.

The Box position itself was a dreadful shambles. A very large number of corpses, Indian, British and Japanese, lay all around and even inside the perimeter, it being impossible to retrieve or bury them. Many bodies which had been buried over previous days had been disinterred by the recent shellfire and lay half exposed and continuing to decompose rapidly.

The lack of water and the impossibility of visiting the latrine left the hill covered with human excrement. The battlefield was also heavily churned and broken up from five days of incessant mortar and artillery fire. The ground was littered with the left-over debris from charred *bashas* and wood piles, as well as the many heaps of used ammunition boxes and thousands upon thousands of empty cartridge cases. It was a horrible and thoroughly unhealthy position, and one which could not be held for much longer.

Morale was also ebbing, particularly in 152 Battalion, which had borne the brunt of the incessant attacks on the church. The remaining soldiers of this Battalion had seen practically every one of their officers either killed or wounded over the last few days. The loss of so many officers would certainly have weighed heavily on the few remaining troops, already stretched thin, bloodied from constant fighting and exhausted by many days without rest. Now these men watched as first the guns and mortars and then the RAP were withdrawn to the far side of the central ridge towards the east. It must have seemed to the remaining men of 152 Battalion that they were being abandoned, left out on their own to face the inevitable when the Japanese resumed their attacks.

But still the remaining officers and men tried their best to maintain the defence.

Major Stewart, the last unwounded officer of 152 Battalion, tried to reorganize his badly depleted Battalion. Since A Company had been practically destroyed, it was decided that the Gurkhas of 153 Battalion would take over the pits from A Company, 152 Battalion around the church. This was stretching an already very thin Battalion even further, but there was no other choice. 'This we did', remarked Major Victor Brookes of 153 Battalion, 'but we were almost reduced to a hollow square. As it was obvious we would be attacked again soon, all the wounded who could crawl or drag themselves joined us on the perimeter ... Those of us who had run out of hand grenades gathered piles of stones to fling when the time came.'[12]

By the end of the day, a further fifty-four men had been admitted to the Field Ambulance with wounds, many of them serious.[13] These casualties were in addition to the many, many more men who had been killed during the day and the already large number of seriously wounded who had been treated over the previous week. The number of wounded would have stretched the resources of a full Field Hospital, let alone a single Field Ambulance, yet Davis and the other doctors continued, almost without sleep, to tend to the wounded. When not treating their patients, the Ambulance staff were constantly looking at ways to expand the footprint of their overstretched hospital. A survey was made of the Kali Bahadur lines to their rear, and a few dugouts were evacuated for use of the wounded and for use as an additional treatment centre.

Later in the afternoon, a wave of RAF Hurricanes flew low over the position and strafed the Japanese, much to the delight of the Brigade troops. This deadly attack convinced the already seriously exhausted Japanese to withdraw from their remaining positions immediately adjacent to the Brigade Box. Some supply drops of water and ammunition were also attempted, but as usual most fell into the jungle just outside the perimeter, presumably to be captured by the waiting Japanese. In any event, no further Japanese attacks were put in through the day, although intermittent shellfire and sniping continued as usual.

At 1723 hrs the Brigade signallers relayed a message to 23 Division: 'Tps very tired (.) doubt ability to resist further sustained attack (.) send help (.) very few offrs'. This was followed shortly thereafter by an even more plaintive message: 'Matter of hours now can I tell tps relief is coming?' These pitiful messages reflect a Brigadier who was effectively done in – he had done everything he possibly could to protect his beleaguered Brigade but he was now at the end of his strength. He had nothing more to give.

* * *

What the British did not know was that, while the Japanese had withdrawn, they were preparing for an even bigger attack. With the newly arrived men of 3rd Battalion 60th Regiment, together with more 75mm artillery, the Japanese were certain that they now had the numbers and the support to allow them to break in and smash the seriously depleted British defenders.

Previous histories have suggested that there was at least some tension if not outright rivalry between the commanders of the 15th and 31st Divisions. Rather than welcoming the recently arrived 15th Division troops when they started to arrive in the vicinity of Sangshak on 24/25 March, the commander of the attacking 31st Division troops wanted his men to continue the attack alone and so gain the glory of destroying the British at Sangshak. There are reports of tense discussions between the commanders of the two Divisions which led to the ridiculous result of the already depleted men of 31 Division continuing to attack alone on the morning of the 26th, even though fresh troops from Matsumura's 60 Regiment were close by. If the Japanese had been able to co-ordinate their attacks, it is unlikely that the beleaguered defenders would have been able to retake and hold the church position, no matter how many counter-attacks were put in or how bravely the men fought.[14]

Whatever the truth of the rivalry between the two Japanese commanders, since 31 Division had failed to secure the church, it was determined that the next attack would be a big one, comprising elements of both Divisions. This new and overwhelming assault was to be launched just before dawn on 27 March, and it was certain to destroy the remaining British and Indian troops and finally deliver the whole village to the Japanese. Lying in their hideouts to the west, north and east of the village, the Japanese infantry snatched some sleep, ate some of the recently captured rations dropped to them by the British planes and made ready for the final assault.

Breakout

Back at Brigade headquarters, and under the shadow of the new installed mountain guns, men took turns pedalling the foot-powered generator to keep the all-important wireless set charged. All of its batteries had been destroyed, and the signallers now relied on manpower to keep the set charged and the last remaining link with higher headquarters open.

As the men slowly pedalled, just after 1800 hrs a message was received, in clear (uncoded), from 23 Division Headquarters.

As the message was taken and written down, an astonished signalman (probably either Charlie Monks[15] or Vic Roden, who were both manning the radio at this time) was said to have immediately exclaimed, 'You can stuff your thoughts, General. What about the bleeding reinforcements!?'[16]

The rest of the Brigade staff, not yet having seen the message, were aghast at this sudden outburst. They thought that the signaller was either drunk on his remaining rum ration or had lost his senses. But then the message was delivered to the Brigadier. It read:

ALPHA ZULU LIMA INDIA' [50 Parachute Brigade's call-sign] THIS IS HOTEL ECHO INDIA [23 Division HQ's call-sign]. FIGHT YOUR WAY OUT SOUTH THEN WEST. AIRCRAFT AND TROOPS ARE ON THE LOOKOUT FOR YOU. ALL OUR THOUGHTS ARE WITH YOU

At first, Hope-Thomson could not believe it. A message this important being sent in clear immediately raised his suspicions. Had the Japanese somehow intercepted their communications and were sending false messages to induce the Brigade to abandon its positions? A quick check back to Headquarters confirmed the veracity of the message. It was genuine.

Hopkinson recalled that the Brigade officers were all surprised by this order. 'It seemed to us that there was really only one course open to us and that was to fight it out where we stood. There had been no thought of a possible withdrawal.' Other officers recounted that, despite the setbacks and the exhaustion, all were committed to fighting on. Rumours had circulated of possible reinforcements, but no one had thought of conducting a withdrawal or a breakout. The whole purpose of a defensive box was to stay put and let the enemy batter itself to death upon your defences.

But this order changed everything. It was no longer to be a 'last ditch' fight to the death, but rather an attempt to withdraw, taking as many men as possible. Hope-Thomson wasted no time and immediately called in his surviving officers to give them the news. He told them that since the Japanese were so close on almost all sides, it would be suicide to try and leave the position as a formed body of troops carrying all their heavy weapons. Instead, 4/5 MLI would provide cover for the withdrawal, and the forward positions of 152 and 153 Battalions would leave in small, lightly-armed groups from about midnight. They would filter through the MLI position and move directly south, which Hope-Thomson assessed as being the direction with the least

Japanese opposition. The withdrawing troops were ordered to thread their way silently past any Japanese patrols and move south for several miles, before doglegging west then north towards the main British position at Imphal. The gunners, mortars and other units would follow, again in small groups, with the MLI bringing up the rear once the rest of the position was clear.

There was however, one significant problem with Hope-Thomson's plan – what should they do with the wounded? As the conference broke up, Bobby Davis entered the HQ to talk with the Brigadier about this. Clearly there were a great many seriously wounded men who could not be moved from the position, even by stretcher. There was nothing that could be done to evacuate them, so they would need to remain where they were, sedated and made as comfortable as possible, until the Japanese arrived. Davis asked for permission to stay and care for the wounded men. But to Hope-Thomson this was out of the question – 'He didn't think it would achieve anything given the Japanese reputation.'[17] The wounded who could walk or be carried would go with them. The rest would have to be left where they were.

Back with 152 Battalion, the 2IC, Major Stewart, started assigning groups of relatively fit men to accompany any walking wounded who had any chance of being able to break out. This included Hopkinson, who had his wounded leg carefully bandaged and made ready for the journey. Elsewhere, hasty bamboo stretchers were being constructed to carry the ten or so stretcher cases who it was decided could be moved and who would leave together with the Battalion.

Surprisingly, one problem was actually locating all of the wounded men. When the Field Ambulance was pulled back to the MLI lines earlier in the day, a great many wounded had been left where they lay in trenches and shell scrapes. While most were carried back, inevitably in the confusion and the ongoing battle, some were left behind. To add to their misery, that evening it rained once more and water seeped everywhere, into the dugouts of the Headquarters and into the operating theatre of the Field Ambulance. Slit trenches occupied by wounded men quickly filled with rain, adding more discomfort and even the threat of drowning to the lot of the already miserable casualties.

Nevertheless, from this point on, all effort was directed at preparing for the withdrawal. Fortunately, apart from an outburst of heavy gunfire at around 2000 hrs, the Japanese obliged by staying generally quiet. The breech blocks of the dependable mountain guns were destroyed and the guns silently dismantled. HE rounds were rammed into the barrels from both ends, blocking them and making the guns unusable. At Brigade HQ, all documents were destroyed, and the Brigade tried to hide or render useless anything that could not be taken with them.

26 March – 'A terrible day, never to be forgotten' 129

To keep up the pretence that they were staying put and ready for a fight, the Brigade engaged in some random firing with what was left of their dwindling ammunition stocks, in order to convince the Japanese that it was 'a normal night' in the British position.

Bill Gollop, who had been hit in the leg and face by grenades while trying to retake the church the day before, was lying in a shell hole with several other wounded men when he heard that the Brigade would be moving out that evening and that the wounded would be carried out on stretchers. 'I didn't believe this', said Gollop, but he sent for his orderly and told him to come and get him as soon as the Battalion was ready to move. It was a wise move on Gollop's part, as in the end several of the stretcher cases who could not be moved were reluctantly given heavy doses of morphine and left in their shell scrapes or the dressing station to await their fate.

Lying on his stretcher and anxiously waiting for his orderly to return, Gollop said he heard strange sounds coming from the Japanese position which sounded more like a 'drunken party' than men readying themselves for another attack. 'Having been in a few drunken parties myself, I should know', said Gollop. 'The Japanese would never admit to this, but the fact that at least 75 per cent of the rum ration dropped to us fell into Japanese territory plus the fact that they did little to cut off the retreating troops does add credence to my supposition.'[18]

The Japanese were not the only ones drinking rum. After the withdrawal orders were given, Trim assembled his remaining officers and told them the news. The conference over, 'Everyone had a drink [of rum], finishing up what little there was in the Mess to prevent it falling into Jap hands and departed to their companies to pass on the orders.'

The officers moved back to their positions and informed their men of the plan. They ordered them to silently destroy everything they could not carry but to not talk about the withdrawal, fearing that JIFs lying just outside the perimeter might hear them and give the plan away.

As the Brigade made its preparations, it appears that sometime after 2000 hrs some of the paratroopers in the forward lines of the perimeter 'jumped the gun' and started to move back towards the MLI positions. The Parachute Battalions noted that there was a 'bottleneck' at the MLI lines, whereas the MLI officers took a much dimmer view of the affair. According to the official MLI War Diary, 'Captain Bessell reported that many men from the Parachute Brigade had again entered his perimeter without orders and that he could not get rid of them. They were seriously inconveniencing the running of his Company because they had filled to overflowing his communication trenches.

He ordered them out at the point of a bayonet but they could not be moved and indeed one of them fired a burst of Sten gun at him.'

This is an illustration of the different ways in which participants can view the same scene. The men of the Parachute Brigade, almost entirely bereft of officers, may just have thought that they were moving to their start positions and preparing for the upcoming withdrawal. To the officers of the MLI, this precipitate movement of troops appeared to be disorganized rabble. Whatever the actual situation, some sympathy should be extended to the exhausted paratroopers, who had been under constant pressure for days. While the MLI officers and men had been fighting constantly, too, they had not borne the brunt of the Japanese attacks and their command structure was relatively intact. Nonetheless, as will be seen, it was the MLI viewpoint that was initially relayed to higher command after the battle, and this may well have contributed to some ugly rumours about the Parachute Brigade which circulated immediately thereafter.

* * *

At 2300 hrs the 3-inch mortars fired their few remaining rounds before they, too, were silently destroyed. The troops of the Mortar Battery were then led out of their position by their GPO (Gun Position Officer) Lieutenant Hepburn down the slope and towards the MLI lines.

As they neared the MLI lines they saw that groups of men in front of them were starting to silently weave through the lines before slipping out of the Box. The sky was moonless, the jungle black, and the men tried their best to remain silent as they moved down the steep slope towards the track and then into the thick jungle to the south of the MLI position. Owing to the darkness, the steep hill and the thick jungle, the men soon broke into small groups, generally of about ten or so, and started to make their way south away from Sangshak.

The dark night was difficult enough for the able-bodied, but doubly so for the accompanying wounded. About ten stretcher cases were gingerly moved down the slope by the hard-pressed stretcher bearers. A further 120 walking wounded hopped or shuffled out of the position as best they could and into the blackness of the jungle beyond.

But that still left another 100 seriously wounded men, sedated and lying in their shell scrapes to wait for the arrival of the Japanese. Most of these men were either close to death or so seriously wounded that there was no prospect of carrying them out. There were also men who, while not close to death, were unconscious and were simply left behind, accidentally forgotten in the darkness and the confusion.

But the majority of the Brigade got away with no further casualties and, amazingly, without alerting the surrounding Japanese besiegers. It was an astonishing feat, and the defenders must have felt a huge sense of relief as they moved into the black, eerie but comparatively safe jungle beyond.

Chapter 13

26 March – Breakout

The withdrawal of the British troops from the Sangshak box and the journey to Imphal is almost a story in itself. In fact, it is several stories, as each of the groups that left Sangshak encountered quite different challenges and dangers on their way back to safety. While the withdrawal was marked by very little fighting, it was no less tense, exhausting and heroic than the defence of Sangshak itself.

The Japanese

At around 0300 hrs the remaining men of 58 Regiment formed up at their jumping-off points on West Hill and in the jungle to the north of what had been the 153 Battalion perimeter. After so many days of bitter fighting and the loss of so many of their comrades, it is hard to imagine what was going through the mind of these soldiers, gripping their rifles and swords and readying themselves for yet another charge and the inevitable hail of bullets and grenades that would meet them. As the preparatory fire from their 75mm guns slackened, the order to charge was given, and they once again set off at a low crouch up the steep slope of East Hill. But this time, something was different. They ran past the forward lines of trenches, now strangely silent, and then past the ruins of demolished *bashas*, burnt, scarred by shrapnel and littered with the debris of days of fighting. Up they moved towards the ruins of the church, where so many of their comrades had been killed in charge after bloody charge, until finally they reached the top of the plateau, to be greeted by a strange silence. The enemy had gone!

To the Japanese, the sudden absence of resistance would initially have been unnerving. Where were the hundreds of British and Indian soldiers who had fought so doggedly over the past week? But surprise was quickly replaced by exhilaration as the attackers realized that the British had gone and the village was now theirs. For the past few days, officers and men had believed that they were the ones in desperate straits, having suffered several nights of incessant fighting and heavy casualties. Little did they suspect that the British forces had suffered similar privations.

To the Japanese, suddenly in complete command of the destroyed West Hill, the only explanation was that the defenders' will had broken and they had simply fled. Why else would they suddenly give up and flee into the jungle? All around them was the litter of five days of fighting and, despite the British orders to destroy all heavy equipment, a large amount of useful war booty remained behind to be scooped up by the grateful Japanese.

Besides the military equipment left behind, the Japanese soon discovered many dead and dying Indian, Gurkha and British soldiers lying in their shallow pits. They also discovered a few who were less seriously wounded but had merely succumbed to exhaustion, fallen asleep and missed the evacuation. These men were quickly rounded up and taken prisoner.

A significant find for the Japanese victors was the body of their highly respected Lieutenant Ban, who had been killed leading the charge in the early morning of 23 March. Uncovering his body, they were very moved by the fact that he had been respectfully buried together with his officer's sword. This small act of military courtesy had a great effect on the Japanese and perhaps explains why the victors did not immediately kill all of the captured wounded soldiers, as had been common Japanese practice in other battles in the theatre. According to Japanese accounts, those wounded men who could be moved were sent back to Field Hospitals, whereas the relatively fit were soon pressed into service, acting as labourers and coolies to carry supplies and equipment. But there were no atrocities carried out by the Japanese on their vanquished foes after this battle.

Exhilaration at victory, however, must quickly have been followed by exhaustion. As the Japanese searched the rest of the abandoned position, and as the adrenaline of the charge seeped away, fatigue would have taken over. Many men will have started to slow down, rest and perhaps eat and sleep, preparing themselves for the inevitable orders to move on northwards. The Japanese were now some five days behind their original schedule, and neither their plans nor their supplies would allow them to rest for long at Sangshak.

Basil Seaton

As the Japanese searched the dead and dying in the early morning gloom, Basil Seaton was startled by being kicked awake by a Japanese soldier. He had fallen asleep in his trench and missed the evacuation! The soldier was as surprised as he was and hesitated momentarily, whereupon Seaton seized his chance and punched him 'below the belt', temporarily disabling the hapless man and giving Seaton just enough time to scuttle out of the position and into the thick undergrowth beyond. He lay there, just outside the perimeter, for what seemed like an age, silently waiting for nightfall and a chance to escape the Sangshak village area. This was a very precarious position. All around, large numbers of Japanese troops could be seen coming and going, searching the entire village and reorganizing themselves. Surely, one of these soldiers or a small patrol was certain to find him, lying so close to the perimeter. But as luck would have it, he lay there undiscovered.

As the daylight faded and darkness descended, Seaton decided to make his move. He got up gingerly, his whole body stiff from lying motionless for the entire day, and still suffering from his wounds. Knowing he could not stay where he was any longer, he quietly pushed aside his cover and started to creep across the dirt track away from Sangshak. But before he could get away, another Japanese soldier suddenly appeared. Seaton quickly got back into his hide, lying still and hoping that the man would move away without seeing him.

But it was not to be. The Japanese soldier noticed a 'body' lying still in the underbrush and moved up to investigate. He placed a hand on Seaton's head, presumably to check if he was alive. But as the man bent over him, Seaton used the only weapon he still possessed, his Para fighting knife. He struck with speed, plunging the blade into the stomach and neck of the astonished soldier. The Japanese soldier fought back, even biting Seaton's knife hand, but after a brief struggle he fell dead. Seaton did not wait to survey his handiwork, knowing that if he was discovered now, with a dead Japanese soldier next to him, he would certainly be killed. He seized his chance, crossed the track and escaped into the jungle as fast as he could while remaining as quiet as possible.

Fortunately, the rest of the Japanese were busy occupying Sangshak and making preparations for their advance north. This is the only explanation why patrols were not immediately sent out to locate and kill Seaton after the Japanese soldier's body was discovered. The general confusion gave him the chance to make a clean break to the south. He would then spend the next three days alone in the jungle, slowly working his way towards the British lines around Imphal. The distance was about 25 miles as the crow flies, but a hard walk even for a fit man, and considerably longer through the jungle and over the hills which were still crawling with the advancing Japanese troops. Besides the pain of the wounds on his face and neck, Seaton's stomach was constantly grumbling through lack of food. Fortunately, he found two grenades on a dead soldier and was able to use them to kill some fish in a stream. Raw jungle fish may not be the most appetizing of meals, but it was a godsend to a starving Basil Seaton. After a lonely three-day march he finally reached British lines, whereupon he was promptly sent off to safety in hospital.[1]

Hope-Thomson and the command team

The Brigade command team made its breakout from Sangshak as a body. The group comprised several of the remaining British officers, including Brigadier Hope-Thomson, Major Gerry Beale[2] (the Brigade Major), Nobby Clark (Quartermaster of 152 Battalion), Dickie Richards and a small party of headquarters soldiers. The total darkness and the moist undergrowth covered them as they slipped quietly through the perimeter, down the southern slope and across the track into the waiting jungle beyond. They continued south until, at about 0300 hrs, when they crossed the Litan track, they heard the sound of gunfire somewhere to their rear. Turning round, they saw a number of fires and numerous lights to the north and east of Sangshak. It was clear to them that the Japanese were now fully in command of the village that they had defended so doggedly for the past week. But there was no time to dwell on the past, and so the party turned back and pushed on.

Despite being the most junior officer of the command team, Dickie Richards was put in charge of navigation. He was known as an extremely skilled outdoorsman, often going off on shooting and fishing trips on his own in the jungles and forests of India, with little more than a rifle and a fishing rod for company. Due to this reputation, the job of navigator naturally fell to him. He was, however, encouraged with good-natured threats of 'castration' from the other officers should he mess it up!

The trek was hard. Not only was the night moonless, but the thick jungle and steep hills made the going treacherous and difficult. It was all too easy to miss your footing or fall into one of the numerous gullies that criss-crossed the area. A few hours into their march, the command team came across two small parties of stretcher-bearers, one carrying the seriously wounded Major Webb and the other carrying Major Richard Gillet. The stretcher-bearers had set off well before the command team but were obviously struggling and slowing down under their loads. The wounded were barely hanging on. Gillet, who had been hit in one of the actions to retake the church, seemed to be barely alive. As Richards went to see how he was faring, the barely conscious Gillet managed to ask him for a cigarette. He also asked to swap his rifle for Richards' revolver. The unspoken implication was clear: Gillet intended to use the revolver on himself if he could not go on or was in danger of capture. Richards put the revolver into Gillet's hands, then took up the heavier rifle and said his goodbyes.

Dickie later heard that Gillet had died almost as soon as he finished his cigarette. In the end, he did not need the revolver. Apparently, his body was buried under a rough stone cairn on the hillside near where he had said goodbye to the command team.

Leaving Gillet with his stretcher-bearers, and unencumbered by wounded men, the command team initially made relatively good progress. Then, about an hour after leaving Gillet, the command party caught up with another group of wounded. This time, the group included Hopkinson, bravely hobbling along, his wounded foot having been double-bandaged to give it some support and protection on the march. It was not enough, however, and his wounds were starting to slow him down. In an effort to give Hopkinson's leg some further support, Richards found a pair of Fox's puttees[3] and tightly wound them around Hoppy's lower leg, already fully covered in plaster and bandages.

The puttees may have provided an additional layer of support, but it was still hopelessly insufficient to cope with the march through the jungle and the scramble over the many hills that separated them from the forward line of British troops at Imphal. Hopkinson put on a brave face and trudged forward as fast as his wounded leg would allow. But no matter how much reinforcement was added to Hoppy's foot, he could not keep up with the pace of the fit men. So the group slowed its advance, reduced to a snail's pace to match Hopkinson's brave but painfully slow gait.

As the command party continued to move south it picked up a few more stragglers, until by late afternoon it had swollen to twenty men – at that time one of the larger groups of Sangshak evacuees. Several of the newcomers were also wounded.

As they made their way gingerly through the jungle, signs that the Japanese were nearby were plain to see. At track junctions, cigarette papers, boot prints and the odd food wrapper were found littering the ground. This clear evidence of enemy nearby added to the stress of the escaping men. Thankfully, however, no Japanese were encountered that day. This was just as well, since the command party had very little ammunition – just a few rounds per rifle and perhaps a grenade or two. If the party met a Japanese patrol, there could be no question of putting up a serious fight. The most that they would be able to do would be to bluff it out by firing a few rounds to keep the enemy's heads down while they tried to escape back into the jungle.

Their lack of speed was not the only problem facing the command group. After a week of meagre food and water rations, now combined with a hot and difficult march, all the men were very hungry and thirsty. When they finally found a small stream which looked clean and clear, they all drank deeply from it in order to quench their thirst. Unfortunately, the water was not as clean as it seemed, and afterwards many of the party suffered from painful stomach cramps and pains, which slowed the team down further still.

Food was also in short supply and desperately needed by the starving men. Richards thought that there must be fish in some of the streams and ponds that dotted the hills, and he resolved to do a 'spot of fishing'. Lacking the rod that usually accompanied him on his pre-war jungle treks, Richards decided to supplement the meagre rations of the group by tossing a grenade into a pond and managed to scoop out a number of stunned small fish. Despite their hunger, not everyone in the party could stomach raw fish. But for those who could, it was a welcome addition of calories, temporarily quietening the rumbling of their shrunken bellies.

One can only wonder about the wisdom of setting off a loud grenade, when large numbers of Japanese troops were somewhere in the surrounding hills. But despite the danger, accounts reveal that a number of the groups who left Sangshak resorted to this form of 'fishing'. Obviously, hunger was a more powerful driver than fear. Also, the men probably knew that a muffled explosion in a stream would be hard to pinpoint by anyone who was not in the immediate vicinity. The potential reward of raw fish was worth the risk.

By the second day out from Sangshak, Hopkinson was clearly having a tough time. The morphine he had been given had now well and truly worn off, and his progress was slow and painful. He gritted his teeth and kept hobbling forward, but it was desperately slow work. He was not, however, the only man showing signs of strain. All of them, already exhausted by a week of bitter fighting, were getting steadily weaker through a combination of lack of food, forced marching over hard terrain and the stress of knowing that two divisions of Japanese soldiers were all around them and between them and safety at Imphal.

But it was Hope-Thomson who seemed to suffer most – not physically but from the strain of the last two weeks. As Dickie Richards recounted, 'For days the Brigadier had been approaching a state of total exhaustion; for him it was not only extended battle fatigue, but also the exceedingly onerous burden of having his Brigade thrust into this invidious situation unprepared. Then for over a week, to watch it ... hacked to death with practically no support from headquarters 4 Corps.'[4]

Few of the survivors said much about Hope-Thomson during the evacuation, but it was clear that he was no longer actively in charge of the Command party. Instead, Colonel Abbot, the Brigade second-in-command, was leading, assisted by Richards and the Brigade Major, Gerry Beale. It is likely that by this time Hope-Thomson was doing little more than passively stumbling behind the command group, somewhat numb, dazed and deep in his own thoughts.

After another 24 hours of moving at the slow pace of the wounded men it was decided to break the party into two groups. The fitter men would move at all speed towards Imphal and warn the waiting British to be on the lookout for returning paratroopers. The wounded and slower men would just have to continue as best they could. While the radio message received from HQ on the evening of 26 March said that 'air and men' would be out looking for them, no one remembered seeing any aircraft searching the hills for them, much less any troops. It was clear that they were on their own and would only reach safety by marching out themselves.

After splitting the party, Richards' group (which included Hopkinson and Hope-Thomson) numbered about ten men. They continued to make painfully slow progress, and it was becoming apparent that Hoppy's wounds were starting to get the better of him. He limped along doggedly, but increasingly slowly. After settling the party down to rest under cover of a ridge outside an abandoned village, Richards and a few of the fitter Indian orderlies went forward to investigate and see if there was any food to scrounge. As they moved towards the village they spotted a large group of Japanese together with mules – probably a re-supply party. Richards flung himself down in the tall grasses on the outskirts of the village, lying doggo and trying not to be seen. But the movement must have been spotted, and the Japanese started firing in their general direction. Fortunately, it was not sustained or accurate fire. It was more in the way of a panicked shot or two fired into the bushes in the hope of scaring any hiding prey into making a run for it. But Richards and his team lay still and did not return fire. After waiting a few minutes, when no shots were returned and nothing seen, the Japanese soon tired of this game and moved on – the need to re-supply their troops obviously more important than searching out a few British stragglers.

After the excitement of the encounter with the Japanese, the next three days reverted to the slow, monotonous and torturous climbing up and down the jungle-clad ridges in the general direction of Imphal. No more Japanese were spotted, and as the immediate danger subsided, the men's thoughts turned inwards – to the battle they had just survived, to their wounds, their exhausted bodies and their empty bellies. But they continued to trudge on.

The party then had what at the time seemed to be a lucky break, stumbling into another abandoned village. Like all Naga villages in this part of Manipur, the villagers had abandoned their homes and escaped into the jungle on the first day of fighting.[5] However, in this one they had inexplicably left some livestock: a few chickens and a pig which had not yet been scooped up by the advancing Japanese. It was a bounty the starving men could not ignore. Despite the obvious danger, the party decided to chance a halt in the village and light a fire in order to have a proper meal. Some inexpert butchery followed, and then chunks of pork were roasted over the open fire. The smell of the cooking meat was like heaven to the starving men – 'the aroma would have made a dead man sniff', was how Richards described it. But while the aroma was heavenly, the meal proved to be a disaster. Whether the meat was undercooked or the men's shrunken stomachs were no longer able to process such rich fare, most of what went down came straight back up again. The party limped out of the village perhaps worse off than when they entered it.

On leaving the village, their pace continued to slow. The wounded men could not keep up, and there was a real fear that they would not be able to make it all the way to Imphal. Then, somewhere ahead in the jungle, Richards heard the yelp of a barking deer. He crept forward silently and spotted the small deer ahead of him in a clearing. Ever the hunter, and with thoughts of a meal of venison foremost in his mind, he raised Gillet's .303 rifle to take a shot at the animal. Aiming carefully, he squeezed the trigger. Click. Nothing happened. He tried again and again, but still nothing happened, and the fortunate deer trotted away, oblivious of the danger he had just escaped.

A plainly frustrated Richards stripped the rifle and discovered that it had a broken firing pin, rendering it useless. So the rifle he had carried through the jungle and over the hills since he swapped his pistol with Gillet had been a dud. Angry at the missed meal, he was also relieved that he had discovered the faulty weapon now and not in the face of a Japanese patrol.

Bad luck continued to dog the Command party; late in the evening of 30 March, Hope-Thomson lost his footing in the dark, hit his head and was very seriously concussed. Clearly dazed, he was barely able to keep going forward. Perhaps importantly for what was to follow, he was still suffering from the effects of the fall when the command team stumbled onto the Imphal plain a day or so later. His depressed and slightly concussed state was to have major consequences for Hope-Thomson and his future career, but at the time the party thought little of it – it was just another injury to add to the already long list suffered by the command team.

At daybreak on 31 March, Richards climbed a tree to scout the land ahead. His perch rewarded him with a clear view of the surrounding area and the welcome observation that they were on the very edge of the Imphal plain. Surely they would soon be picked up by forward British patrols. Knowing that safety was not too far away, the remaining men sat in a group and looked through their meagre possessions. They found an old razor blade and tried to scrape away the scraggly beards they had grown over the past week. They tidied themselves up as best they could, partly out of pride, but also so they would be recognized as British troops and not accidentally shot at by edgy troops on the front line.

Stumbling out of the jungle, they were soon stopped by an armoured column on the Litan-Imphal Road at about noon. They were immediately whisked to a nearby defensive position, where the front-line troops shared their rations and looked after the dazed men. But they didn't rest there long. Hoppy and the other wounded men were taken straight to hospital, while Colonel Abbot and Captain Richards were taken to 23 Division HQ to be debriefed by General Ouvry Roberts.

Hope-Thomson did not join the debrief party but was also taken immediately to hospital, where he was diagnosed with 'nervous exhaustion'. The men of the Parachute Brigade would never see Hope-Thomson again, nor would they learn what had happened to him until much later. He was soon sent to India, where he remained in hospital for several weeks before his 'posting order' came through. He was ordered to return immediately to England and was reduced to his substantive rank of Lieutenant Colonel. It was a callous and ignominious end for an officer who, despite his faults, had commanded the Brigade through its most deadly trial at Sangshak to the best of his ability and to the very end of his personal strength and courage. His sudden removal, without any notification or explanation, was a complete surprise to his officers and men. It would also be the catalyst for a series of vicious and insidious rumours about Hope-Thomson and the Brigade which the officers of 50 Parachute Brigade would work for years to dispel.

4/5 Mahratta Light Infantry

The officers and men of 4/5 MLI had a tough but very different evacuation experience to that of the command party.

Upon receiving the orders to evacuate, the MLI officers went around their troops and gave a detailed plan to each platoon. Trim was determined to keep his men together as far as possible. Accordingly, when the order to move was given, they were to break out and stick together in parties of no less than platoon size (about thirty men). Inevitably, smaller groups split off as a result of getting lost in the dark or being slowed down by wounds, but by and large the Battalion stayed relatively coherent throughout the withdrawal. This was in marked contrast to the men of the parachute battalions, who very quickly fragmented into very small groups. Unlike the Mahrattas, the paratroopers were often in groups of fewer than ten, and incredibly, many men made their way back to Imphal either individually or in pairs.

But despite the clear orders from their officers, there was nevertheless some confusion as the men started to leave their trenches. Some immediately lost their footing in the dark and fell down the 10ft embankment just beyond their forward pits and onto the track between the village and the jungle. Even Trim himself almost toppled over the side of the embankment. Luckily, one of his men was able to grab his web equipment, and he was spared a nasty fall. Despite the initial confusion, thankfully they were not discovered by the enemy and all managed to collect themselves for the move south.

The evacuation plan was simplicity itself, so that everyone in the Battalion could understand and remember it. They were initially to march directly south until dawn (at about 0600 hrs) before making a sharp turn to the west. They would then continue in a generally westward direction until they hit the Imphal plain. The plan was sound, but by 0300 hrs the men were dog-tired, and when a short halt was called, several of them instantly fell asleep, only to be woken sometime later by the cold in the middle of the night.

The next day saw heavy going through elephant grass and then marshy ground, before having to repeatedly ascend and descend the numerous 4,000ft ridges that were the most common feature of this part of Manipur. Constantly tired and hungry, the Mahrattas suffered, in turn, from the heat while they climbed during the day and then the creeping cold when they lay up at night on the jungle floor, without even a blanket or coat to protect them.

During the march, the Mahratta officers were constantly worried about the danger of meeting Japanese patrols. While the men still carried their arms, they would not have been able to put up any kind of serious resistance if a fight ensued. To mitigate this threat, small teams of scouts were often sent out to probe ahead of the main platoon groups and warn of any enemy activity. The Battalion also had a rough plan of action if they were surprised or bumped an enemy patrol. Upon contact, the forward platoon would immediately turn towards the Japanese and charge at them, firing and yelling as they went. It was hoped that this aggressive manoeuvre would shock the surprised Japanese and give the remaining platoons time to move to the flank and provide covering fire, further confusing the enemy. Under cover of this supporting fire, the forward platoon would withdraw, and then the remainder of the following men would leapfrog backwards and away from the Japanese.

Thankfully, the Mahrattas never had cause to deploy this 'action on contact' plan, as none of the MLI groups met any serious resistance. Nevertheless, the forward deployment of scouts proved its worth when, on the second day out from Sangshak, the scouts heard the noise of a small group of enemy coming up the track. Major McConnell, up forward with the scout party, heard what he thought sounded like someone trying to drive cattle (which may well have been the case, given Mutaguchi's ill-conceived plan to supply his troops with rations 'on the hoof'). McConnell and the scouts froze, hoping that the Japanese would pass them by. They all did so except for a couple walking some way behind the main party. A very brave Japanese officer, accompanied by a single JIF soldier, was walking along the track and suddenly spotted one of the scouts. Instead of shooting, the Japanese officer coolly held up one hand as if to signal the scout to stop and then called out in Urdu, '*Fire mat karo*' ('Don't fire/don't shoot'). He then motioned with his arms for the Mahrattas to put down their weapons. The MLI scouts were taken completely by surprise at this display and froze, staring at the Japanese officer facing them. It took a well-aimed shot from Captain Steele, who had just arrived on the scene, to wake the men, whereupon the Bren gunner also opened up and put a burst of fire into the Japanese officer and his JIF aide, killing them both. Realizing the danger they were in, the MLI troops then quickly crossed the track and made off into the jungle as fast as they could, before any Japanese reinforcements returned to investigate the noise.

The rest of the Mahrattas' journey out of the hills was relatively uneventful. Reports tell of tiredness by day and cold at night as the men tried to snatch a few hours' sleep. The climbing up and down the many hills was hard on exhausted men who had little in the way of food except a single tin each of emergency rations. But after no further encounters with the enemy, the MLI groups emerged from the jungle and onto the edge of the Imphal plain on 29 March. The forward elements of the Battalion were met by two Lee tanks of 7 Cavalry Regiment, who must have been very surprised to see a British unit emerge from the jungle into what they believed was the forward edge of their own lines. Once recovered from their shock, the Cavalry soldiers greeted the Mahrattas warmly, before ferrying them to the safety of the nearby Waithou Box.

The Mahrattas had handled the withdrawal magnificently and returned to British lines in relatively good order. Trim would have been justifiably pleased with the efforts of his men as he was taken away by jeep to be debriefed back at HQ 23 Brigade.

Return to Imphal

The withdrawal from Sangshak was not a classic, set-piece, disciplined military manoeuvre. Reports show that it very quickly fragmented into a series of mini-escapes, each with its own hardships and challenges. The fact that it worked, however, and that so many men got away to safety was testament to the grit, character and determination of all of the men who were evacuated from Sangshak. The escape, while not particularly orderly or pretty, should be remembered with a sense of awe that men who had already endured so much over the preceding weeks could still find the strength to go on, sometimes alone and without any assistance from higher command, and make it back to the comparative safety of the British lines.

With the main elements of 50 Parachute Brigade arriving at various locations around Imphal between 29 and 31 March, one would have expected them to have been pulled out of the line and sent to a rear area to rest and re-equip. However, unlike later wars, in which a unit which had seen as much combat as 50 Brigade would have been sent immediately to safety to recuperate, in the Second World War such units were often kept close to the front, re-equipped with whatever was at hand and then sent straight back into action as soon as possible.

It should also be remembered that just as the men of 50 Parachute Brigade were reaching Imphal, the entire Manipur region had erupted in fierce fighting between the British Indian Army and the three divisions of the Mutaguchi's Fifteenth Army. April was the high point of the Japanese offensive, which would see both the bitter defence of Kohima and continued vicious fighting south of Imphal itself. There was simply no time to dwell on the battles of the past when the focus had to be the many battles taking place right now.

With no prospect of rest, the remaining fit men of the Parachute Brigade were sent to be the nearby 'Catfish' Box, where they would be re-equipped before being sent back into action. By 7 April the Brigade's total strength was just under 1,500 men (62 British officers, 56 British other ranks and 1,327 Indian/Gurkha troops), and this number included a large number of men, such as Lieutenant Colonel Hopkinson, who had been wounded and were now recovering in hospital.

Over the past week of fighting around Sangshak and Sheldon's Corner, almost 600 of the Brigade's officers and men had either died or been seriously wounded.

Victor Brookes recalled what happened when the Brigade reached the safety of the Imphal plain:

When we reformed in Imphal we received no thanks or recognition for what we had done at Sangshak. The battle of Imphal had begun and the whole incident at Sangshak was thankfully swept under the carpet and forgotten as soon as possible.[6]

Chapter 14

The Prisoners

It is remarkable that so many groups of men were able to slip out from under the very noses of an imminent Japanese attack at Sangshak and thread their way back to Imphal. A withdrawal, particularly when still actively engaged with the enemy, is regarded as one of the most complex and difficult military manoeuvres. The fact that so many of the survivors of 50 Parachute Brigade were able to get away is remarkable and testament to the skill, training and grit of the officers and men of the Brigade. But it is also true that the survivors had more than a little luck as well.

However, not all the defenders were so lucky, and a very great many of them, perhaps inevitably, found their way into captivity. In all, it appears that at least 100–200 Indian soldiers became prisoners of war within the first few days after the Sangshak battle. Brigade personnel returns dated 7 April 1944 counted 410 men as officially 'missing'. But this was likely to be an overestimate, as the Brigade often marked down a man as 'missing' unless it was positively known that he had been killed or wounded. Thus many men who had been initially marked as missing on the Brigade roll had probably already been killed.

Nonetheless, we know that quite a number of Indian troops were captured. Approximately seventy-three Indian troops from 152 Battalion alone were made prisoner, and another twenty-five from 4/5 MLI. If we add some further men from 153 Battalion and the independent Brigade units, we can estimate that somewhere between 150 and 200 men were captured at some stage after the Sangshak battle.

As would be expected, the majority were captured within the first day or two after the breakout from Sangshak. A few were caught in the position itself, having failed to be woken up by their comrades and inadvertently left behind. More were rounded up in the hills around Sangshak within the next two days. As these small groups were often leaderless, with neither a senior NCO nor an officer in charge, it is likely that they had no compass or map and would inevitably have become lost or disorientated in the dark and in the jungle. With no commander to drive them on, it is also possible that some allowed exhaustion to get the better of them and rested longer than they should have, with the inevitable result that they were found by the advancing Japanese troops.

But whatever the reason, many were picked up by Japanese patrols and immediately pressed into service, hauling supplies and stores for the Japanese as they continued their advance towards Kohima and Imphal.

A consistent theme of all reports is that the Japanese tended to treat the captured Indian soldiers fairly well. This was in stark contrast to earlier campaigns, when Japanese brutality towards their captured foes was legendary. In other theatres, and even at other times in Burma, captured British soldiers could expect to be shot out of hand, beheaded or even used for instant bayonet practice by Japanese soldiers who did not want to be weighed down by prisoners.

Atrocities and mistreatment of captives at the hands of victorious Japanese soldiers was not merely a feature of the early stages of the war. As recently as the diversionary Ha-Go Operation and the famous 'Battle of the Admin Box' in February 1944, reports had told of IJA troops bursting into the Indian hospital lines and proceeding to shoot and bayonet to death thirty-one patients and four doctors.[1] Such behaviour was standard practice for advancing Japanese troops, thus their relatively humane treatment of the Sangshak captives was a remarkable exception.

One explanation for the lenient treatment of the Sangshak PoWs is that the Japanese were moved by the honourable way which the British treated their enemy war dead at Sangshak, epitomized by the burial of the Japanese officer with his sword. While this could perhaps explain the actions of the Japanese during the immediate aftermath of the capture of Sangshak, it seems a less plausible explanation the further removed we are from the battle in both time and space. This also does not explain the almost uniformly decent treatment of Indian PoWs during this part of the campaign.

One explanation is that the Japanese may have regarded the captured Indian soldiers rather differently to their British officers. While the British were clearly the enemy, their Indian troops may have been seen as something less – acting under duress, perhaps, or forced to fight by their British masters – rather than as highly motivated and willing combatants. While that belief was clearly a misreading of the complex reasons why Indian troops fought (and wilful blindness to the superb fight put up by the Indian troops over the preceding week), this way of thinking meshed with the official Japanese reason for the U-Go campaign – to liberate a portion of India and support the Indians in rising up against their colonial masters.

The presence of INA troops assisting the Japanese may also have had some effect on Japanese behaviour at the beginning of the U-Go campaign. While the INA was not used as an independent fighting unit, elements certainly accompanied the forward Japanese troops. It is possible that this close contact with INA soldiers either made the Japanese look at the Indian troops they captured slightly more favourably, or that intercession by INA soldiers moderated Japanese treatment of these captured enemies.

A more prosaic but more compelling reason may have been that the awful logistical predicament that the Japanese found themselves in forced them to use whatever source of labour was available. Surviving PoWs recounted how they had to haul goods, carry supplies and perform the myriad manual tasks required by the IJA as it moved rapidly through difficult and inhospitable terrain.

Whatever the reason, capture did not lead to immediate execution, and most new Indian PoWs either became coolies or were sent to assist at the forward field hospital at Litan, several miles south of Sangshak. That these men were kept labouring close to the front line meant they had a chance to escape, evidenced by the fact that almost immediately after capture many found a way to give their captors the slip and reach the British lines.

* * *

Two such men that were able to escape were Naiks Chand and Singh, junior NCOs from 152 Battalion, who became separated from the rest of their comrades in the dark soon after the breakout from Sangshak. After wandering alone, the two hapless NCOs were soon picked up by a Japanese patrol in the early hours immediately following the breakout. But captivity did not agree with them, nor did the idea of acting as coolies for the Japanese, and so, less than fourteen hours after being captured, they slipped away from their Japanese guards while they were sleeping. They then worked their way up and down the hills of Manipur, alone, until they eventually found their way into the arms of friendly forces at Yaingangporpi, some nine miles south-west of Litan.

Fourteen hours from capture to escape appears to have been something of a record, but reports show that most men taken prisoner escaped from their captors between two days and two weeks after capture. Most successful escapes occurred during the confusion of actual fighting, but a number of Indian troops were also able to slip off into the jungle during quiet times when they were collecting water or hauling stores. It appeared that the Japanese had neither the time nor the manpower to closely monitor their captives, and thus the majority of the men captured by the Japanese managed to escape relatively easily.

There were many stories of grit and determination displayed by the captives, but that of Havildar Mohd Ashraf bears repeating. It was a tale so astounding that upon his return to the British lines he was awarded a 'Mention in Despatches' for his exploits.

Havildar Mohd Ashraf was an NCO clerk of 152 Battalion and, like several of his comrades, was picked up in the immediate aftermath of the Sangshak battle and then pressed into service, labouring like most of his fellows. After about three days, and by now thoroughly sick of acting as a coolie for the Japanese, he seized his chance and made off into the jungle, easily eluding his captors. Unfortunately, his freedom did not last long, for he was soon recaptured by another group of Japanese soldiers.

Amazingly, however, this time he was not destined to resume work as a labourer. We don't know what story he told his new captors, but it must have been convincing, since soon afterwards he was informed that henceforth he was to be a card-carrying member of the INA. Even more improbably, despite having been an enemy soldier just several days previously, the Japanese now gave him a weapon!

The record is also silent on whether he was actually forced to fight against other Indian troops, but three days later he escaped yet again, this time taking another four Indian soldiers with him. Unlike the rest of his 50 Brigade comrades who were striking roughly westwards towards Imphal, Havildar Mohd Ashraf decided that it would be better to proceed north-east towards Kohima and the railhead at Dimapur beyond. He thought it would be less likely that the Japanese were looking for stragglers in this direction.

Although they moved quietly through the jungle, it looked as though the escapees' luck had run out when they bumped into another Japanese patrol also making its way towards Kohima. What Havildar Ashraf did not know was that Kohima was destined to witness one of the most intense and biggest battles of the entire U-Go campaign, and large numbers of Japanese soldiers from the 31st Division were at this time making their way towards the place.

Unlike his previous encounters, this time the Japanese patrol did not hesitate and immediately opened fire with automatic weapons. The escape party went to ground, but instead of returning fire, Havildar Ashraf was quick-thinking enough to wave his INA badge at the Japanese and yell out that they were INA soldiers. Somehow this ruse worked, and the firing stopped. After a quick interrogation, the Japanese expressed themselves satisfied with their story, and they were allowed to proceed on their way. Less than a day later, Ashraf and his small party reached friendly lines.

The recommendation for his award noted that not only had Havildar Mohd Ashraf displayed great courage and coolness, but also that he managed to bring back a great deal of intelligence about the Japanese which was later found to be extremely accurate and useful.

C Company, 152 Battalion

While most of the captured men managed to escape quite quickly after capture, escapees continued to straggle back to Imphal throughout the rest of April. Amazingly, and after almost a whole month in captivity, on 20 April twenty-four troops from C Company, 152 Battalion, long feared lost, found their way back to friendly lines.

All of the escapees were junior soldiers who had been picked up by the Japanese in the aftermath of C Company's stand on Hill 7378 at Sheldon's Corner. With the return of these men, it was now clear that the battle at Hill 7378 had not resulted in the total loss of all British personnel. Up to this point, the British believed that Major Fuller and his C Company had fought to the bitter end and had all died defending the position. What actually happened, however, was that with his ammunition almost spent and most of his men dead, Fuller had decided to attempt a breakout, in the hope of getting as many men as possible out of the position and back to safety. Unfortunately, the breakout was unsuccessful, with a number of men stumbling and falling into a previously hidden crevices in the hill and most of the rest being killed by the attackers. The survivors of the attempt, nearly a platoon's worth of men, were soon captured as the Japanese swarmed over Hill 7378, and they became PoWs for the best part of a month.

Immediately after capture, the C Company soldiers were marched east towards the Chindwin River. They then spent a week at Pushing, the Japanese initial staging area east of the river. Like most PoWs at this time, they were relatively well treated and were employed in menial tasks and for hauling and carrying stores.

A week later, after Sangshak was taken, the men were moved up to Ukhrul and then, a week later, on to Litan. It was in the confusion of the move south towards Litan that they were able to slip out of Japanese lines and make their way to safety. They were initially questioned by the British (possibly suspecting them of being JIFs), but when their bona fides was established, they were released for medical treatment and eventually reunited with their comrades in 152 Battalion. The return of the C Company men ended the longest stretch of captivity endured by any of the British troops captured during the Sangshak battle.

Lieutenant Robin Kynoch-Shand

It is notable that very few British soldiers or officers were captured at Sangshak. As can be seen from the reports of stretcher parties labouring to

The Prisoners 149

move seriously wounded British officers, the Brigade made every effort to evacuate them, irrespective of their wounds. Stories of Japanese atrocities in every Asian theatre since the beginning of the war convinced the British that the fate of any captured British soldier would be a horrific death, probably at the end of a bayonet or by way of decapitation.

Nevertheless, one British officer was captured. Lieutenant Robin Kynoch-Shand was the sole British officer from Sangshak to find himself at the mercy of the Japanese.

A contemporary photograph of Kynoch-Shand shows a very young and handsome officer, proudly sporting his officer's peaked cap emblazoned with his para wings and cocked at a jaunty angle. Educated at the prestigious Loretto School in Edinburgh, where he was a member of the rugby team, and enlisting shortly after leaving school, Kynoch-Shand was a mere twenty-one years old at the time of the battle. Nevertheless, he had already been in the Army for two years, quickly working his way through the ranks and rising from Private to Lieutenant.

Kynoch-Shand was one of the few unwounded officers from 153 Battalion at the time of the withdrawal. He managed to slip out of Sangshak along with the rest of his battalion but somehow became separated from them. Then, on 27 March, he was captured by a Japanese patrol. Dragged back to the patrol's higher Battalion headquarters, Kynoch-Shand had his hands bound behind his back, his boots removed and a rope passed from his bound feet up his back to his tied hands. Kneeling and tied up thus, he was roughly questioned by the Japanese, all the while being threatened with swords, bayonets and pistols.

The official record notes that he did not tell his captors anything. With night closing in, and running out of patience with their mute captive, the Japanese had a large fire prepared and placed Kynoch-Shand uncomfortably close to it without any water, with the aim of sweating the answers to their questions out of him. This is where he stayed for the entire night, dripping with sweat and with his hands and feet cramping in his tightening bonds. At about 0400 hrs on 28 March, he had his foot bindings cut, and with his hands still tightly tied behind him, was ordered to march out with his captors. Dehydrated from his night beside the fire, Kynoch-Shand got to his feet shakily and hobbled in the dark after his captors on his sore bare feet.

Just before dawn, his group was moving along a typical jungle track hugging the mountainside. To one side was a steep cutting sloping directly upwards towards the summit; on the other side was the '*khudside*', a precipitous drop straight down into the valley and the jungle below. Seizing his chance, Kynoch-Shand threw himself off the side of the track and down the hill. Shots rang out, but he was falling fast, further and further away, until he was out of sight of his captors. In the pre-morning gloom, and with their prisoner so far down the steep embankment, the Japanese fired a few more desultory shots before moving off – no one was going to waste their time making the dangerous descent to find him.

Kynoch-Shand was lucky. He had suffered scrapes and cuts in his fall, but nothing was broken. His hands remained tied behind his back, however, and try as he might he was unable to get them free. There were still Japanese nearby, so he remained motionless for several hours until he was sure that they had all gone and he was unseen. Then, with his hands behind him becoming numb, he got gingerly onto his tender bare feet and started to make his way slowly south-west towards the Imphal plain.

For three days he travelled alone, until a Naga tribesman luckily found him and cut his hands free. He then spent a few more days alone in the jungle until, both injured and increasingly weak from sickness, on 5 April he stumbled into the outskirts of Imphal. While he had made his way to safety he was so badly affected by his injuries that he was unable to return to his Battalion and was quickly evacuated by air back to India for medical treatment.

His escape was an amazing feat of grit and determination. For his 'initiative, courage and endurance' as well as his refusal to submit to the enemy's questions, Kynoch-Shand was recommended for and received an immediate Military Cross.[2]

Sadly, however, this was not the end of the story. Having recovered from his wounds, Kynoch-Shand soon rejoined 153 Battalion and participated in the first, and only, large-scale parachute drop that 50 Parachute Brigade attempted during the war – to silence enemy coastal guns at Elephant Point outside Rangoon on 1 May 1945. While leading an attack of assault pioneers against a particularly tough Japanese bunker, Kynoch-Shand was shot dead in one of the last encounters of the war in Burma. He was just twenty-two years old.

Chapter 15

The Aftermath

The Battle of Sangshak had an effect on both the British and the Japanese out of all proportion to the number of men involved, the casualties, its size or its geographical scope. While it would only become clear in the weeks and months following the battle, Sangshak would prove to have an important effect on both British and Japanese fortunes and the ultimate outcome of the entire U-Go campaign.

For the Japanese, the stubborn British defence caused a delay to Mutaguchi's plans from which he never recovered. With significant elements of both the 15 and 31 Divisions unexpectedly focussed on a single British Brigade trapped on a hilltop village for over a week, they fell further and further behind their timetable to cut the Manipur Road and strike north to occupy Kohima and Dimapur. It was a delay that would have deadly consequences and was arguably a major reason why they eventually lost the campaign. In a post-war interview with officers of the Japanese 31 Division it was admitted:

> Although Sangshak was outside its operational boundaries, [the left assault unit of the Division] believed it could quickly inflict an overwhelming defeat on the enemy and the decision was made to attack on 22 March. The task proved much more difficult than had been estimated ... The fact that the unit lost some 16 per cent of its strength and spent five days in the Sangshak engagement undoubtedly had an adverse effect on the final operation at Kohima.[1]

The Japanese commanders instinctively knew the importance of momentum in battle, the crucial need to keep pushing forward, to overwhelm your enemy and never give him time to pause, regroup and, crucially, think. They had used these tactics with great success again and again in the campaigns to take Malaya, Singapore and Burma. Mutaguchi and his Divisional commanders had all participated in these battles, so their decision to keep attacking a relatively minor outpost, wasting day after day and precious resources, is hard to understand. Why did they keep throwing themselves at the hard nut of Sangshak rather than just bypassing it and moving swiftly to their objectives?

Why waste several regiments on an under-strength Parachute Brigade on an isolated hilltop, rather than racing to take the infinitely more important positions of Kohima and Dimapur?

To be charitable, perhaps the commanders of 31 Division were concerned that they might be left exposed if they merely bypassed 50 Parachute Brigade. This could have been a consideration, but it is unlikely to have been the dominant one, particularly since Japanese tactics regularly called for infiltrating large bodies of troops through enemy lines and accepting that there might be some risk to their lines of supply in doing so. In any event, as we have seen, the Japanese had almost no lines of supply available to them for Operation U-Go; all supplies were carried in by the front-line troops or captured from the enemy. As such, the argument that the Japanese were worried about threats to their lines of communication does not make any sense.

Perhaps the answer lay partially in the character of the Japanese infantry. A contemporary American intelligence analysis of the Japanese Army in Burma noted that the Japanese infantrymen and small groups are tenacious and had 'bulldog determination to carry out a mission, even to annihilation'. It went on to say that 'discipline, lack of imagination and fatalism drives them on despite losses'.[2]

This was a commonly held belief among both Allied soldiers and commanders. Slim noted that 'The Japanese were ruthless and bold as ants while their designs went well, but if those plans were disturbed or thrown out – ant-like again – they fell into confusion, were slow to readjust themselves, and invariably clung too long to their original schemes.'[3]

While Slim grudgingly admired the tenacity and spirit of the individual Japanese fighting man, he was scathing in his assessment of their commanders, who continued doggedly to attack the same objective time and time again, even when it was clear that it was pointless to do so. He believed that the reason for such actions stemmed from a combination of 'unquenchable military optimism' and a lack of moral courage – the inability to admit to a mistake, with the resultant loss of face that it would necessarily entail.

Yet another reason for the wasteful delay at Sangshak was probably old-fashioned competition and jealousy between the Divisional commanders. Japanese commanders were notorious for seeking battlefield glory, and perhaps an isolated British unit at Sangshak was just too attractive for the commander of 31 Division to pass up. The well-known historian of the Burma campaign, Louis Allen, seems to believe that this was at least partly the reason why 58 Regiment (of 31 Division) first attacked the British outside of their divisional boundaries, and then continued to attack them even though it quickly became clear that this was going to be a sizeable undertaking swallowing up precious time, men and resources.[4]

But whatever the reasoning behind besieging Sangshak, the result was that the week-long delay caused an irreplaceable drain on Mutaguchi's already precarious supply arrangements. The few Allied airdrops which found their way into the hands of his grateful soldiers were never enough to make up for the prodigious expenditure of ammunition in the repeated attacks against the British. Nor were they sufficient to replace their dwindling food stocks – which even at the beginning of the operation were little more than survival rations. And critically, no amount of war booty could replace the casualties. Estimates vary between 500 and 1,000 Japanese soldiers killed or wounded,[5] and these men were simply irreplaceable. No troops would be able to make their way across the Chindwin and over the hills of Manipur to bolster the depleted 58 Regiment or any of the other units deployed at Sangshak.

By June 1944, Mutaguchi's forces had been totally defeated, and the last few sick and starving survivors slowly retreated out of Manipur and back into Burma from where they had come. Operation U-Go had failed completely, and the Japanese were unable to mount a similar operation in Burma again for the rest of the war. It had, however, been a near-run thing, particularly at the start of the Operation, when the Japanese were at their freshest and the British were initially shocked at the scale and speed of the operation. It was at this critical early stage that the loss of the best part of one Regiment of highly trained and experienced Japanese troops at Sangshak would have fatal consequences for Mutaguchi's plans and ambitions.

* * *

To the British, the delay was a godsend. While the onslaught at Sangshak was unexpected and came as a great shock to both the Parachute Brigade and its higher command, it gave the British an unexpected but much-needed breathing space. The crucial week allowed them to airlift the best part of an entire division from the Arakan in Burma back to the Imphal plain and instal them in defensive positions before the worst of the Japanese offensive broke over them. It also allowed British units time to make their way into the strategically vital position of Kohima and set up a hasty defence before the Japanese arrived in full force. Kohima, the gateway to the all-important railhead at Dimapur, would eventually be the scene of some of the fiercest fighting of the entire U-Go campaign. If the Japanese had been able to capture Kohima and Dimapur beyond, it is very likely that the British would have been unable to re-supply their armies in and around Imphal, and this might have resulted in their being defeated. As it was, the British only just managed to beat the Japanese to Kohima, and it was the delay brought about by the men of 50 Parachute Brigade that contributed, at least in part, to helping the British to beat them to the punch.

While the importance of the delay is clear with the benefit of hindsight, in April 1944 the contribution of 50 Parachute Brigade was less obvious to either the commanders or men of the 23rd Indian Division. As the remnants of the Brigade staggered back into various forward positions surrounding Imphal, often wounded, weak and thoroughly bedraggled, a pernicious rumour started to do the rounds of the Division and even the whole of IV Corps. A whispering campaign began, claiming that the Paratroopers had failed in their first encounter with the enemy. They were 'green' and 'inexperienced' troops, went the rumour, and it was for this reason that the Brigade had come off second best. The rumour mill also focused on the location of the defence, claiming that the siting of the Box at Sangshak was a mistake and the result of poor tactics and poor commanders. There were even whispers that the paratroopers 'had run away'.

The rumours were fanned by a message which was apparently radioed from higher command to all units around Imphal to keep a look out for 'stragglers' coming back from Sangshak – with the implication that such men were not a formed body of troops but a broken, retreating gaggle. These allegations were plainly false, a terrible slur on soldiers who had fought bravely and tenaciously against incredible odds and an insult that would rankle with survivors for many years after the event.

It is hard to know exactly where the rumours came from or how they started. Part of their genesis, however, might lie in the methods that senior Divisional officers used to debrief the incoming refugees from Sangshak. Another simple cause could be the order in which the defenders arrived back at Imphal – the earlier returnees being able to give their version of the story before it could be verified by the rest of the Brigade.

As some of the first to arrive back at Imphal (from 29 March) and in relatively good order, Lieutenant Colonel Trim and his men of the 4/5 MLI were also among the first to be interviewed by Major General Roberts and senior commanders of 23 Division. Immediately on reaching Imphal, Trim was whisked away by carrier to be debriefed. Following this, on 30 March, two days before Hope-Thomson's party even arrived at the edge of the Imphal plain, Roberts visited the commanders and men of 4/5 MLI and congratulated them on 'the fine show that the Battalion had put up'.

We don't know the contents of the debrief, but it is likely that Trim, if not deliberately exaggerating the contributions of his Battalion, at least depicted his soldiers' efforts in the most favourable light possible. On the one hand, that is as it should be; a commander should be proud of his men, particularly after they have got through such an exacting challenge. However, it also appears likely that at the same time he was possibly, even if subtly or subconsciously, running down the paratroopers, their contribution to the battle and most importantly, their commander.

This conclusion is based on three pieces of evidence, namely the timing of the debriefs, the contents of the 4/5 MLI War Diary (in particular, the comments about 152 Battalion leaving their positions early prior to the breakout and having to be forced out of the MLI positions almost at gun point) and the fact that the MLI troops received a comparatively greater number of honours and awards after the battle than all the rest of the 50 Parachute Brigade troops. This included Trim himself being recommended for a Distinguished Service Order (DSO) on 24 May, only to have it upgraded to an Order of the British Empire (OBE) – a significantly more important honour. None of the other Battalion Commanders or senior officers from the Parachute Brigade received any award for their part in the defence of Sangshak, despite the fact that their Battalions bore the brunt of the Japanese attacks for the whole of the siege.[6]

Another factor was that in those first days of April the senior officers of 50 Parachute Brigade were simply not in a position to defend themselves. The small group of 50 Brigade officers had only just made their way to the edge of the Imphal plain on 31 March, several days after 4/5 MLI reached Imphal. Hope-Thomson, in a concussed and dazed state, was immediately sent to hospital and never seen again by the Brigade. While he quickly recovered, he was nevertheless sent home to England, reduced to his substantive rank of Lieutenant Colonel and had the notation 'nervous exhaustion' added to his service record.

Hope-Thomson's collapse generated an enormous amount of controversy several decades later, when histories of the Burma campaign started to be published. The earliest accounts were very unflattering to him, essentially claiming that he had cracked up under pressure. Some of the more fanciful, and completely untrue, narratives claimed that Hope-Thomson was seen drawing his toothpaste tube from his webbing and aiming it at the enemy, mistaking it for his revolver!

In response, the surviving Brigade officers put up a valiant defence of their former commander, corresponding constantly and in some cases quite aggressively with historians, to get them to retract or amend their accounts of the battle and to paint their much-loved commander in a more sympathetic light.

The truth, however, is that Hope-Thomson did suffer a short collapse during the battle. While he quickly recovered, at least sufficiently to maintain a semblance of command, he would continue to deteriorate over the next few days until finally, by the time he returned to Imphal, he was in no fit state to lead the Brigade, much less defend its reputation to senior officers. He needed complete rest, and the official medical diagnosis of 'nervous exhaustion' would, in the end, prove to be accurate.

While it may have seemed harsh and unfair to Hope-Thomson that he was sent home and reduced in rank, he was very soon on the mend and back commanding front-line units. He fought in Europe, where he won another DSO and was then awarded an OBE in 1950. He would continue to serve in the Army for many years after the war, leading troops again in Malaya and eventually retiring with his previous rank of Brigadier. Hope-Thomson was a serious, capable and thoroughly professional soldier who should be remembered for the many things that he did well at Sangshak rather than the brief breakdown which has unfortunately come to dominate any discussion of his career.

Another key Brigade officer, Lieutenant Colonel Hopkinson, was also sent to hospital, to have his leg wounds treated. While there he was tasked to write a report of his Battalion's actions at Sangshak. This was a very well written and balanced report in three parts – the events at Sheldon's Corner, the defence of Sangshak and the withdrawal to Imphal. The report detailed very fairly the contributions of all of the units in the Brigade. Unfortunately, it was probably delivered too late to stop the rumour mill from starting to turn. In any event, by the time it was completed it was probably given scant attention by senior commanders, their focus now very firmly fixed on the all-out battle with the Japanese Army which was raging all around them.

Instead of recognizing the effect of timing and the wider context of the battle of Imphal, Seaman places special blame for the rumours on senior Divisional officers. He is particularly scathing about Lieutenant General Scoones, then commanding general of IV Corps (the higher headquarters of both 23 Division and 50 Parachute Brigade), and about his official report and later *History of the War in Burma*, in which he painted the paratroopers in a somewhat unfavourable light. Seaman says that Scoones was at least aware of Japanese preparations prior to 15 March 1944 but did not adequately inform the Parachute Brigade – effectively 'dropping them in it'. He is also critical of Scoones' subtle misrepresentation in his later writings of the relative strengths of the combatants, the skill or otherwise of Hope-Thomson and the fighting qualities of the men.

In Seaman's view, the nasty rumours about 50 Parachute Brigade were started in order to 'cover up' the failure of Scoones and other senior commanders to warn Hope-Thomson about the imminent Japanese attacks:

It is impossible to avoid the conclusion that the 50th Indian Parachute Brigade and its commander had been made the scapegoats for the errors and omissions of those above them. In the nature of the role for which its men had volunteered, as parachute troops, they expected no favours from the enemy; from their own, however, they merited a fair judgement. This they were denied.[7]

Seaman's arguments are not convincing. While senior British officers were aware that the Japanese were moving men up to the Chindwin River in late February 1944, no one suspected that they would try to move two Divisions across the mountains and jungles of Manipur to try and take Imphal from the north. Right up until the time that the Brigade was attacked at Sheldon's Corner, no one in higher command, and certainly not the commander of 23 Division or Scoones himself, suspected that anything more than raiding parties would come from this direction. There is simply no evidence to support Seaman's allegations. He and other Brigade officers may have felt under-appreciated, but there is nothing to prove allegations of conspiracy or cover up.

* * *

In any event, these arguments were for the future. In April 1944, the immediate priorities of the Brigade were to reconstitute its men and re-equip itself so that it could be put back into the fight. By early April 1944, finding themselves allocated to the Winkle Box on the Imphal plain, the Brigade was much reduced, particularly in relation to junior and mid-ranking officers. In 152 Battalion there were only two officers fit enough to exercise command and they were desperately trying to reorganize their now largely leaderless men. Meanwhile, 153 Battalion was little better off. Colonel Abbot, assuming command of the much-depleted Brigade, should have been able to better defend the Brigade's reputation, but to be charitable, perhaps he was too busy trying to re-form and re-equip his shattered Brigade to deal with rumour and scuttlebutt. Alternatively, perhaps, he too was exhausted following the ordeal that he had just survived. In any event, reports showed that the Brigade lacked almost every item of equipment needed to function as a fighting unit. Even such fundamental equipment as .303 rifles and Bren guns was only received in small quantities from 4 April onwards. It was likely that it was these vital matters were occupying Colonel Abbott's mind, rather than dealing with rumour and scandal.

* * *

At the end of August 1944, reputations were mended and hurt pride somewhat mollified by the issue of General Slim's Special Order of the Day dated 31 August and addressed to the 50 Parachute Brigade. It read:

> Your parachute Brigade bore the first brunt of the enemy's powerful flanking attack, and by their staunchness gave the garrison of Imphal the vital time required to adjust their defences. To the officers and men of the 50th Parachute Brigade I send my congratulations. The Fourteenth Army has inflicted on the Japanese the greatest defeat his Army has yet suffered.

Slim's Special Order made it clear to all that the efforts of 50 Parachute Brigade at Sangshak were of vital importance to the entire British defence at Imphal. Far from 'running away', the Brigade's steadfast defence had cost the enemy dearly and helped secure the eventual British victory. The Special Order was a welcome vindication of all the officers and men of the Parachute Brigade.

Slim maintained his view that the defence of Sangshak gave his XIV Army valuable time to strengthen their defences. In a message to the Indian Parachute Brigade Association years later he said, 'I shall always remember the days you gained for the XIV Army, at a critical time, by the magnificent stand at Sangshak.'[8]

Eighty years on – what does Sangshak mean to us now?

The Battle of Sangshak was a little-known encounter in an important but now dimly remembered campaign in 1944. Some have referred to it as a 'sideshow within a sideshow'.[9] Like the entire Imphal campaign, Sangshak was quickly forgotten by the general public, and even by the Army, fixated as it was on the titanic struggles occurring in Europe at that time, particularly the D-Day landings of June 1944.

However, with the passing of time, more people have now come to recognize just how significant the Imphal campaign was to the eventual defeat of Japan. After Imphal, Japan was no longer in a position to go on the offensive in Burma, and a newly confident Indian Army, well led and superbly trained, was able to strike back and push the Japanese down the entire length of the country, until Rangoon was eventually liberated in May 1945.

The key strategic impact of Sangshak was the vital five-day delay that it imposed on the Japanese. This was crucial to the British defence of Imphal and, while little understood at the time, was rightly recognized by Slim in his Special Order of the Day as a critical factor in the eventual British success.

Sangshak also demonstrated just how far the British and Indian troops had come in terms of tackling the Japanese since 1942. No longer would they simply retreat in the face of significant enemy forces, but they would stand and fight, supplied from the air, where they stood. While the airdrops did not always go according to plan, Sangshak nevertheless showed for the first time that well trained and highly motivated Indian troops were more than capable of meeting and defeating the best of the Japanese Army in the jungle. Perhaps the final words should be reserved for Hope-Thomson himself, who said:

> But what the hell! It's all an old story now and, apart from you historians, who gives a damn whether we did well or ill? The few who remember, and know what it was like, are all old men now.[10]

But with all due respect to Brigadier Hope-Thomson, he is wrong. By any measure, the officers and men of 50 Indian Parachute Brigade performed admirably and courageously at Sangshak. Their stand set the tone for the British defence in the months to come and for their eventual victory over the Japanese. It was a magnificent stand in a crucial battle and one that deserves never to be forgotten.

Appendix A

Ranks

The rank structure of the Indian Army during the Second World War was a mixture of traditional British Army ranks and a number of local ranks peculiar to the Indian Army.

There were also distinctions between various types of officers – British Army Officers (BO), holding the King's Commission, and Indian Army Officers who were Viceroy Commissioned Officers (VCO).

Ranks with their British Army and Indian Army equivalents are as follows:

Enlisted Men

British Army	Indian Army
Private (PTE)	Sepoy/Rifleman
Lance Corporal (LCPL)	Lance Naik
Corporal (CPL)	Naik
Sergeant (SGT)	Havildar
Warrant Officer 2nd Class – CSM	Havildar Major
Warrant Officer 1st Class – RSM	

Note: Gurkha private soldiers were always referred to as 'Riflemen' and never as 'Sepoys', as was common in some Indian Regiments.

Officers

British Army	Indian Army
Lieutenant (LT)	Jemadar
Captain (CAPT)	Subedar
Major (MAJ)	Subedar Major
Lieutenant Colonel (LTCOL)	
Colonel (COL)	
Brigadier (BRIG)	

Appendix B

Key Personnel

50 Parachute Brigade Headquarters Staff

BRIG Julian 'Tim' Hope-Thomson	Commanding Officer
COL Bernard Abbott	2IC
MAJ Gerry Beale	Brigade Major
CAPT 'Dickie' Richards	Intelligence Officer
CAPT Lester Allen	Intelligence Officer
MAJ (John) Ball*	OC MMG Coy
CAPT Alan Lewis	MMG Coy
CAPT Roger Sylvester	Brigade Supply and Transport Officer
LT Robin de la Haye*	OC Defence Platoon

80 Field Ambulance

LTCOL Bobby Davis	Regimental Medical Officer
Jack Hyslop	Surgical team
Harry Pozner	Anaesthetist

Brigade Signals Section

CAPT Eric Buirski	OC Signals section
LT Maurice G. Bell	2IC Signals section
SGT S.G. Yardley	Senior NCO

411 (P) Fd Sqn [Engineers]

| CAPT McClune | OC |

152 Indian Parachute Battalion

LTCOL Paul 'Hoppy' Hopkinson	Commanding Officer
CAPT T. Monaghan	Adjutant
MAJ Gillett*	OC A Coy
MAJ John Fuller*	OC C Coy

CAPT Thomas Roseby*	C Coy 2IC
LT Andrew Faul*	C Coy
Havildar Makmud Din*	C Coy
LT R. Bolton*	C Coy
LT H. Easton	C Coy
CAPT A.G. Rangaraj	Medical Officer
LT Basil Seaton	A Coy
Havildar Mohd Ali	A Coy, 5 Platoon
LT Alan Cowell	A Coy, 5 Platoon
CAPT John Sanderson	
CAPT John Weaver	Transport Officer

*KIA

153 Indian Parachute Battalion

LTCOL R. Willis	Commanding Officer 153 Bn
CAPT Eric Neild	Medical Officer
LT Harold 'Bones' Hammond-Seaman	
LT Robin Kynoch-Shand	
MAJ Victor Brookes	
MAJ Jimmy Roberts	OC A Coy
Subadar Dudhjang Ghale	A Coy
CAPT David Little	

4/5 Mahratta Light Infantry

LTCOL Jack (Jackie) Harold Trim	Commanding Officer 4/5 MLI
MAJ William Mackay	2IC 4/5 MLI
MAJ Steele	OC D Coy
LT Khurray	D Coy

15 (Jellum) Mountain Battery

MAJ Robert John Penton Lock*	Battery Commander
LT J.G. Kidd	
LT Malhotra	

D Troop, 582 Bty, 158 Regt RA

MAJ Jack Smith*	Battery Commander
LT Hepburn	GPO

Notes

Chapter 2
1. Neild, *With Pegasus in India* p53
2. Neild – *Airborne Reminiscences* p264
3. *Pegasus Journal*, June 1992
4. David Atkins *The Forgotten Major* p89. The original poem is by Frances Croft Cornford entitled *On Rupert Brooke* – 'A young Apollo, golden-haired/ stands dreaming on the verge of strife/ Magnificently unprepared/ For the long littleness of life.'
5. *Operational Training Instruction 50 (P) Bde*
6. '*Khud*' is an Indian word for a deep ravine or chasm. Falling '*khudside*' was something to be avoided but which unfortunately befell a great many jeeps and vehicles throughout this area of Manipur.

Chapter 3
1. Allen, *Burma: The Longest War* p152
2. Bond, p109
3. Slim, p612
4. *Four Samurai* p249
5. *Burma Operations Record, Fifteenth Army* p111
6. *Tactics and Strategy of the Japanese Army,* para 15
7. *Burma Operation Records, Fifteenth Army* p112
8. The story of the INA and the motivations for individual Indian soldiers to join it deserves serious consideration on its own but is beyond the scope of this book. In summary, the reasons why an individual Indian soldier would join the JIFS were various, but many had little choice after they fell into Japanese hands following the surrender of Singapore. Whatever their reasons for joining, these men were roundly hated by Indian Army troops during the Burma campaign, and little mercy was extended to captured JIFS.
9. Quoted in Evans, *Imphal – Flower on a Lofty Height* p111
10. *Tales by Japanese Soldiers* p158

Chapter 4
1. Sheldon's Corner was named after another British engineer serving under Major Finch, Captain W.L. Sheldon, as the road was built from Litan to Sangshak, and then on to Nungshangkong, with local labour. Sheldon was supported by Andrew Arthur, a 13-year-old Sangshak native who served as his interpreter and relayed to the author the story about how the corner got its name.
2. 23 Division War Diary
3. 'Mutual reinforcing' or 'mutual support' are military terms which refer to a situation in which the fire of one unit can effectively cover the approaches to a neighbouring unit.

164 Fight Your Way Out

The effect is that an enemy must contend with not only the unit to its immediate front but also the fire from its neighbouring units, making it a much more difficult object of attack.

4. Hope-Thomson's recollections p3
5. *Valour Enshrined* p420
6. Terrance Lane, IWM Oral History, No 24657 Reel 7
7. Lieutenant Gollop - email to Rajeshwor
8. Hope-Thomson recollections p3
9. *Valour Enshrined* p417
10. 23 Div War Diary, 19 Mar 44
11. Neild p60
12. *The Battle at Sheldon's Corner* – Lieutenant Colonel Hopkinson
13. *The Battle at Sheldon's Corner* – Lieutenant Colonel Hopkinson

Chapter 5
1. Slim, *Defeat into Victory* p29
2. WO 373/33/152 – Award of MM to Lance Naik Desai
3. WO 373/33/58 – Award of MC to Jemadar Desai
4. Seaman, Harry, loc 1045 – Curiously, no mention of this British soldier is found in any of the official British accounts, nor does Lieutenant Easton mention it when he returns to the Brigade.
5. Twenty-four men of C Company would be captured around Hill 7378. They were initially sent to Pushing but were then sent forward to Ukhrul and other locations to act as labourers for the Japanese, hauling supplies and carrying the wounded. Most would eventually make their way back to British lines over the course of the following month.
6. WO 373/34245 – Award of MC to Subedar Shripat Vishwashrao
7. *Valour Enshrined* p423
8. Neild p60
9. 23 Div War Diary, 20 Mar 44
10. 23 Div Operation Instruction 10 dated 20 Mar 44
11. *The History of the Indian Mountain Artillery*
12. A type of Burmese knife, typically with a blade about 7–8ins long
13. MLI War Diary – 20 March 1944
14. MLI War Diary – 20 March 1944
15. Major John Weaver, Interview

Chapter 6
1. After the war, there was much discussion about whether Sangshak was suitable as a defensive location and whether this was yet another example of Hope-Thomson's incompetence. However, at the time it was considered a good position, with participants including Dickie Richards declaring that 'tactically [it was] very well sited' – *Forgotten Voices of the Second World War* p166
2. *Battle at SANGSHAK 1944 War Diary Report* – Lieutenant Colonel Hopkinson
3. Account of the Battle at Sheldon's Corner – Lieutenant Colonel Hopkinson
4. Neild p62
5. *History of the Indian Mountain Artillery* p352
6. Neild p62

Notes

Chapter 7
1. *Burma Operations Record, Fifteenth Army* p119
2. *The Battle at Sheldon's Corner* – Lieutenant Colonel Hopkinson
3. 4/5 MLI War Diary 22 March 44
4. The 15cwt truck was the main light truck available to British troops in India. Cwt is the abbreviation of 'hundredweight', equal to 112 pounds or just over 50kg. Thus the 15cwt truck had a capacity of approximately 750kg
5. MLI War Diary
6. Neild – *Airborne Reminiscences* p259
7. Neild – *With Pegasus in India* p63

Chapter 8
1. *Tales by Japanese Soldiers* p158
2. *The Battle at Sangshak* – Lieutenant Colonel Hopkinson
3. Neild p63
4. Trim's recollections

Chapter 9
1. 23 Div War Diary, 23 March 1944
2. Roger Sylvester's recollections
3. Hatton's recollections
4. Maurice Bell – 'Sangshak Snippets'
5. *The Battle at Sangshak* – Lieutenant Colonel Hopkinson
6. Captain Pozner was later awarded an MC for his work at Sangshak and for his care of the wounded during the withdrawal.
7. Maurice Bell – 'Sangshak Snippets'

Chapter 10
1. Maurice Bell – 'Sangshak Snippets'
2. WD HQ 23 Ind Div
3. 23 Div War Diary – Orders Dictated to OC 2/1 Punjab at 0715 hrs on 22 Mar 44
4. Admissions to the Field Ambulance on 24 March 1944: British Officers – 3, British Other Ranks – 6, VCO and Indian/Gurkha Other Ranks – 56. Total – 65
5. Max Arthur, Obituary: Major Tom Monaghan, *Independent* 22 Oct 2011
6. WO373-33-51 – Cowell MC Citation
7. WO-373-33 – Cowell MC Citation
8. WO373-33-51 – Cowell MC Citation

Chapter 11
1. Gollop recollections
2. Gollop recollections
3. Sangshak – Lieutenant Colonel Hopkinson
4. Letter, Hope-Thomson to Allen 29 Jan 1986
5. Letter, Hope-Thomson to JR Dent & Sons, 4 Mar 1986
6. Hope-Thomson recollections
7. Hopkinson
8. Susumi Nishida 'The Last Drop of Water' in The Burma Campaign Society newsletter, September 2005

166 Fight Your Way Out

Chapter 12
1. Hope-Thomson recollections
2. Neild, *With Pegasus in India* p66
3. Lieutenant Colonel Hopkinson
4. Lieutenant Colonel Hopkinson
5. Lieutenant Om Prakash Malhotra would recover from his wounds and have an extremely successful military career, eventually becoming the Chief of Army Staff of the Indian Army in 1978.
6. The 'colours' of a regiment are the flags, standards or guidons which traditionally marked the rallying point for a regiment in battle. They also represent the honour of a regiment,t and as such it is regarded as a great point of shame if they are captured by the enemy.
7. 15 Mountain Battery War Diary, 31 March 1944
8. WO 373/33/202 and WO 373/33/203 – Mohan Lal and Sarwan Das medal recommendations
9. Major Jimmy Roberts, OC of A Company 153 Battalion was an extremely well respected and experienced officer who had already won an MC for an operational parachute drop in northern Burma in 1942. After the war he became an accomplished mountaineer.
10. WO33-373-76 – Jemadar Dudhjang Ghale MC Recommendation
11. Hope-Thomson recollections
12. Victor Brookes, *Games & War* p3
13. Admissions during the 26th were: British officers – 5, British Other Ranks – 3, VCO and Indian/Gurkha Other Ranks – 46. Total – 54
14. See Allen pp217–18
15. Corporal Monks would survive Sangshak and later earn the Distinguished Conduct Medal for gallantry in action in another desperate fight in May 1944 while accompanying another Gurkha unit as a signaller
16. L.F. Richards, *Humour in Uniform – It can be a life saver* p142
17. Hope-Thomson recollections
18. Bill Gollop recollections

Chapter 13
1. Seaton would be awarded a Mention in Despatches for this action. His CO had recommended him for an MC since this was the second time he had been put forward for an MID, but for whatever reason, he only received another MID.
2. The Brigade Major was the 'chief of staff' of a Brigade, reporting to the Brigadier and overseeing many of the administrative and operational sections of the Brigade.
3. A puttee is a long strip of cloth, like a bandage, which is used to cover a soldier's lower leg and give it some protection from mud and undergrowth. They were almost ubiquitous in the First World War but by now were seldom used.
4. Richards *The Bloody Battle at Sangshak* p71
5. The plight of the Naga villages is rarely discussed, but the villagers suffered for months, hiding in the jungle with little food or supplies. Many of them spent months there before they thought it safe enough to return to their often destroyed villages. Nevertheless, survivor stories abound with tales of Naga villagers helping lost and wounded men, giving them much needed food and supplies when they themselves had so very little.
6. Victor Brookes, *Games and War* p5

Chapter 14
1. Allen p183
2. WO-373-33-78 – Kynoch-Shand MC recommendation

Chapter 15
1. *Burma Operations Record, Fifteenth Army* p119
2. *Tactics and Strategy of the Japanese Army*, p25
3. Slim *Defeat Into Victory* p 612
4. Louis Allen, *Burma: The Longest War* pp218–19
5. Kojima Noboru '*Valley of Heroes – the Operation to Conquer Imphal*' estimates 58 Regiment losses as 499 casualties, including more than half of the company and platoon commanders in 2 and 3 Battalions (pp 155–6). British Official History estimates Japanese casualties at 580, of which 220 were killed (p 237).
6. The sole exception was Lieutenant Colonel Bobby Davis, the Brigade Medical Officer, who was awarded the Distinguished Service Order.
7. Seaman at n1989
8. Dickie Richards' account of the Battle of Sangshak – Paradata
9. Victor Dawes
10. Hope-Thomson 'Some personal notes on the battle of Sangshak'

Bibliography

War Diaries & Reports
WO/172/4338 War Diary 23 Division
WO/172/4420 War Diary 50 Indian Parachute Brigade
WO/172/5063 War Diary 152 Indian Parachute Battalion
WO/172/4949 War Diary 4/5 Mahratta Light Infantry
WO/172/4849 War Diary 15(J) Indian Mountain Battery
WO/172/5323 War Diary 411 (RB) Parachute Squadron (IE)
Battle at SANGSHAK 1944 War Diary Report by Lieutenant Colonel Paul Hopkinson
Report on the Actions in the Area Sangshak by Lieutenant Colonel Jack Trim (23 Div War Diary)

Books
Abhyankan, M.G. *Valour Enshrined – A History of the Maratha Light Infantry 1768–1947* (1960) Orient Longman
Allen, Louis *Burma: The Longest War 1941–45* (1984) Phoenix Press paperback 2000 edition
Arthur, Max *Forgotten Voices of the Second World War* (2004) Ebury Press, Kindle
Atkins, David *The Forgotten Major* (1989) The Toat Press
Barkawi, Tarak *Soldiers of Empire* (2017) *Cambridge University Press*
Bond, Brian (ed.). *British and Japanese Military Leadership in the Far Eastern War*, 1941–45 (2012) *Routledge*
Butler, Sir James (ed.) *History of the Second World War, Vol III The War Against Japan* (1962) HM Stationery Office
Evans, Sir Geoffrey *Imphal: A Flower on Lofty Heights* (1962) Macmillan & Co
Graham, Brigadier C.A.L. *The History of the Indian Mountain Artillery* (1957) Aldershot, Gale & Polden Ltd
Kazuo Tamayama & John Nunnery *Tales by Japanese Soldiers* (2000) Cassell & Co
Lyman, Robert *A War of Empires Japan, India, Burma & Britain 1941–45* (2021) Osprey
Moreman, Tim *The Jungle, Japanese and the British Armies at War, 1941–1945* (2005) Routledge
Neild, Eric *With Pegasus in India. The Story of 153 Gurkha Parachute Battalion* (1990) The Battery Press
Seaman, Harry *The Battle at Sangshak: Prelude to Kohima* (1989) Pen & Sword Books, Kindle
Slim, Viscount William *Defeat into Victory, Battling Japan in Burma and India 1942–1945* (1956) Cooper Square Press edition 2000
Swinson, Arthur *Four Samurai* (1968) Hutchinson & Co

Personal Accounts and Articles

Arthur, Andrew 'Sangshak', correspondence with the author, 12 Aug 2022
Bell, Maurice 'Sangshak Snippets', correspondence with Rajeshwor Yumnam
Brookes, Victor 'Games & War', British Library, Mss Eur C770: 1944
Glass, Sir Leslie 'The Brigade Major's Story', letter to Louis Allen 13 Feb 1986
Hirakubo, Masao, Oral Interview, Imperial War Museum, Object number 80033030
Hope-Thomson, M.R.J. 'Some Personal Notes on the Battle of Sangshak', Letter to Louis Allen 1987
Neild, F.G. (Eric) 'Indian Airborne Reminiscences', *Royal Journal of the Army Medical Corps*, 1 Dec 1948
Susumi Nishida 'The Last Drop of Water', *The Burma Campaign Society Newsletter* September 2005
Seaton, Basil email to Rajeshwor Yumnam, 17 Jan 2010
Pitt, Michael Walter, 1993, Oral History, Imperial War Museum Item No. 13237 (Reel 3)
Richards, L.F. 'Dickie' 'Humour in Uniform – It can be a Life Saver', *Pegasus Journal*, Dec 1987
—— 'The Bloody Battle of Sangshak' SOAS Burma Archive
Weaver, John, Oral History and Interviews, conducted by Sam Thompson, early 2000
Yardley, S.G. 'Pegasus in India', *Pegasus Journal*, April 1988

Official Documents

Headquarters, United States Army Japan 'Burma Operations Record: 15th Army Operations in Imphal Area and withdrawal to Northern Burma' 1957
Lieutenant-General William Slim, 'Special Order of the Day', 31 August 1944
United States Military Observer Group in India, 'Tactics and Strategy of the Japanese Army in the Burma Campaign from Nov 1943 to Sept 1944', October 1944
Operational Training Instruction 50 (P) Bde [Undated – likely Dec 1943], Paradata
War Cabinet, Joint Intelligence Sub-Committee report 'Japanese Intentions', 12 Jan 1944. National Archives CAB 79/69

Medal recommendations

WO373/80/349: OBE – Lieutenant Colonel H. Trim
WO 373/33/152: MM – Lance Naik Desai
WO 373/33/58: MC – Jemadar Desai
WO 373/34/245: MC – Subedar Shripat Vishwashrao
WO373/33/51: MC – Lieutenant Cowell
WO 373/32/46: MC – Subedar Singh
WO 373/33/202: IDSM – Havildar Mohan Lal
WO 373/33/203: IDSM – Havildar Sarwan Das
WO33/373/76: MC – Jemadar Dudhjang Ghale
WO373/33/78: MC – Lieutenant Kynoch-Shand

Acknowledgements

One of the great delights in preparing this book was corresponding with a great many people and experts who had either previously looked at this battle or whose family members had participated in it. I have found everyone I contacted unfailingly polite, helpful and enthusiastic in helping me with this project.

Special thanks must go to Robert Lyman, Saul David and Tarak Barkawi. Dr Lyman will not know it, but it was his works that first got me interested in the Burma campaign and inspired me to write. He then was gracious enough to put me in touch with both Saul David, who kindly agreed to write the Foreword, and Professor Barkawi, who probably knows more about the Sangshak battle than any other contemporary historian. Heartfelt thanks to all of you.

The Twittersphere also uncovered its treasures. Thanks to James McKemy for information about his grandfather, David Little (on 'loan' to 50 Parachute Brigade just in time to take part in the battle) and to Sam Thompson for the amazing set of interviews which he had conducted with Major John Weaver. What a find those interviews were!

As most of this book was written during the COVID pandemic, its completion would have been impossible without the unflagging and sustained assistance of my London-based research assistant, Dr Kevin Jones. Kevin told me when we first discussed the project that he had a 'knack' for uncovering surprising things in the archive and he was true to his word!

Finally, my eternal gratitude goes to my long-suffering wife Sasha, and to my children, who have had to put up with me 'tippitytappitying' all day long for months on end.

Index

15 Division (IJA), 17, 21
  and tension with 31 Division, 126
15 Mountain Battery, 54, 68, 84, *see also* Mountain Batteries
151 Battalion, 7
152 Battalion (Indian), 7, 26, 62, 65, 72–3
153 Battalion (Gurkha), 7, 35, 66
154 Battalion (Gurkha), 7
2/1 Punjab Rifles, 100–1
23 Division, 24
  and orders to defend Sangshak, 64
31 Division (IJA), 1, 3–4, 17, 21
  and tension with 15 Division, 126
33 Division (IJA), 1, 17
4/5 Mahratta Light Infantry (4/5 MLI), 24–5
  and withdrawal from Sangshak, 140–2
411 (Royal Bombay) Field Engineers, 11
49 Brigade, 23
50 (P) Bde, *see* 50 Indian Parachute Brigade
50 Indian Parachute Brigade (50 (P) Bde), 4, 7, 14
  and defences 88
  and water and supply 89
  and order to withdraw, 128
  and controversy, 154
  and Order of Battle, 7, 9, 11
58 Regiment (31 Division IJA), 19, 21, 78, 115
582 Battery RA, 50, 78, 109
60 Regiment, 21
711 Field Company, 68
75mm Mountain Gun (IJA), 92, 97

Abbott, Colonel (2IC 50 P Bde), 55, 137, 157

Advanced jungle Training, 5
Airdrops, 57–8, 62, 65
  and failure of, 93, 96, 111
Ali, Havildar Mohd, 103–4
Allen, Captain Lester (Bde IO), 85
Ammunition, usage, 89–90, 95
Arakan, 5
Ashraf, Havildar Mohd (152 Bn), 147
Assam, 4
Atkins, David, 8, *see also The Forgotten Major*

Badger Hill, 26, 55
  and withdrawal from, 62, 65, 72–3
Ball, Major (MMG Coy), 98
Ban, Lieutenant (58 Regt IJA), 82, 133
  and burial of 86
Banzai Charge, 81–2, 116
Barbed wire, lack of, 90
Bashas, 27
Batta, 6
Battle of the Admin Box, 145
Beale, Major Gerry (Brigade Major), 135, 137
Bell, Maurice, 94, 99
Bolton, Lieutenant Ronald (C Coy 153 Bn), 38
Bose, Subhas Chandra, 20, *see also* Indian National Army
Box, description of 27
Brookes, Major Victor (153 Bn), 125, 143

C Company, 152 Bn, 26–39
  and overrun, 46
  and prisoners, 148
Campbellpore, 6
Chindit, 5, 16–17

172   Fight Your Way Out

Chindwin River, 1, 15
Church (American Baptist Church), 61, 67, 105, 106
   and order to abandon, 107
   and Japanese take control, 116
   and recapture, 123
Communications, 62
   and failure at night 68
Cowell, Lieutenant Alan (152 Bn), 65, 75, 103–5

Das, Havildar Sarwan (15 MtnBty), 118, 121
Davis, Lieutenant Colonel Bobby (Bde RMO), 67, 80, 102
De la Haye, Lieutenant Robin (Defence Platoon), 117
Defeat into Victory, 16, 43, *see also* Slim
Delhi, 4
Desai, Jemadar Laxuman (A Coy 4/5 MLI), 44–5, 48
Desai, Lance Naik Appa (A Coy 4/5 MLI), 45
Dimapur, 4, 153
Din, Havildar Makmud (C Coy 153 Bn), 37–8
Divisional boundaries (Japanese), 71–2, 152

Easton, Lieutenant (C Coy 152 Bn), 46–7
Elephant Point, 150
Elephants, 96–7

Faul, Lieutenant Andrew (C Coy 152 Bn), 30, 36, 42
Field Allowance, *see Bata*
Field Ambulance, 67, 80, 103
Fight Your Way Out message, 127
Finch, Major John, 12, *see* Finches Corner
Finches Corner, 12, 25, 76
Food on the Hoof, 17, 126, *see* Japanese logistics and supply
Fuller, Major John (C Coy 152 Bn), 6, 27–39, 41

Gammon, 26, 69
Gaydon, Captain (MMG), 104

Ghale, Jemadar (153 Bn), 122
Ghayal, Lieutenant (152 Bn), 40
Gillet, Major, (A Coy 152 Bn), 33, 116, 135
Gollop, Lieutenant Bill (A Coy 152 Bn), 29–30, 77, 106, 129
Grenade dischargers, 31
Gurkhas, 7–8, 82

Hatton, Captain (582 Bty), 87
Hill 7378, 24, 27–39
   and overrun, 46
Hindu soldiers, 7
Hirakubo Maso, Lieutenant, 1–2
Holland, Major (A Coy 4.5 MLI), 34, 42–6, 48
Hope-Thomson, Brigadier Richard Julian 'Tim', 4, 32, 51, 107
   and choice of defensive position, 53
   and criticism of defensive position, 74
   and diagnosis of 'nervous exhaustion', 140
   and exhaustion, 88
   and nervous collapse, 111–13, 155–6
   and order to hold at all costs, 116
   and returned to England, 140
   and withdrawal from Sangshak, 135, 137
Hopkinson, Lieutenant Colonel Paul 'Hoppy', 7, 26, 32, 40, 49, 113
   and church counter-attack, 117
   and withdrawal wounded, 136
   and Report, 156
Hoppy, *see* Hopkinson
HQ Defence Platoon, 11
Hurricane fighter-bomber, 98–9, 111

Imperial Japanese Army (IJA), 1, 14
Imphal– Kohima Road, 2, *see also* Manipur Road
INA, *see* India National Army
Inada, Major General (IJA), 18
Indian National Army, 20, 83, 145–6

Japanese, 1, 14, *see also* Imperial Japanese Army
   and aggressive spirit, 37

and dress and equipment, 5, 10
and logistics and supply, 1–2, 17, 126, 153, *see also* Food on the Hoof
Japanese artillery, 19, *see also* 75mm mountain gun
Japanese infantryman, 14, 18, 114, 152
JIFS (Japanese Indian Fifth Columnists), *see* Indian National Army

Kameyama, Captain Shosaku (58 Regt IJA), 21, 82–3, *see* 58 Regiment
Kawabe, General Masakazu (IJA), 16
Khali Bahadur, 24–5, 53, 66, 74, 77
Khudside, 12, 149
Khurray, Lieutenant (4/5 MLI), 97, 102, 109–10
Kidd, Lieutenant (15 Mtn Bty), 92, 121
Kidney Camp, 25, 29, 50–1, 56
Kohima, 2, 5, 17, 153
Kuki, 12
Kukri, 11, 82
Kynoch-Shand, Lieutenant Robin, 148–50

Lal, Havildar Mohan (15 Mtn Bty), 84, 121–2
Lane, Terrance, 28
Lewis, Captain (MMG), 104
Litan, 54, 100–1
Lock, Major John (15 Mtn Bty), 54, 92, 107, 118–19

Machine Gun Company (50 P Bde), 11, 25, 64
Malhotra, Lieutenant (15 Mtn Bty), 118
Manipur road, 23, 64, *see also* Imphal–Kohima road
Manipur, 2, 4, 11
Map controversy, 85–6
Marco Polo Bridge Incident, 16
Matsumura, Lieutenant Colonel (60 Regt, IJA), 114
McLune, Captain (711 Field Company), 61, 107
Medical support, 79–80
MLI, *see* 4/5 Mahratta Light Infantry
Monaghan, Captain Tom (152 Bn), 42, 103

Monsoon, 3, 15
Mountain Batteries, 54, *see also* 15 Mountain Battery
Mules, 54, 89, 98
Muslim soldiers, 7
Mutaguchi, Lieutenant General Renya, 14, 16–17, 151, *see also* Operation U-Go
and Marco Polo Bridge incident, 16
and plan to invade India, 15,18
and Special order of the Day, 20

Naga, 12
Neild, Captain Eric (MO 153 Bn), 52, 79–80, 83
Nervous collapse controversy, 111–13, *see* Hope-Thomson
New Guinea roadblock, 40, 42
New Guinea, 26–39
Nishida, Susumi (58 Regt IJA), 113–16

Operation Ha-Go, 145
Operation U-Go
and delay, 151
and development of, 14–15
and failure, 153
and logistics and supplies, 1–2, 14, 17
and order of battle, 17
and terrain, 11–12
Operation 21, 15–16, *see also* Operation U-Go

Parachuting, 6
Phosphorus burns, 110
Pozner, Captain (MO), 80
Prisoners, 144
and Japanese treatment of, 145
Pushing, 24, 29
Pyara, Lieutenant, 32

Rangaraj, Captain A.G. (152 Bn MO), 79
Richards, Captain 'Dicky', 55, 61, 93, 135
Ringway, 4
Roberts, Major General Ouvry, 23, 25–6, 140, 154
Roberts, Major Jimmy (A Coy 153 Bn), 122

Roseby, Captain (C Coy, 152 Bn), 41
Rum ration, 111

Sangshak, 53
   and active defence, 75
   and breakout from, 132
   and choice of defensive position, 53, 61
   and criticism of Hope-Thomson's decision, 74
   and delay, 158
   and digging 74
   and relief attempt, 101
   and terrain, 60
   and water points, 60, 63, 74
Sato, Lieutenant General (31 Division IJA), 72
Seaman, Lieutenant Harry, 46
   and C Coy overrun, 46–47
   and 'cover up', 156–7
   and map controversy, 85–6
Seaton, Lieutenant Basil (A Coy 152 Bn), 87–8
   and escape from Sangshak, 133–4
   and wounded, 88
Sheldon's Corner, 23–39
Slim, Lieutenant General, William 'Bill', 16, 43
   and Chindits, 17
   and impression of Japanese Infantry, 152
   and Special Order of the Day, 158
Smith, Major (582 Bty), 64, 119
Steele, Captain (D Coy 4/5 MLI), 33, 75, 119, 142
Stewart, Major (152 Bn), 125, 128
Streamer message, 99–100
Stuart Light Tank, 101
Sylvester, Captain Roger (Supply Officer), 87

The Forgotten Major, 8
Tojo, Prime Minister Hideki, 18
Trim, Lieutenant Colonel Jack, 24, 32, 56, 84, 154–5

Ukhrul, 4, 31, 35, 61

V Force, 21, 24, 29
Vishwashrao, Subedar Shripat (A Coy 4/5 MLI), 45, 48–9

Weaver, Lieutenant John (153 Bn), 37
Willis, Lieutenant Colonel (153 Bn), 8, 89
Wingate, General Orde, 16, *see* Chindits

Zaman, Havildar Khan (152 Bn), 106